D0806327

Humanity
Is
Trying

Humanity
— Is —
Trying

Experiments in Living with Grief, Finding Connection, and Resisting Easy Answers

Jason Gots

HANOVER
SQUARE
PRESS

HANOVER
SQUARE
PRESS™

Recycling programs
for this product may
not exist in your area.

ISBN-13: 978-1-335-65294-2

Humanity Is Trying: Experiments in Living with Grief, Finding Connection, and Resisting Easy Answers

Copyright © 2022 by Jason Gots

All rights reserved. No part of this book may be used or reproduced in any manner whatsoever
without written permission except in the case of brief quotations embodied in critical articles and
reviews.

This publication contains opinions and ideas of the author. It is intended for informational and
educational purposes only. The reader should seek the services of a competent professional for
expert assistance or professional advice. Reference to any organization, publication or website does
not constitute or imply an endorsement by the author or the publisher. The author and the publisher
specifically disclaim any and all liability arising directly or indirectly from the use or application of
any information contained in this publication.

Hanover Square Press
22 Adelaide St. West, 41st Floor
Toronto, Ontario M5H 4E3, Canada
HanoverSqPress.com
BookClubbish.com

Printed in U.S.A.

For John, who wasn't afraid of his dreams.
For Meri, who wasn't afraid of the world.
And for everyone who lives somewhere in between.

Contents

I went to the coast the other day... I went to just, to look at the sea, and look at the sky... And I was standing on the edge of the land... And I realized that, you know it's just this piece of land... And on top of this piece of land it's just populated by this kind of noise. Humanity, we've built these cities, and we just tell these stories to each other about who we are and what we do...

It's just stories.

And I stood there and I watched the water come in and go out on the land and I thought, "This is real."

And everything, the way we structure ourselves, our power structures within our families, the way we fall in love—it's just stories that we tell. It's just narrative. And I understand this because I'm a teller of stories. I understand how important they are. I'm in love with stories, of course.

And I thought: "Well, if you want to make a change, you just need to change the narrative."

—Kae Tempest on *Think Again*—*a* Big Think *podcast*

Here's How This Book was Supposed to Begin

I'm in the East Asian Reading Room on the tenth floor of NYU's Bobst Library, a building I entered maybe once in four years as an undergrad here almost thirty years ago, and then only to read—and then, on impulse, steal—a single book.

I still have it. It's a slim, business-blue volume about (and containing) William Blake's illustrations to the Book of Job, that strange, more ancient myth that somehow found its way into the Hebrew Bible, where it sits nestled between Esther and Psalms, squatting uneasily alongside much later, less enigmatic material as if hoping nobody will notice.

I can understand why Blake was drawn to this story. Like his own "prophetic writings," it radiates symbolic power and defies easy interpretation. Job is a rich, happy shepherd with a wife, kids, and many fat sheep. He is known throughout the land as a God-loving guy whose blessings are the result of his piousness and prayer. This gives Satan an idea.

"Pssst," he says to God. *"It's nice that Job loves you and all…but*

how do you know he's not playing you for a chump? What if you took away the wife, the kids, and all the fat sheep? What then?"

An easy mark, apparently, God takes the bet and Job's whole world falls to pieces. As Blake draws it, he's left miserably scrabbling around in the dust while one fair-weather friend after another comes by to gloat. *"What happened to the sheep, Job? Where's that pretty wife of yours? Guess all the piousness didn't pay off, after all?"*

Then God shows up inside a "whirlwind," which I picture as a more robust version of one of those "dust devils" I occasionally saw in New Mexico, during grad school, wending their way across the sandy turf between the piñon bushes. Job, not surprisingly, is pissed: *"What the hell, God? I thought we had a deal!"* This reaction is proof of the Devil's hypothesis: Job's just in it for the goodies. Love? *Please.* He's a player, just like the rest of them.

God whirls off somewhere, leaving Job to reflect. There in the dust, Job leaves his rage behind and arrives at something like acceptance. The tears fall hot and thick. *"God!"* he cries, *"I was ungrateful! I took my blessings for granted! Please forgive me!"* In an act of mercy, God puts Job's life back together (new wife, new kids, new sheep). And Job lives happily ever after.

It feels right to be writing this book here, overlooking Washington Square Park—my first home in New York City (I lived in NYU's Hayden Hall on Washington Square East) and the epicenter of my own fat sheep moment—those years when I was first, most fully myself before the fall that is adulthood and all the things after, so many things gained and blighted and shattered and lost until, sitting there in the dust, you breathe it all in and calmly assemble the pieces into something new. Something you think you can live with.

And here's where you have to be careful. Put anything together in any order and it becomes a story. And stories, like songs, get stuck in your head. The insistent melody of narrative plays on repeat until the life it frames starts to fade; the way it felt to be nine years old is swallowed up by a single photograph of yourself at a Burger King birthday party, wearing a bent paper crown. And when this happens, it's easy to forget two things: that the story is your own creation, and that no story's ever complete.

That's how this one was supposed to begin: Washington Square framed from above in the big picture windows of the East Asian Reading Room. A lofty perspective on this place of great symbolic meaning. Instead I'm at ground level, in the Starbucks across the street, with a flavorless turkey bacon and egg white sandwich. The Office of Alumni Giving (which hasn't opened yet) needs to send an email to the Library Privileges window (which opened late) stating that I donated the $275 that allows me reading privileges. Instead of the reverent silence and shelves lined with Buddhist texts I'd imagined as the backdrop to these ruminations, I've got Starbucks' auto-tuned R & B.

How apt that this story about abrupt plot twists and endings and how they derail us should itself begin with a derailment. That it should start by forcing me to adapt to a new reality less perfect than the one I had planned.

This is a book about two people I loved and lost too early. It's also about mourning. To the extent that life becomes a struggle between the stories we try to tell and the rewrites the world throws back at us—each sudden change in the narrative is a kind of trauma. It's a shock to our expectations. And trauma needs to be processed, or mourned. We can't shrug it off, rail against it, or power through without consequences.

This is true both of big, dramatic changes like death and of smaller ones—the more manageable revisions of everyday life. A relationship fails. A pandemic obliterates your carefully cultivated daily workout routine. You end up starting your memoir in a Starbucks. The degree of trauma depends on how attached you are to any given story line. And where there's trauma, its hold on your life can only be loosened by seeing it clearly, fully, and compassionately enough to move on. In other words, by mourning.

Twenty-five hundred years before I stole that library book, Buddhism had captured this thought in its "second noble truth"—that the origin of human suffering is *tanha*: variously translated into English from Pali (the ancient, Sanskrit-related language spoken by Siddhārtha Gautama, the historical figure known as the Buddha) as *thirst*, *desire*, or *greed*. For modern-day Americans (like me), this idea can be tough to swallow. In our culture, ambition is a sacred value. It's what drives us to attempt the kinds of things that have tended to make it into our history books. It's the desire that produces growth under capitalism, through grand entrepreneurial visions and private purchases. Anything that questions the natural law of desire is at best considered marginal, at worst a flirtation with heresy.

The problem with *tanha*, though, isn't so much in *wanting* things as in the habit of pursuing those desires in every area of our lives without question, which leads to the stubborn refusal to let go of their fruits, even after they're long lost or transformed beyond recognition.

Job starts his story in a state of innocence: success, happiness, and God's love are all he's ever known. Like Adam and Eve in the Garden, he lives outside of narrative time—in a place where nothing ever changes. The Devil's bet is something new: a plot twist. It kick-starts the story's causal chain by spinning Job's cozy world into chaos and confusion. Job is understandably shocked and outraged. Life isn't supposed to work this way! Indeed, God's behavior seems to defy even God's own standards of decency: Job has done everything right, gone above and beyond the necessary prayers and sacrifices...what's he being punished for?

Fair enough. But let's put the injustice aside for a moment. What shouldn't have happened *has* happened. Now, in the aftermath, *tanha* is the origin of Job's suffering. He can't adjust to his new story. He's thirsty for a reality that no longer exists.

The story's tragicomic ending—Job surrounded by a shiny new family that for all its happiness and prosperity can't possibly erase his (or our) memory of the wife and kids he lost—is a song of experience. On the other side of the *tanha* and all the suffering it caused him, Job seems to have arrived at a state of acceptance. The Bible doesn't fill in the psychological blanks, of course, but through Blake's drawings I see Job as older, wiser, transformed by his mourning. Innocence, once lost, can never be regained, so he can't unsee the narrative threads of his own past. But maybe God's arbitrary and brutal rewrites have loosened his attachments to any one draft. If stories are the inevitable human condition, they're also always subject to change.

I'm looking at a photo on my iPhone. A digital photo I took of a framed, physical photo in my parents' house in Florida. In it, my sister, Meri, and I sit together on a swing in the woods next to the house we grew up in, in Bethesda, Maryland. It's fall, the most perfect season in that densely wooded place. Meri must be around three years old, which would make me six or seven. I'm smiling from the heart and looking off meaningfully into the distance, my round face framed by a ten-dollar Hair Cuttery bowl cut. Meri's smile is warier, her intelligent eyes locked on someone or something outside of the frame. We're both grasping the steel chains of the swing, my body behind hers: protective, older-brotherly. Like all the photos we have from that time, it's sepia-toned, which adds a nostalgic sheen like the feeling I always get from '70s pop music—everything bright and sunny, oversaturated and just out of reach.

This photo is one of a series. The locations and quality suggest the work of a professional, but our expressions are so natural that this person, whoever they were, clearly managed to put us both at ease. In another one, we're laughing our heads off and Meri's delight is so complete, so whole-body that it makes me grin every time I see it. I love these pictures because there's nothing overly posed or composed about them.

Contrast this series with a family studio portrait we have from the Reagan '80s in which we look like an aspiring First Family: Mom in a red power suit with huge, padded shoulders; Dad towering presidentially above her; Meri in the most presentable version that Mom could squeeze her into of the horsey frontier look she favored at the time; me in a blue blazer that must have been bought for the occasion and a more mature, Spock-like upgrade of the aforementioned bowl cut. All of us perfectly composed, tense, and lifeless.

I prefer the series to the portrait, but both of them are fictions. Each tells a story that's only partially true. The first is a story of uncomplicated happiness, the second of uncomplicated material success. But life's complicated, always. Just ask Job.

Another photo that's burned into my memory: my best friend John Mastny with a Franz Liszt haircut, balancing on one leg by his mother's grand piano. He's shirtless and his sculpted, trapezoidal torso, muscular neck, and Nijinsky-like gaze into the infinite distance are all evidence of the single-minded passion for dance that possessed him at the time. Sometimes when I'm missing him most I want to dig this photo out of its album, tear it to shreds and erase its memory. I want to obliterate every image, every story, every beautiful fiction that stands between him and me.

Narrative memory exists because it helps us survive. Storytelling reduces our lives to manageable causal chains. It helps us to learn from the past and shape the future. But evolution's cleverest tricks are often the ones most guilty of overreach. Where in the story of her tragic end is the sound of my sister's voice? Where in all the newspaper articles about the promising dancer shot dead in the street can I find, once again, what it was like to make my best friend laugh?

The antidote to the seemingly inescapable gravity of narrative is connection. There are so many ways of looking for it. All of them are messy. All involve getting lost before stumbling upon some new way forward.

One is dialogue itself. In the five years before I started writing this book, through the podcast *Think Again*, which I hosted and produced, I had roughly two hundred dialogues with some of the wisest scientists, artists, and thinkers living today. Those conversations opened new connections for myself and the audience—doorways into being more fully alive.

They stay with me, talking back to my life, provoking and guiding me. Bits of them will almost certainly find their way into this book.

A key element of *Think Again* was surprise; together the guest and I encountered and discussed an idea we hadn't prepared for in advance. It destabilized the conversation, pushing us into the unknown, into the potential for something new to happen.

In writing this book I'm sure to lose my way again, many times over. I'll do it in the hope of getting underneath the stories that sometimes disconnect me. And for you, the reader, it's my hope that these detours—and any discoveries they lead to—may be of some help in your own pursuit of connection.

I'm in the library now, for real this time. Emails were sent. An ID card was made. I sit by a window that is four feet wide by twelve feet high and through it I can see the bright white rooftops of the redbrick town houses on Washington Square North. Below them, students move slowly in their winter coats along the winding paths of the park, visible without detail through a screen of mostly leafless trees. Birds, which I wouldn't have noticed thirty years ago and whose names (having spent most of my adult life in this city, more interested in buildings and the people inside them) I still don't know, are everywhere. A bright blue one flutters up into the uppermost branches of the tree nearest my window. Behind the town houses, a massive, tan, art deco building asserts itself like a temple to the gods of early twentieth-century American ambition. Next to the bird, it's ridiculous. Pompous old structure! Check your story of triumph. Nothing lasts forever and there are no real endings.

Part 1

Yes, but—

It's 8 p.m., May 26, 2017, and I'm in a yurt. This is the first yurt I've ever been in, and by comparison to its ancient cousins, from which its name derives, those portable roundhouses my wife Demet's Turkish ancestors lugged from encampment to encampment across the Central Asian steppes, this one is luxurious. It's wooden and spacious, stained a deep butterscotch color made more butterscotch still by the play of the candlelight from the altar and the cloth runway that leads from it to the yurt's midpoint, where the "water ceremony" takes place.

It's so easy to slip into wry parody here, as Ariel Levy did in her *New Yorker* description of a Brooklyn ayahuasca ceremony—a burlesque of lost hipsters and New Age sad sacks vomiting all over one another—because when you observe the scene from a critical distance there are so many targets for snarky judgment. The altar in this yurt is a syncretic jumble of artifacts and symbols from New Age spirituality and various indigenous American traditions. Eagle feathers? Check. Dream catchers? Aplenty. There's even a rose quartz crystal ball. The walls are hung with psychedelic black light paintings of luminous plants, jaguars, snakes, and elderly wisewomen—imagery traditionally associated with ayahuasca. They strike my tightly wound critical sensibilities as incredibly "cheesy," the kind of thing that might hang alongside a Jethro Tull poster. They're for sale, and they aren't cheap.

Twenty-eight of us are crowded along the walls of the room. That's five or six too many. Everyone is wedged uncomfortably into their own personal comfort pod consisting of a camping mattress or a yoga mat, some blankets, a pillow, and some reassuring item of personal significance. In my case it's a big *mala*—a string of Tibetan Buddhist prayer beads I find reassuring both because Buddhist ideas and practices have become an important part of my life and because they're made of beautiful, richly grained wood. Wood is from trees, trees are from nature, and worrying at these beads with my fingers reminds me that I'm not just a judgmental, isolated brain that won't shut up. I'm matter, and as such, I'm connected to everything.

Each of us has brought whatever seemed necessary to accompany us on a two-night journey that might or might not involve vomiting, diarrhea, weeping, sweating, chills, strange visions of travel through the "sacred geometry" of fractal worlds, painful encounters with the past, communication with what seem to be benevolent alien entities, and more.

This is my first experience with the powerful psychedelic brew ayahuasca, made from a leaf and a vine of Amazonian origin. Let's get botanical and biochemical for a moment: *Psychotria viridis*—the leaf (also known as Chacruna)—contains dimethyltryptamine (DMT). DMT is a powerful psychedelic molecule that the body metabolizes almost instantly. That means its effects, while intense, don't last very long. Smoking DMT, for example, frequently causes people to feel that they've traveled to another dimension, but the whole trip lasts less than ten minutes. *Banisteriopsis caapi*—the ayahuasca vine with which the leaf is brewed for many hours to make the ayahuasca potion we'll take—contains a monoamine oxidase inhibitor (MAOI) that allows the body to absorb the DMT more slowly, over the course of four hours or so. This gives you enough time to build a ceremony around the experience, as many indigenous Amazonian tribes have done, along with more recent would-be shamans around the world.

While there's evidence that humans have been using psychoactive plants and fungi ceremonially for thousands of years, and while indigenous Amazonians do have an ancient history of plant medicine ceremonies, some anthropologists think the vine and leaf brew may be less than a century old. The group I'm sitting with wouldn't want to hear this. They're religiously committed to the belief that the drink is a millennia-old gift to humanity from the spirits of the plants themselves.

We're somewhere in the Catskill Mountains, about an hour outside of New York City. This is the heart of what my Jewish grandparents (on my dad's side) knew as the Borscht Belt, where comics with bow ties told one-liners punctuated by the ba-dum-bum-chhh! of the accompanying snare drum. Not far from here there are still active ultraorthodox Jewish summer colonies, everyone roaming around in their long black frock coats, hats, and floor-length skirts, somehow surviving (and enjoying?) the summer sun. This knowledge rattles around in one sub-basement of my consciousness as other levels fall under the spell of the bittersweet, viscous liquid.

The group I'm with is run by a young white woman, the widow of a Central American shaman who, it is rumored, was murdered by a rival shaman. Traditional shamanism, as opposed to the sanitized New Age version, often involves spiritual and/ or actual warfare. I've learned all this in whispers from returning participants in the hours leading up to the ceremony. Along with all the syncretic artifacts and the persistent mental images of Henny Youngman ("ba-dum-bum-chhh!"), this sinister backstory would cast a kind of pall over my evening if it weren't for the undeniable power of the *medicina* itself. I don't know what

Ariel Levy drank, but as soon as I start to feel ayahuasca's influence it becomes impossible to laugh this experience off.

It's difficult for anthropologists and hopeless for an amateur like me to try to untangle all the layers of culture at play here. *Medicina*—one name for the ayahuasca brew—is a Spanish colonial overlay on what seem to be older concepts, like the idea that the spirit of ayahuasca is a wise, benevolent-yet-tough-as-nails grandmother who will force you to confront profound truths about yourself and the world. The spirit is also, somehow, that of a jaguar and/or a giant snake, images that inspire awe and a sense of our inability to control the outcome of the journey.

Whatever their origin, I come to see these icons as cautionary tales against the natural tendency to respond with fear to these intense experiences—to fight or try to run from them. Cling too tightly to your existing perspective or to any desired outcome and you're in for a very rough ride. Awe and respect are what you need here. Trust and submission.

Myths and symbolism are the waters I like to swim in, but the people leading this particular ceremony seem to believe, literally, that the plants are sentient beings trying to communicate with us. I try not to get too hung up on this as the debate that ensues in my head is fussy and alienating: *Where exactly would this spirit be? On what evidence do you believe plants are sentient?* etc. This drags me out of the moment and into the irritating mindset of pre-Enlightenment philosophers quibbling over the exact location of the soul in the human body. The heart? The pineal gland?

Like everybody else, I'm here for a reason. Several reasons, I guess. The *medicina*, I've been told, has the power of release. The "purging" can take the aforementioned forms of vomiting, crying, sweating, etc., but the idea is that stuck parts of yourself get unstuck. I know a little bit about what this means from Buddhism. In Buddhist psychology, *tanha* (thirst, greed, desire) leads to *upādāna* (grasping, clinging, attachment). We cling greedily to the things we want in life and also (less intuitively obvious) to the things we don't want. Can I love museum art without finding black light paintings cheesy? Where would Batman be without his Joker?

If *tanha* is the force of attraction, *upādāna* is the active cause of suffering. It's the choice we make to hold on to a thing, resisting the fundamental nature of reality: impermanence and change. It's Job trying to argue with the whirlwind. *Upādāna* is often a choice driven by fear: the fear of facing something you don't want to deal with, the fear of losing something you don't want to lose, the fear of not getting something you think you need or want. Most of us would agree that fear is not the force we want governing our lives. But rationalization is one of humanity's greatest storytelling gifts; we're geniuses at explaining away our own worst motives.

When questioned, the clinging ego becomes a master rhetorician—the Perry Mason of bullshit excuses. It clings for dear life to clinging itself. *This tension keeps me on my toes*, it argues. *It is discipline in the face of disorder. It's how civilization arose from the muck! Why, the opposite of what you call "clinging" is sloth! Passivity! Fatalism!*

Applying Buddhist ideas and meditative practices in my own life, I've seen that fear and clinging are the enemies of connection and flow. And that acceptance—the opposite of *upādāna*—isn't the enemy of action. Whether you're trying to maintain an exercise routine, build a city, or even (if it comes to that) do battle with an enemy, connection and flow will get you better results than fear, every time.

Over the next forty-eight hours in the yurt, ayahuasca will make this even more viscerally plain. Novelist Elif Shafak has said: "there is too much information, less knowledge, and even less wisdom" in the world today. On ayahuasca, I'll feel what it's like when that order is reversed.

It's three in the morning on May 28—the second night of my two-night journey—and I'm talking to my sister, Meri.

It's been two years since she died and in all this time I've cried for her only twice: once while writing a poem full of details about her I'd forgotten until I wrote them down, and once while reading the poem aloud at her memorial. The tears stopped there. I don't know why this is, and it bugs me. I wonder if I'm still stuck in an earlier, unfinished story. Whether the death, years before, of my friend John and the way life hurtled on indifferently afterward has robbed me of my natural ability to mourn.

There are other possibilities, of course. For her last decade or so my sister was relegated by phantom limb pain and opioids to a kind of limbo, a half-life. She'd been stuck in quicksand, trying not to struggle too much, imperceptibly but surely sinking. Maybe I'd been mourning her loss on a slow drip for years.

Or maybe the slow, tragic arc of her adult life and death—the stupid, maudlin story I kept retelling of high hopes dashed, of my white horse arriving too late to the rescue—had muffled her voice in my memory.

As beginning meditators learn quickly, the mind is rarely at rest. Most of the time, as we go about our business, we have no idea what it's up to—chattering away, for example, about dinner plans and grocery logistics while simultaneously replaying some decades-old argument with Mom about nutrition. For years I'd been anxious about my sister. I'd known she was struggling and that her husband—a man with a truckload of his own baggage—was in no position to help her. I'd been twisting like a butterfly on my little pin of guilt because I couldn't come up with the right words or, like Alexander with his brutal solution to the Gordian Knot, the mad, bold stroke that would save her. As kids, we'd secretly chiseled through the wall between our closets and installed a six-inch length of galvanized pipe for late-night gossip, going so far as to seal around the edges with a silicone that never quite dried. I can't remember anything we talked about through that tube, but I remember the feeling. The intimacy and connection we didn't have words for yet, that bond that never lets go of you, no matter which way the plot points lead.

Like the grandmother it's supposed to be, ayahuasca has a way of seeing right through you. It takes you directly to the heart of your deeper preoccupations and poses tough questions: "What's so terrible that you just can't face it? What if your anguish is a waste of time because this unsolvable problem isn't yours to solve? What if, instead of guilt and shame, you wallowed in the love you feel for this person?" Friday night's journey had been murky and unpleasant, but the second night, the ayahuasca speaks clearly, pushing me gently to take action. I try whispering to Meri aloud:

I love you. I'm so sorry I couldn't help you. Maybe we should have staged an intervention. Gotten you off the meds. I just didn't know the right thing to do.

I'm crying now, telling myself (or being told by the ayahuasca) to relax more deeply into my sister's presence. Not to let guilt come between us.

I miss you, Meri. I love you!

The part of me that resists tears, always, begins to clamp down on my emotions and I talk back to it gently, reassuringly. *Go ahead and cry. There's nothing to be afraid of.* In a very real sense, for the first time since her death, Meri's there with me. I'm not psychotically detached from reality or anything but I am somehow able to allow myself to feel her presence.

It's a mysterious thing, being in the presence of someone you know so well. It's a polyphonic song composed of their energy and yours—the facial expressions, bodily rhythms, and all the unspoken understandings and assumptions that pass between you. And there's something else: a third voice or harmonic that's an emergent property of your coming together, a sound that exists nowhere else in the world. When you lose someone you love, that third voice might be what you miss the most.

It's okay. Stop it. There was nothing else you could have done. I feel her there, forgiving me. And I understand that what I really want isn't absolution. I want the courage to hear that third voice clearly. Purely. Not, as Hamlet puts it, "sicklied o'er with the pale cast of thought."

Everyone in my family is overly attached to reasoning and reasonableness. We think critically and we think (and talk) too much. Personally, I waste an enormous amount of time and energy dwelling on past and future possibilities. I second- and third-guess every decision before and after the fact. In young adulthood I almost went to China to teach English. Then I became curious about Taiwan's relative openness and worried about China's authoritarianism. Then I remembered my lifelong love of Japanese food and culture, and firmly decided to teach in Tokyo. On further research, Osaka started looking like the hipper sibling—Brooklyn to Tokyo's Manhattan—and I was filled with anxious doubt about the Tokyo teaching contract I'd signed. Ultimately I was so paralyzed by the proliferation of options and all the good reasons for choosing or rejecting any one of them, that I decided not to go anywhere at all.

Buddhism has this concept of mind-states or mental factors (*citta*). Western Buddhist teachers often talk about being in a certain "mind," like the mind (*citta*) of doubt about whether you look okay in this Hawaiian shirt, or the citta of really, really wanting to see the latest Martin Scorsese movie. I've come to think of the relentless critical/rational voice in my head as the "yes, but—" citta. At do-or-die moments (the heat of sexual passion, say, or the birth of my only child) this *citta* shows up like Socrates to ask, "Yes, but—where exactly is this headed?" Or "Yes, but—how do you know that what you're feeling right now is what you're *supposed* to be feeling?" In other words, it ruins everything.

Ayahuasca—more powerfully than other psychedelics I've taken (which is most of them)—uses every imaginable strategy (what Buddhism would call "skillful means") to deactivate the "yes, but—" mind. Sometimes it propagates overthinking to the point of absurdity or nauseating intensity, until it collapses upon itself. This can take the form of internal chatter or terrifying abstract visuals that force the rational mind to give up and allow a simpler, more emotionally direct *citta* to take over. This process seems to happen at light speed and—bypassing the rational mind as it does—is as hard to explain as a dream. But the effect is what I imagine people mean by *faith*. Exhausted with your babbling inner professor, you submit to what your body and your cellular memory know to be true. Knowledge gives way to wisdom.

As facilitated by ayahuasca, the process is always about remembering things you've forgotten or talked your way out of dealing with. It can mean accessing raw emotions like sorrow, loneliness, gratitude, or love, or getting a sudden flash of insight into a relationship or a decision you've been struggling with. After the initial turmoil and the act of reconnection, you're left with a deep sense of relief from a heavy burden you've been carrying—sometimes for many, many years without conscious awareness. It feels like medicine for the soul.

By three in the morning on that second night I am fully in this place. The suffocating tobacco incense, the foul-smelling water they periodically spray around the room (to induce nausea, perhaps), the drums and the singing and the sighs and cries of my fellow travelers, the candlelight, the black light posters, the pervasive reek of vomit—this entire yurt has become a living, breathing organism. Nothing is separate, estranged from me. And everything that happens here is exactly, only what needs to happen.

Talking to Meri, I understand in a flash just how pernicious words can be. I've been so wrapped up in Meri's life story that I've lost touch with the sister I know in my bones—the one I don't ever have to bury. It's a choice I've been making out of fear, to oversimplify her life so I don't have to feel her loss. And this ongoing act of cowardice is doing me harm. I'm left with two bits of insight that seem contradict one another: a distrust of words that borders on contempt and the idea that I have to write something for Meri. That words might help me find my way back to her.

There's an ancient meditation practice devoted to the cultivation of a *citta* called *mettā*. *Mettā* is often translated from Pali as "loving-kindness," a lofty, alienating compound that totally fails to capture the sense of *mettā* as I've come to understand it through reading, dharma talks, and practice. *Mettā* is a state of open acceptance—an orientation of friendly welcome toward the world and our own experience, no matter how unpleasant or undesirable it may seem. In traditional *mettā* practice you mentally recite a series of phrases—some variation on "May you be happy. May you be healthy. May you be safe. May you be free." You start by sending these wishes to yourself, sticking with the meditation for however long it takes to achieve a stable relationship of friendly welcome with yourself. It takes some of us much longer than others.

Over time you extend the practice outward: first to a beloved benefactor, then to a friend, then to a "neutral" acquaintance, then to someone you've been in conflict with, and ultimately to "all beings everywhere."

As the conversation with Meri fades out, but still under the ayahuasca's effects, I slip into a kind of spontaneous *mettā* meditation. Instead of the traditional formula, one simple, repeated phrase comes to my mind—an unconscious paraphrase of a line from Rumi's most famous poem: "Welcome, friend. Welcome, friend…" This mantra is an antidote to the "yes, but—" mind, a kind of spell of protection for whenever overthinking threatens to divide me from myself. Instead of twisting on the pin, I'll welcome in the guilt, the shame, the confusion, the sorrow.

All the things I'm afraid of, all the stories I cling to, even the critical mind itself: one by one, like the ocean I'll absorb them and transmute them, through acceptance, into love.

Yes, but—
Yes, but—
Yes. Yes. Yes.

The Explainers

For years, Meri and I had a running joke—an imitation of our mom telling us how to find something in the house that was always some variation on:

> *It's in the hall closet. To the left of the kitchen, down the stairs, to the right. The closet directly across from the bathroom. On the second shelf from the top, behind the duvet cover, in the lower left-hand corner of the shelf, catercorner from the Christmas boxes. If it were any more obvious, it would bite you!*

If she tried to explain the location of your nose, Mom's elaborate instructions would confuse you to the point of defeat.

I come from a family of explainers. Of rational categorizers and problem solvers hardwired to analyze, dissect, elucidate, and educate. Long before the term *mansplaining* was coined, Gotsplaining was a gender-neutral pastime for us: Want to make a Gots happy? Just stop and ask them for directions.

And like every talent, the explanatory gift is a double-edged sword.

My dad's dad, Joseph Gots, was a scientist. PhD educated on the GI bill in the golden years for American Jews after World

War II, he became a microbiologist and professor at the University of Pennsylvania medical school. After the double helix was discovered in 1953, he metamorphosed along with all the other microbiologists into a geneticist. I remember visiting his lab sometime in the '80s and seeing dot matrix printouts of nucleotide sequences. An early adopter (though late in life) of computers, Joe could beat the early chess programs on his Apple IIe. He also programmed from scratch what may have been the first ever computerized final exam at UPenn.

While many of his colleagues at Cold Spring Harbor Laboratory, like the corn geneticist Barbara McClintock, won Nobel Prizes, that particular honor passed him by. But he was a beloved professor. Over the course of his career, he won multiple teaching awards and was remembered fondly for stunts—like throwing a handful of worms onto his students during his yearly lecture on parasitology—that might get him fired today. When a blood clot obstructed the flow of oxygen to his brain and he collapsed during a lecture in the winter of 1993-94, it was his students who saved his life with a procedure that was new at the time, using an enzyme to break up a clot in a major artery in his brain.

Even before the stroke, I knew Joe as a man of few words. His prodigious explanatory gifts were relegated to the classroom and our yearly Passover seder—that very lengthy explanation of Jewish suffering, illustrated with food. His relative silence at home might have had something to do with the fact that his wife, my "Mom Mom" Selma, was one of the world's most enthusiastic talkers—an epicurean humanist and world traveler who had a strong opinion about everything. "Coffee?" she announced every single time I drank a cup of coffee in her presence, "I don't really see the point. To me, coffee is just a hot drink."

Mom Mom's point of view, which Meri and I inherited pretty much unadulterated, rested on two pillars: the importance of education and the idea that life is for enjoying through travel, good conversation with friends, and the beauty of art and nature. Money was useful—and to be used judiciously—as a means to these ends, but worthless in itself and contemptible as a life pursuit. The same went for fancy cars and clothes and meals and houses. When my dad left these values behind for the lifestyle of an '80s businessman—for the Mercedes, the walk-in closet full of seasonal suits, and the big, suburban house—I bet she never stopped explaining to him and my mother how unnecessary, how extravagant it all was. Depending on the audience, a charming, worldly explainer like Mom Mom can quickly turn into a nuisance.

Toward the end of Selma's life we talked for hours on the phone, mostly about what a disappointment the world had become for her. After her escape (with her mom) at five years old from anti-Semitic Poland, singing "God Bless America" all the way across the Atlantic to cheer up the rest of the huddled refugees, America's triumphant role in the defeat of Hitler, and the early promise of globalism, it seemed to her that everything had gone straight downhill. The nail in the coffin was 9/11; with the fall of the Twin Towers, the story arc of humanity had bent irrevocably toward tragedy.

In response to her deepening pessimism, I often ended up taking the position of Voltaire's *Candide* that the best any of us can do right now is to tend to our own garden—that we can cultivate small-scale beauty and goodness and hope that it spreads. A kind of "trickle-up" theory of human progress. Even then, I only half believed it. Like her, both Meri and I were big-picture thinkers, born to connect the dots on a larger scale (while missing many of the details). The explanatory gene pushed us to seek shared understanding and common humanity, and left us irritable and confused when things fell apart. Try as we might to fiddle while Rome burned, the song wouldn't be a happy one.

In my family, explainers live on a spectrum from big-picture to detail-oriented. My dad and I are more the former, as were

Mom Mom and Meri. We're extroverted and we want to tend to all the gardens at once. Pop Pop—with his charismatic lecturing on the one hand and his meticulous, incremental lab work on the other—was probably somewhere in the middle. My mom's detail-oriented, to an extraordinary degree. This was an endless source of frustration for her in our household; she could never understand why no one could remember how to do or where to find anything, in spite of her exhaustive instructions.

She's an enigma, my mom—a practical, rational explainer on the outside with depths of inner thought and feeling that, as far as I know, have never been shared with another living soul. She started out as an English major; I still have her copies of Henry James's *The Portrait of a Lady* and (my favorite as a middle schooler) *What Maisie Knew*, full of detail-oriented notes like "theme of snow—pp. 23, 47, 126, 139, 250." But after college, she decided that if English came so naturally to her, it couldn't be worth pursuing. I don't think it's going out on a limb to read this as a Catholic distrust of pleasure. Eve followed her bliss, after all, and look where that led her. So Mom applied to medical school and became an ophthalmologist.

For most of my childhood she was also an amateur scholar of the Holocaust, her bookshelves filled with massive tomes on Treblinka, Nazi doctors, and Goebbels's propaganda machine. Maybe this had something to do with being an Italian Catholic married to a Jew, a big problem for her parents at the time of the wedding (though, people being what they are, they soon decided that *this* particular Jew was the one exception to the rule). Whatever the case, unlike us more extroverted big-picture types, Mom has always pursued her intellectual passions without fanfare, zealously, and totally alone.

Even more than she'd once loved literature, Mom came to love ophthalmology and her patients. She practiced for a couple of years in Maryland while I was a toddler, and was by all accounts an excellent and beloved doctor. But when my father decided to start a business, she left medical practice for good to help him manage it. For a big-picture explainer like me or Meri—driven as we are to seek one grand purpose in life—this would have led to an identity crisis. Detail-oriented as she was, Mom just sharpened her tools and spent the next four decades tending the garden she'd landed in. Not without complaint...but if there was ever any second-guessing, we never heard it. Good Catholic that she was, maybe virtue lay in sacrifice.

One fallacy to which all explainers are especially vulnerable is the appeal to common sense. I might be considered the flaky one in my family but we're all quick to strike a levelheaded tone, a tone that implies that there's one, and only one simple, clear, correct way to understand whatever is currently under discussion. Philosopher of mind Daniel Dennett likes to poke fun at "the 'surely' operator," as in "*Surely* what we're *really* saying here is that..." The surely operator, one among many tools of explanatory rhetoric, coerces the listener into dismissing their doubts and agreeing with you. Since agreement is what explainers like Meri and I crave most of all, we're so often guilty of the appeal to common sense that we can end up falling under its spell, believing that the world divides neatly into the sensible folks and the crazies. *Surely* any belief that "there are two kinds of people..." is a dangerous threat to learning and growth. It's what psychologist Carol Dweck calls a "fixed" rather than a "growth" mindset, one that assumes that human qualities like intelligence and temperament are innate and unchangeable.

But most often in our family the explanatory tone is just that—a tone. A rhetorical flourish. We speak with bravado but are open to convincing alternatives. To the uninitiated, this can be overwhelming. Well into young adulthood I sat in furious silence or stammered in rage at the dinner table as my dad and my sister debated politics. I was appalled by their certainty, by all the definitive opinions they seemed to have on issues I saw as impossibly, irresolvably complex, like the Israeli-Palestinian conflict. More anxious and emotional than my sister, I was as confused by this kind of sparring as I was by boys' smack talk on the playground. Born into a family of rational explainers, I'd spend many years wandering before I found my own voice, and I remain wary to this day of bravado and certainty, especially in myself.

I understand now how this game of opinions is supposed to work. Opinions are like scientific hypotheses: you take a position, test it in conversation, await the responses, and gather the data. It's a brand of scientific skepticism; you maintain your position until it's disproved. When it works, it's a tough but spirited approach to learning. If everyone's playing in good faith, no one takes any position too seriously and debate leads, over time, to a shared body of knowledge.

But just like science, this form of rational argument is vulnerable to corruption. Sometimes we're seduced by our own rhetoric. Sometimes we're overpowered by the fluency or confidence of the person we're talking to. Sometimes we cling to an idea because the ego doesn't like to be proven wrong. In these ways and many more, a hypothesis can harden into a law without proper testing or peer review. This is how skepticism collapses into cynicism.

My dad's a doctor, too. He specialized in general surgery but decided after his hundredth hernia operation that sewing people together was just well-paid, highly specialized manual drudgery. In 1979 he and my mom branched out, coauthoring a book called *Caring for Your Unborn Child*. It was a big hit—the must-have book for pregnant moms that year. I once saw a video of them both on *The Phil Donahue Show* during the book tour; my younger, hipper parents calmly reassuring a mom-to-be in the studio audience that smoking a joint probably wouldn't harm her baby.

Next, swept up in the entrepreneurial fever of the early Reagan '80s, my big-picture adventurer of a dad decided to start a business: National Medical Advisory Service.

Over the years NMAS and its spin-off companies have helped doctors, landlords, pharmaceutical companies, Dow Chemical, and others argue in court that there was no clear causal link between something they had done or failed to do, and people's claims of having gotten sick or died because of it. In many of these cases my dad acted as an expert witness in defense of the alleged abusers. In a film like *Erin Brockovich*—or in any film about this kind of thing, actually—this puts him squarely on the side of capital-*E* Evil, with my mom back at the office in the role of lead henchwoman.

Reality is often more complicated than *Erin Brockovich*, but not always. I suspect that many people over the years did in fact get sick or die because of the actions of my parents' clients. Many of them couldn't afford expensive lawyers or expert witnesses like my father. These cases are fought in an adversarial system of tort law that isn't especially concerned with scientific truth or advancing human understanding. Self-interested parties and their lawyers do battle over huge cash payouts, sometimes in a just cause, sometimes not.

As an expert witness, my dad comes in as the voice of reason, a vetted explainer drawing on his scientific and medical understanding. He's there to say either "we know that this doesn't cause that" or "we don't have enough evidence to know that this causes that." Because you can't do clinical trials exposing random volunteers to cancers or mesothelioma or black lung, say, and because exposure to asbestos or creosote or whatever often happens in the course of people's daily lives—lives in which they're exposed to a thousand other potentially harmful things—scientific proof is often hard to come by, and reasonable doubt reasonably easy to cast.

At the same time, America's litigious culture encourages not only innocent victims but also unscrupulous lawyers and con artists to sue big companies for huge amounts of money in hopes of winning a big jackpot. Even when they settle (as they often do), the payouts can be enormous.

So from the scientific training of his youth—summers spent at Cold Spring Harbor playing in Barbara McClintock's cornfields and bumping elbows with James Watson, one of the discoverers of the double helix, my dad ends up on the witness stand, using his explanatory powers on behalf of big players in a morally ambiguous arena. I love and respect my dad, and know him to be a man of integrity. I believe that he does this work as honestly as anybody can. But all those years of labor on one side of an adversarial system are a recipe for cynicism.

Once, while I was in grad school in New Mexico, I went to a talk my dad gave about multiple chemical sensitivity syndrome. The subject of a litigation boom in the '90s, MCS is an umbrella diagnosis. It groups a wide range of people with a wide range of symptoms—everything from chronic headaches to respiratory failure—claiming that they suffer from a rare sensitivity to a wide range of chemicals.

In the talk, my dad explained to an audience (including a number of people on respirators who had come in protest) that MCS had little basis in scientific fact. Here, he said, you have all these people with different complaints in different environments being treated by a newly arisen cottage industry of doctors from special clinics featuring hydrotherapy and other scientifically untested practices—doctors who would diagnose one and all as suffering from MCS and testify accordingly in court, helping their patients win millions of dollars while guaranteeing themselves a steady stream of future MCS patients in the process.

My dad sounded pretty convincing. After all, even if some of these people were actually injured by chemicals, lumping them all together seemed like a stretch—except as a legal strategy. And with all of the variables, how could anyone prove (or even convincingly demonstrate) that many of these cases weren't psychosomatic? Western medicine has finally caught up to Chinese, Indian, and many other ancient medical systems in understanding that mental distress often manifests in debilitating physical symptoms. We now acknowledge that the mind has a deep and mysterious power over the body. Wasn't it possible that the cause of these patients' symptoms was fear—of chemicals, of the workplace, or even of life itself?

After the talk, I was approached by a woman whose close friend, she told me, had suffered for many years from a sensitivity to the smell of the copy machine while working at a company you've probably heard of. For decades, with the help of my father and experts like him, the company had denied any legal responsibility. Ultimately her friend had died of complications, penniless and embittered. Was I happy, she wondered, about the fact that this "blood money" had put me through college?

For thirty seconds, I was speechless. Finally, I managed to stammer out something like: "I'm so sorry about your friend. But I can't really speak for my father. Um, maybe you should talk to him? He's right there." The encounter shook me because it brought home the human costs of my father's work—work that had, indeed, paid for my expensive private college and was now paying for grad school. Suppose her friend *had* been killed by the copy machine? Did my father speak for objective medical truth—if such a thing even exists—or were there equally legitimate and convincing medical experts out there with opposing opinions, experts this woman's friend just couldn't find or afford? I had never really bothered to investigate. This was the soil I was planted in; what did that say about me?

So this was my sister's and my birthright and cultural framework. We were born into science and rational argument and we saw them used to ambiguous ends. Meri grew up trusting in it all more than I did. From an early age she was a zealous believer in science, democracy, and the fight for social justice. She believed in a rational, manageable, intelligible world. I grew up hungry to know the world and myself, but skeptical of the available instruments and the conclusions they led to.

Neither of us had the whole picture. Every story, every explanation, is a lie of convenience. And it carries within it the seeds of its own undoing.

As a child, Meri was that thing that should never be named: a person of great potential. The idea of potential generates fantasies and expectations that have little to do with the contours of real life. It forecloses on all possibilities that don't fit the model. I should know: I was a child of great potential, too. At forty-seven years old, I'm still getting over it.

I was only three and a half when Meri was born in the bicentennial year of 1976. On the advice of a book about how to keep your firstborn from having homicidal thoughts about the new baby, I guess, my parents tasked me with coming up with a middle name. From a much-loved collection of tiny Beatrix Potter books, I painstakingly selected the name "Jemima Puddle-Duck." It was immediately shot down. At preschool the next morning I discovered that a book had mysteriously appeared in my cubby. It was called *The Three Robbers*. The main character was a robber-thwarting little girl named Tiffany. At that age the world is full of signs, and "Tiffany" sounded nice, so I went home and announced that my sister would thenceforth be known as Meredith Tiffany Gots.

I was reportedly a good-natured, easygoing kid. I loved climbing things and making up jokes, like this one—from a kindergarten class trip to the Chesapeake Bay:

Me: What do you call a seagull that lives in the bay?
Teacher: What?
Me: A bagel!

From the beginning, Meri was the opposite: stubborn, willful, intense—prone to fits of bawling and rage, especially at

RONALD GOTS

Jason gestures toward the future. Meri gnaws on an eggbeater.

weddings and birthday parties. Meri, Meri, Quite Contrary. In retrospect, her hardheadedness protected her from childhood trauma I had no defenses against. But in adulthood it would end up doing her a great deal of harm.

My childhood dream was to become a singer in musicals. I have a recording of myself at five years old belting out "Tomorrow" from *Little Orphan Annie* and "Over the Rainbow" from *The Wizard of Oz*. As early as elementary school Meri decided she would one day be the president of the United States. Well into high school her bookshelves were filled with dog-eared tomes like Carl Sandburg's multivolume biography of Lincoln and *The Autobiography of Eleanor Roosevelt*.

One summer when she was twelve, Meri became a vegetarian. She might not have been the first twelve-year-old in history to swear off meat, but she was probably the first to do so instantly and permanently out of compassion for a lobster. Clowning around on vacation, my dad set our soon-to-be dinner scrabbling helplessly around on the linoleum kitchen floor. Maybe it was his casual disregard for its life—the sudden horror of seeing a death sentence used as a sight gag—but Meri turned red, burst into tears, and screamed that she was done, forever, with eating animals.

This was 1988, my parents were East Coast Republicans, and my mom, in charge of most of our meals, was Italian-American; the childhood dinner I remember best was called "meat rolls." So vegetarianism, in my parents' minds, meant slow starvation on flavorless tofu.

Mom—who has a very hard head of her own—shot back that this vegetarianism thing would happen over her dead body. There was no way, she insisted, to get enough protein to grow to adulthood without meat. There was no way she was going to cook two separate meals every night. She talked and talked. But after that night, Meri never ate meat again.

This is as good a place as any to flag the central cliché-because-it's-true of all memoirs: that memory is a slippery thing. Here's how my mother remembers the story:

The lobster patio meal was at home, spring of 1988. Each of us got a whole lobster on a plate. We were seated at a table on our deck and Meri sat so low on the patio chair that she was eye level with the lobster's head and antennae, looking directly into its face. The lobster scrambling on the floor was at a Nantucket restaurant, several years earlier.

Mom's the detail person. Her memory's much better than mine. But we're all unreliable narrators of our own lives.

In later years I'd dream of becoming an actor, a writer, a director, a professor, a '90s singer-songwriter, a rabbi, a psychologist, a cartoonist, and many other things when I grew up. I'm still dreaming.

By contrast, Meri wasn't one to let go of any dream lightly. But the cancer that nearly killed her at twelve and the experimental operation that saved her life ended her presidential aspirations. After that, she only ever wanted to be one thing: a doctor.

In June of 1988, soon after she gave up meat, Meri started having leg pains. Always one to hurtle headlong through life disregarding scrapes, bruises, and even minor broken bones, Meri ignored the pain at first. Eventually it got so intense that walking became a problem, and my parents took her in for an X-ray.

It turned out she had an osteosarcoma (a bone cancer) in the joint of her right leg. It was serious and growing fast. The typical course of treatment at the time included heavy chemotherapy, radiation, and—if both failed to eradicate the cancer—amputation.

Losing your leg in early adolescence is better than death, of course, but it's not great. Contrary and fierce as she was, Meri could handle the vomiting, the hair loss, even the stares of passing visitors as they walked by her on the cancer ward by cracking morbid jokes and cursing like a sailor. But neither she nor my parents was ready to accept the loss of her leg before she'd even had her first kiss.

In spite of all the treatment, though, the cancer was putting up a serious fight. After three specialists told them that amputation was the only option, my parents sought out a fourth opinion from an orthopedic surgeon in Washington, DC, named Martin Malawer. He had invented a new, experimental procedure that involved removing the knee joint, some of the tibia (shinbone) containing the tumor, and some of the femur (thighbone) above the knee. The knee joint was then replaced with a titanium hinge that was anchored with posts in the femur and the tibia but not cemented (to allow for growth and adjustment). This left Meri's kneecap, skin, and the majority of her leg intact. As she grew, they'd have to go in periodically, turn a bolt, and lengthen the hinge. After all the talk of amputation, it sounded like a miracle. The experiment worked: Meri got to keep her own leg and the cancer never came back.

But there was a catch. The average American walks three thousand to four thousand steps a day and each step Meri took put the stress of gravity on the prosthetic joint. Without cement, the prosthesis (which was eleven inches long) tended to wobble a bit, wearing away the bones into which its posts were anchored. When it got too loose—as Meri's did a couple of times between middle school and medical school—the prosthesis could be re-anchored. But there's only so much bone there to wear through.

The titanium joint saw her through the formative years of adolescence and college, but in the middle of her third year at USC medical school, Meri wore through the last of the femur and the leg had to be amputated just above the knee. She took it in stride, telling me excitedly over the phone about the $30,000 programmable "C-Leg" her insurance had reluctantly paid for, an engineering marvel that could auto-adjust to different gaits for skiing, hiking, and other adventures. Nothing like this had existed when she was in middle school, and Meri felt like she and her birth leg had had a good run.

Soon after the amputation, Meri started waking up at night in excruciating pain—white-hot shooting pain in the foot and lower leg that no longer existed. Persisting even in the daytime, the pain made it difficult to do her medical rotations, and only high-dose prescription opioids could keep it at bay. USC was not equipped or willing to adapt to Meri's changing situation, and between the effects of the medication and the difficulty of hiking all over the school's large campus—even on the marvel-ous C-Leg—Meri just couldn't keep up. She left USC and de-ferred indefinitely the dream of being a physician.

For the next decade she would follow her psychiatrist husband (who we'll call Theodore) from state to state, devoting herself mainly to her garden and her dog, Cali. Meri never did things by half measures, so this meant total head-heart devotion: informal studies in animal training, nutrition, and botany, and hours of loving attention each day to Cali and her plants. It was a dedicated, hardworking life. But from the standpoint of the child of great potential, and the girl who couldn't easily let go of dreams, there was a pervasive—and mostly unspoken—sense of failure. It manifested some nights in heavy drinking and fits of rage at her husband, who was busy struggling with many demons of his own, and as far as anyone in the family could tell just did his best to get on with his career.

More turning points in the arc of the story: Meri decided to get a master's in public health at the University of Virginia. She thought of becoming an "elder advocate," fighting on behalf of elderly people abused by their caregivers. It's a more common problem than you might think. And it seemed just the right fit for Meri, already a zealous protector of the defenseless long before she met that final lobster.

She got the degree, but couldn't hold down a job or a volunteer gig anywhere. I think it was the meds. Throughout those years (as I later learned) she was a severe insomniac, watching reality TV shows like *The Dog Whisperer* until three or four in the morning. She would also periodically slip into what I think of as "fugue states." More than once on a family vacation in those years, my parents and I saw her dissociate from her surroundings, repeating herself and not making much sense. We thought it might be meds on their own, or their interaction with alcohol. We talked to her about it a few times—sometimes gently, sometimes gravely—but never to much effect.

Between these unmanageable, unpredictable struggles and her total investment in garden and dog, Meri had habituated to a different reality than that of the working world. Every new avenue she explored, every attempt she made to network or market herself through social media, every one of the hundreds of job applications she put in over those years ultimately came to nothing, landing her back at home.

More narrative twists: a betrayal. A divorce. A reluctant move down to Florida to live ten minutes from our folks, at least until she got back on her one natural foot and a better-fitting prosthetic one. A change of meds—to methadone, which solved some problems and introduced others. And which ultimately may have killed her.

In Florida, the fugue states became rarer, but the insomnia continued. In the backyard of the little rented house where she lived alone with Cali, she planted a mango tree for my son, her nephew, and climbed up on a wobbly stepladder to put up a zip line for him. More than once she protected her neighbor from an abusive boyfriend—cursing him out, calling the police, and giving her neighbor a couch to sleep on. In my mind Meri is forever like one of those ants carrying ten times its body weight—always ascending or descending stairs and ladders, defiantly carrying some impossible burden. And sometimes—literally and figuratively—toppling under its weight.

Proud and independent-minded since toddlerhood, Meri hated her situation. Living so close to my parents, completely dependent on them for food and rent, and spending so much time with their friends (who knew and held opinions about her story) was a bitter pill to swallow. Naturally, she sometimes withdrew. After the first few months in Florida, it wasn't unusual for my parents to hear nothing from my sister for a couple of days. I talked to her once a week at most, feigning interest in the latest details about her battle with the aphids or Cali's slight hearing loss, and walking a tightrope between protecting her emotional security and trying to support her toward a more complete life.

Then, in March of 2015, Mom heard nothing from Meri for four days straight—not even a text. She stopped by her house and found Meri in bed, where she'd been lying, dead, for the past four days.

From the standpoint of a medical examiner, four days is a

very long time. An autopsy told us little—was this an accidental overdose? An interaction of the various meds she was on?

Or was it the first thing that came to my mind: a suicide?

But when I came from New York to help empty Meri's house,
I noticed that she hadn't left extra food or water out for Cali.
Even in the deepest, blackest pit of despair, I told myself, there's
no way she wouldn't have provided for her dog.

I was always a horrible science student, in part because I was
a horrible math student. I had no patience for checking my
arithmetic, understood very little of algebra and geometry, and
crashed definitively, once and for all, on the rocky shoals of
precalculus. I remember the sensation of thousands of bees in
my head as my seventh grade math teacher once again tried to
explain to me the unit circle in after-school tutoring. I remember all her calm, hopeful attempts: "It's really very simple…we
begin with…" and then, each time, the rising drone of the bees,
the vacant, anxious nodding of my head, and always, finally the
admission that I just didn't get it. I remember her barely contained rage at my stupidity or pigheaded refusal to understand.

In seventh grade biology I met a similar Waterloo while dis-
secting a fetal pig. Bored and confused, I put its tail on a tooth-
pick and walked around saying, "Hors d'oeuvres?" After class,
the very earnest, nature-loving teacher took me aside and explained through clenched teeth that I would be getting an F for
the assignment, and probably for the semester.

But growing up in a science-minded family, I did learn a
couple things. I learned to respect scientific curiosity and the
investigative spirit. I learned to think critically—to ask questions and seek out answers. I was taught to believe that reality
can be divided neatly between dubious, subjective claims and
objective truths.

For some questions, science has all the answers. If you want
to live on Mars or cure polio, put your money on science. For

others—like how to manage chronic pain or live a meaningful life—its answers are incomplete, inadequate, and sometimes
deadly. At a moment in American history when our scientific
understanding of the world is under attack from both sides—with
anti-vaxxers (mostly on the political left until COVID complicated the picture) and climate change deniers (mostly on the
right), when a president deliberately undermined people's ability
to sort fact from fiction with Twitter rants about "fake news" and
paid disinformation campaigns on social media, it feels strange,
even a little dangerous to plant a flag for a less rational approach
to life. But that's exactly what I feel compelled to do.

So much of our lived experience is subjective. The difficult
question of who I am and what I should do with my life's brief
span is not answerable by science. Likewise the question of how
to live with a terrible loss. These questions are answerable only
with words that the scientific skepticism I grew up with would
find embarrassingly vague and sentimental: heart, connection,
presence, love. And I've come to understand that we deny ourselves access to these quieter, more subtle ways of knowing at
our own peril.

More than one scientific thinker (science writer James Gleick,
for example, and primatologist Frans De Waal, an important re-
searcher into the evolutionary basis of cooperation) has told me
explicitly that scientific skepticism at its best is a form of humility—an acknowledgment of everything science doesn't yet (and
may never) know. To paraphrase Wittgenstein, whereof science
and fact cannot yet speak, there they should remain silent. But
in my childhood home the voice of science and reason, of order
and inflexible discipline spoke so loudly, so arrogantly, with so
little respect for the mysterious spaces between things, that my
coming-of-age became a kind of course correction toward chaos,
messiness, and organicity.

Meri pushed back in her own ways, demanding elbow room
to live her own life on her own terms. But when the organiz-

ing principle of that life broke down, Meri's story stopped making sense and—for so many reasons—she couldn't write a new one. And stuck as the rest of us Gotses were in our own rigid explanations of things, none of us could figure out exactly how to help her.

Raised in a family of explainers, I've become obsessed with all the ways our explanations fall short. Sometimes uncertainty is an answer in itself. Sometimes, when reason and science disappoint, you go looking for answers in unlikely places.

Had she lived, I don't know what language Meri might have found to talk about some of the things we were taught to dismiss. My life, especially in these past five years since her death, has been all about finding those words, writing my way into those invisible spaces.

Take spiritual growth, for example. There are so many good reasons to be skeptical of the current wellness industry—so many self-interested peddlers out there of mindfulness snake oil and Instagram enlightenment. There's undeniable truth in the argument—made most convincingly (and hilariously) perhaps by Ruth Whippman in her book *The Pursuit of Happiness*—that pop spirituality in America is often an extension of our cultural selfishness and insularity, and that it plays right into the hands of corporations eager to shift responsibility for our increasingly precarious professional lives onto "The Start-Up of You."

But Buddhist thought and meditation, ayahuasca, and art have led me on a path that started with personal pain and led naturally outward. They've helped me grieve the loss of my friend John and my sister, face the verbal, emotional, and sometimes physical violence of my childhood home, and turn from these long-nursed inner wounds outward toward love and care for my family and the rest of humanity. There's no objective way to prove all this, no science that can account for it, so I struggle every day to believe that it's as true as the double helix or evolution. But I think that's a battle worth fighting: the soul's demand for space in the quantified world.

Psychology prides itself on the ability to develop nuanced questionnaires (called "instruments") to learn something objectively true about happiness (for example) or personality. In these tests, you agree, disagree, or remain neutral about statements such as "I am more or less content with my life." However well designed they may be, all these studies are compromised by the fact that things like happiness and personality aren't definable or quantifiable.

In recent years, for example, laboratories around the world have been doing MRI studies of meditators' brains to determine whether or not (and in what dosage) meditation "works"— whether by thickening myelin in the cerebral cortex or by some other means. But neuroscientific models are a woefully inadequate proxy for the experience of meditation or the way it changes a person.

It's not that psychologists are stupid—some may be, but many are not and they understand these limitations. Still, they press on with the work of trying to make the subjective objective because that's the only way you can turn the ambiguous, nuanced, inexpressibly complex experience of the self into science. This work may yield some useful insights. It may provide valuable ammunition for policy makers trying to make space for wellness in school curriculums. But it also inevitably reinforces the belief that we can only truly know things from the outside in. And that anything we can't yet objectively prove, isn't real.

Art doesn't have to explain itself, at least not until the poor artist has to go on a podcast to promote her book or record or exhibition. There's something magical about the fact that since the very beginning of human culture, and long after the Age of Reason, we have always made these strange artifacts of our inner lives: songs, poems, paintings, stories, dance. There's something profoundly beautiful about our stubborn refusal to stop making these things in spite of their apparent uselessness and inexplicability. If the school board is threatening to cut your funding, there are ways to defend and explain the value of art, but first, art just *is*: one of us makes it and others come along and relate to it, subjectively and idiosyncratically. As such, art is honest because it speaks to what we all are on the inside: strange and inexplicable. Unreliable and beautiful.

Tracy Edwards, British captain of the first all-female team to race a yacht around the world back in 1989, told me that she's noticed a positive shift in the world since her racing days—that people are talking much more openly now about their inner lives than they did back then, trying to heal wounds her generation was taught to ignore. Having suffered stoically through a clinical depression at the height of her racing career, she's become a fierce advocate since for psychological openness and health.

I think whatever language we invent as we navigate the treacherous waters of learning to talk about ourselves—of learning to *be* ourselves with all of our nuanced differences and commonalities—it cannot be the language of explanation, or not entirely. It might have more in common with art. Explanation—so useful in the lab and the courtroom—is always, also, justification and defense. And like the ocean swallowing up expensive beachfront property, it takes its territory stealthily, inch by inch.

The human spirit shouldn't have to live in fear of dismissal, condemnation, or death by numbers. It should be celebrated as the wild space it is—loved for its changeability and what religious studies scholar (and my old friend) Jeffrey Israel, along with his mentor Martha Nussbaum, would call "human vulnerability." Finding this subjective language and learning to give it voice, I believe, is at least as important to our happiness and the survival of the species as is reasoning our way toward objective truth.

Blackberrying

Nobody in the lane, and nothing, nothing but blackberries,
Blackberries on either side, though on the right mainly,
A blackberry alley, going down in hooks, and a sea
Somewhere at the end of it, heaving.

      —Sylvia Plath, "Blackberrying"

The bushes are taller than we are. Toughened and gnarled by the salty winds that blow across the island, each clinging stubbornly to its little scrap of earth. The paths wind on forever, circuitous and unmarked. It's not important where they're headed. Where we're headed. Mom and Dad are with us and they must know the way back. Also, we feel safe here, as if the island itself were an unsmiling but benevolent relative, a great-aunt or something who, though we saw her once a year at most, would kill to protect us. Here and there the branches reach exploratory tendrils across the path, looking to rejoin their estranged cousins and return to thicket, but the island is well loved and these paths are quietly, sedulously pruned by the historical society—mostly older ladies who, like nuns betrothed to Jesus, have bound their lives to this place.

Meri and I aren't aware of any of that. All we know—the

single object of a mindfulness so intense any yogi might envy it—is the hunt for berries. Our restless eyes scan the base of the scrub bushes for thorny, hairy blackberry vines. Or higher up, the distinctive ovoid leaves of blueberry bushes, easily confused with waxy bayberry (good for candle making, but inedible) and tough to spot in this visually noisy place, even when the berries are abundant. Let's wander there again, Meri, directionless yet purposeful. Swallowed up by nature and safe.

There's a crucial turning point in the story of the Buddha's enlightenment. After studying under a series of ascetic yogis, mastering their disciplines of self-denial to the point where each announces he's got nothing left to teach the young adept, Siddhārtha realizes he still hasn't found what he's looking for. All this fasting and holding of yogic poses past the point of white-hot pain has taught him self-discipline, but it hasn't shown him a way out of human suffering. Suddenly he's transported in memory to a moment from his childhood: an experience of simple, perfect joy in the shade of a tree, watching his father at work in the fields. This, he decides, is the right *citta* for meditation toward spiritual freedom.

Berry picking in Nantucket is my *mettā citta*, my childhood memory of perfect welcome and connection—to myself, to the earth, and to my family. Wandering through the brambles, Meri and I are at the fulcrum of purpose and discovery, of making things happen and letting them happen. It's a balance I've been trying to regain, one way or another, ever since.

We hunt blueberries and blackberries, but blackberries are the real prize. They develop late in August and, thinner-skinned than blueberries, they only last a week or two at peak fatness and sweetness before withering or bursting or being eaten by robins, crows, or red-winged blackbirds. We're not always on vacation at the right moment to catch them. So when we are, we're on a mission.

When we find a vine, we both scramble to get to it, shoving and jostling each other for the best berries, arguing about whose picks are the biggest and juiciest. Tempting as it is to try to strip-mine them all at once, you have to be gentle removing each berry from the vine. They're delicate. But no matter how careful we are, our fingers always end up ink-stained with that rare, rich purple. It's vivid and holy, like *tekhelet*, the turquoise ink of a mollusk ancient Jews used to dye the fringes of their holy garments, its source lost to history for fourteen hundred years, and the snail itself never rediscovered.

If we're lucky, we end up with bucketsful of berries. From the blueberries, Dad will make muffins or pancakes for the next few days. The blackberries are too precious to wait for. On the way home, even before they're washed, we'll steal a few, scarfing them down on the sly (because we know it's unsanitary and selfish).

It's a feeling of absolute power, this berry hunting. Although we're kids and dependent in so many other areas of our lives, we're experts at this. We're fully capable of coming home victorious, having provided—if not sustenance, exactly—a substantial treat for the whole family. The roles are reversed; we're the ones feeding Mom and Dad, instead of the other way around.

On this island, so many tables are turned. The stress of our Bethesda homelife dissolves into an ache in memory—*as thin of substance as the air*—and we are free. Though they often bring some work with them, vacation frees Mom and Dad, too, from all that rushing around to the office and the extracurricular activities of their busy, suburban kids. Mom isn't tasked with keeping us civilized and punctual while running a company in Dad's frequent absence as he travels cross-country on business trips. On the island, Meri and I don't live in terror of getting any grade below an A. We get all the sleep we could wish for.

Each day is an unpredictable adventure. There's just so much slack in the system.

In ordinary life, we struggle for control of the narrative. We whine and argue and stifle and clutch at any scrap of sense or selfhood that promises even momentary relief. Here, there's no linear narrative at all. The story spreads out in every direction.

If we feel like it, we might go crabbing. Dad will take the rusty, clattering old crab trap down from the attic. Ingenious device! A pyramidal cage that blossoms into a flat, star-shaped surface then suddenly, at the flick of a wrist, snaps back into shape. Crabs are not the brightest, and with the help of this marvelous invention they're very easy to trap. The creeks run under the road, concealed by tall, salt meadow cordgrass. We park a little ways back and walk to the culvert.

If you watch the water long and carefully enough, opening the hand of thought, the murkiness becomes legible. Here and there you might see a crab clinging to a bridge post. Another one furtively exploring the creek floor. Overcast days are the best.

The center of the trap is a square, and onto its grid you tie a sturdy piece of fish with kitchen twine. A chunk of some deep-sea dweller like halibut or swordfish, dislocated in these brackish shallows. You lower the trap gently into the water so as not to startle the crabs. You feel it hit the silt with a soft thud, then you let its sides drift open to the bottom. The bit of fish sits there in the middle, its thinner tissues swaying like ribbons in the current. The visuals are enticing, but maybe just the smell is enough. Soon a crab crawls cautiously out onto the grid, too dim to notice that something's awry—that the ground it walks on is never quite this shiny or orderly. You wait for two or three to gather, then SNAP! Up and into the bucket. Grab them from behind or else you get pinched.

In Douglas Adams's *The Hitchhiker's Guide to the Galaxy*, the towel is the most useful and versatile object in the universe. On the island, it's the bucket. We use buckets for everything. Crabs, mussels, berries. Meri and I build a pulley-and-bucket mechanism on our bunk bed to hoist up snacks and secret messages.

Unlike blackberrying, crabbing needs a lot of scaffolding from Dad. He understands the subtleties of timing better than we do. He has the patience not to snap the trap shut at the first sign of a crab. Some are tiny and aren't worth keeping, but Meri and I can't always tell the difference. Here, we work together. We hunt in a pack. And if the catch goes well we'll have something truly miraculous: a whole dinner we didn't have to buy in a restaurant or a grocery store.

Mom mostly waits these trips out at home. Not her scene, crouching on a bridge in the summer sun, beset by flies and gnats. She never could stand camping. Mom is what my occupational therapist friend Ed would call a bit *sensory*—hypersensitive to touch. In the comfort of the living room, she patiently assembles a two-thousand-piece puzzle on the coffee table, a bag of pretzels beside her and a glass of iced tea. Or else she sits on the patio in a chaise longue, reading a biography or a mystery. Like her, I'll never need much more than a good book to be happy.

The thing about the island is this: everyone's free to be themselves, so nobody's Self gets too much in the way. Here we're effortlessly whole, in spite of our radical differences.

Back home, nothing is effortless. For Mom, there's the unrelenting pressure she puts on herself to make sure we turn out okay. That we don't put our elbows on the table ("Mabel!") or slurp our milk. That we are utterly silent in church. That our schoolwork is neat and our clothing and hair presentable. It's not that these expectations are inherently outrageous, but the anxiety and perfectionism behind them bind our daily lives impossibly tight. And this has unintended consequences.

Because life is messy, and because Mom is so often left in charge, alone with the terrifying possibility that we are both, in fact, hopeless and it's all her fault, she is often possessed by terrifying fits of rage. Triggered by a shirt hung wrong in the closet or one of us running late for school she turns into one of those furies that fly screeching through Dante's Wood of Suicides: destructive and inconsolable. I learn to go quiet. To make myself small. To wait for the first sign of calm and then try to crack a joke.

And where appeasement doesn't work, I learn to armor myself with words, strategic intransigence, little acts of rebellion. Tasked with doing the dishes, I do them so slowly and incompetently that Mom has to shove me aside and take over. I refuse to learn even the most basic principles of organizing my time or my binder, so that well into high school important things get crumpled, forgotten, or lost.

Meri fights back more directly, more bravely, so she wins herself more territory. She learns quickly to keep her own counsel, gains sovereignty but also a deep distrust, a difficulty letting other people in.

On Nantucket, though, we're more open. We stretch out like Walt Whitman's narrator in *Leaves of Grass*: *"I loafe and invite my soul/I lean and loafe at my ease...observing a spear of summer grass."* Laziness here isn't the enemy of productivity. Activity and rest flow naturally, one into the other, and no one bothers about where one ends and the other begins.

Even without grades to worry about, we are industrious, Meri and I. We turn the attic into a clubhouse, decorating it with watercolors of birds. We brave the fierce and murky waters of Madaket Beach, learning to dive directly into the waves or ride them to the top, twisting our backs at just the right moment to avoid a dizzying slap in the face. We hunt, sometimes for five hours straight, for mussels and hermit crabs on Jetties Beach. In my dad's hands, the mussels become bouillabaisse and in ours the hermit crabs turn into temporary pets. One time we find a conch shell whose hermit crab occupant, given so much space, so much freedom to stretch out and be itself, has grown to the size of a small lobster.

* * *

Some summers we'd bring friends or extended family along, and later on boyfriends and girlfriends, sharing with the people we loved this alternate reality where everyone was welcome. We'd drive into town and giggle as the cobblestones rattled our butts and our teeth, kid-splaining to every newcomer that the smooth, round stones had once been ballast in the whaling ships.

This was once a whaling island, the setting of *Moby Dick*. Once upon a time in this place grim-faced men left their gray-shingled houses, setting off for possible death in search of spermaceti and ambergris. They passed the long days between hunts making scrimshaw on whale bones and teeth. Captains' wives paced on the widow's walks on top of their houses, scanning the indifferent ocean with a telescope for some sign of their husbands' return, the way we scan the horizons of our lives, finding faith or despair at the point where our vision starts to falter.

This was a place of industry, especially for the whalers who clambered off ships into the glorified dinghies from which they tossed the harpoons. And for the women at home, spinning wool and making candles and just trying to keep everyone alive through the long winters. Famine, sickness, and death thrived in this place like blackberries. A raw scramble for survival and wealth before the systems had settled into their present, all-encompassing form. Before the walls of the crab trap were visible.

On TV in our summerhouse as the afternoon waned, Robin Leach would explain in his posh, nasal accent that this island was now a "playground of the rich and famous." He'd take us on an aerial tour of Ralph Lauren's massive compound and lavish fulsome praise on Nantucket's coveted luxuries, including $800 "lighthouse baskets" adorned with scrimshaw. We would learn that in the semiotics of class, Nantucket meant money. Old, white Protestant money, for the most part. Starbucks was once a whaling family. So were Folger and Macy. They and their forbears had murdered and exiled the Wampanoag people who lived here first. Nowadays people flew to the island in their private jets. Docked their yachts in town. Dined in exclusive restaurants. Opted first for desirable homes in 'Sconset, the island's oldest village, and if that wasn't possible, scooped up some acreage and built their own. Whenever I think about Nantucket now it passes first through this lens of privilege. It's lost its innocence. But for Meri and me in childhood it might as well have been a cabin in the woods. It might have been a raft on the Mississippi River.

What lives there in memory is the feeling of bobbing like a cork on the ocean, just past the breaking waves. What lives there are the painted turtles in the hidden pond we once discovered, hundreds of them poking their heads up to snap at the bread we threw while dragonflies hovered like sentries nearby. What lives there is Dad chopping potatoes for clam chowder, happy and expansive on the differences between quahogs and steamers and littlenecks.

What lives there is the continuity of this place over years and years of summers, in spite of all the changes in our lives… a day on the beach just before I graduated college: me, a girl I loved at the time, and Meri, all three of us on LSD, totally absorbed in each pebble and seashell and understanding Huxley's vision of "infinity in a flower." The seagulls—so rude and assertive—still cawing in my memory for potato chips. The line at the ice cream shop and the smell of fresh-baked waffle cones. The cheeky wooden sign with the direction and distance from Main Street to Pitcairn and Moscow and Bombay and Rome. Mom in her Ray-Ban aviators on the grass mat under the beach umbrella, Dad in a floppy bucket hat reading Clive Cussler or Dick Francis, Meri and I taking turns burying each other in the sand and fighting about the sand in our eyes or our mouths or our hair. Mom knowing the sand would end up all over the house yet miraculously, somehow letting it go.

What lives there is the possibility of home. For American grown-ups, vacation's a fantasyland—something frivolous you do to escape your real life. But were we ever more real, more alive, or more whole than we were for those two weeks a year?

Wrong Discipline

In a dharma talk I went to in Brooklyn, Lama Rod Owens, a Buddhist teacher and coauthor of the book *Radical Dharma: Talking Race, Love, and Liberation*, talked about his walk from the subway to the meditation center where the event was taking place. As a big, Black man, he said, he was conscious in the streets of this gentrified neighborhood of the reactions of the white people he passed. In some of their faces and bodies he sensed fear or intimidation, and this unspoken interaction caused him pain. He wasn't a mind reader, he said. It wasn't relevant what exactly each person was thinking—what mattered was that in America just his physical presence in that neighborhood meant something.

"Everything has to be mourned," he said. "Even that three-block walk from the subway. Everything has to be mourned."

Those words have stayed with me since.

In his 2013 book *The Trauma of Everyday Life*, Buddhist psychiatrist Mark Epstein makes a related point:

Some traumas—loss, death, accidents, disease, and abuse—are explicit; others—like the emotional deprivation of an unloved child—are more subtle; and some, like my own feelings of estrangement, seem to come from nowhere.

To my grandparents' generation, the idea of "everyday trauma" would sound ridiculous—yet another proof of the preciousness and oversensitivity of "these kids today." Given some of the hardships they and their parents had to endure—poverty, immigration to a strange, new country, anti-Semitism on Dad's side and anti-Italian bigotry on Mom's—it's easy to understand how a survivalist mentality took hold of them and to some extent was passed on to their children. In the midst of trauma and existential threat, there isn't much time to process your feelings. But while survivalism is sometimes expedient, inevitable even, it's also a form of internalized violence—a brutality to the self. It's a recipe for survival, but not necessarily for health and happiness.

America's can-do, forward-thinking, sometimes aggressively optimistic culture is itself a form of survivalism learned through historical trauma. The idea that "everything has to be mourned" demands instead that we slow down long enough to process the pain of living. It's another way of expressing the core idea of Buddhism as captured in the Four Noble Truths, which, like the history of slavery and systemic racism, can be very tough for some Americans to swallow.

1) At the core of our lives, there's a constant, ambient hum of suffering that comes from dissatisfaction. The Pali word for this, *dukkha*, is a compound that literally means "bad fit." Most of the time, our view of the world, or what we expect from the world, poorly fits the world as it is.

2) The cause of that dissatisfaction is the fact that everything is impermanent, but we tend to act as if it isn't. We live our lives grasping on to things, experiences, and people for dear life or else trying to escape them. While running around on our various desire-driven missions, we miss many things worth noticing, including the moment-to-moment experience of our own lives. Even when we're happy, it's often part

of this cycle of grasping and avoidance that keeps bringing us back to grief.

3) It doesn't have to be like this. It's possible to escape this *dukkha*.

4) The way out of *dukkha* is to change our relationship with the world and ourselves.

The fourth truth, unpacked, becomes the Buddha's Eightfold Path to freedom through understanding these teachings, living ethically, and training the mind and heart through meditation to stop reacting unconsciously, thereby clearing our perspective to see reality as it is: impermanent and interconnected.

But this shift in perspective doesn't happen in an instant. Everything has to be mourned. Every bit of *dukkha*—and *trauma* is as good a word as any for *dukkha*'s lingering effects on us— lives on in the mind, heart, and body until/unless it can be seen, transformed, and released. This goes for historical trauma, too—like the anxieties and fears that linger on in families as the legacy of survivalism.

Unprocessed traumas big and little interrupt the flow of our lives, causing us to overreact to present experience based on the past. We fight or flee or cling. An unloved child becomes an adult who demands an all-encompassing love no partner can possibly give. An abused child grows up to abuse her own children, set off by the slightest sign of laziness or disrespect…the same fears that triggered her parent.

Present-day trauma researchers and therapists including Bessel van der Kolk and Resmaa Menakem think of *trauma* as a fear-based reaction to experience that lives on in the body, brain, and mind, and whose effects depend not only on the intensity and frequency of the experience but also on the sensitivity of the individual. In his book *My Grandmother's Hands: Racialized*

Trauma and the Pathway to Mending Our Hearts and Bodies, Menakem writes:

> *We typically think of trauma as the result of a specific and deeply
> painful event, such as a serious accident, an attack, or the news of
> someone's death. That may be the case sometimes, but trauma can
> also be the body's response to a long sequence of smaller wounds.
> It can be a response to anything that it experiences as too much,
> too soon, or too fast... Two bodies may respond very differently to
> the same experience. If you and a friend are at a Fourth of July
> celebration and a firecracker explodes at your feet, your body may
> forget about the incident within minutes, while your friend may
> go on to be terrified by loud, sudden noises for years afterward.
> When two siblings suffer the same childhood abuse, one may heal
> fully during adolescence, while the other may get stuck and live
> with painful trauma for decades.*

I use the lens of trauma in this book to try and understand
parts of my sister's story and parts of my own. For some, it may
seem an unlikely approach: after all, Meri and I were raised with
significant financial and social privilege in one of the wealthi-
est countries in the world. We never experienced the horrors
of war, homelessness, or (as far as I know) sexual abuse. We
were never targets of racism or xenophobia. We grew up in a
two-parent household untouched by incarceration or psychiatric illness destabilizing enough to get anyone hospitalized. In a
spreadsheet of human suffering, we might occupy the "low to
very moderate" column.

In applying the concept of trauma to our lives, I don't want to
minimize the atrocities others have experienced; I want to argue
that for most people life is characterized by *dukkha*—by what
Hamlet calls the "thousand natural shocks that flesh is heir to,"
and that so much of our experience while being alive depends
on how we respond to those shocks, beginning with whether

we're willing to acknowledge them at all. Accepting trauma as a universal human condition is a stance of compassion not only toward myself and my sister, but toward everyone.

While the metaphysics of karma and enlightenment may be even harder than the Four Noble Truths for modern minds to accept, many of the Buddha's teachings are surprisingly pragmatic insights into human psychology. Whether or not we've been taught to admit it, we all suffer. Much of that suffering is our own doing. Sometimes we can change the world, but not always: science can't yet end old age, sickness, or death (and the possibility of eventually doing so introduces a Pandora's box full of potential new forms of *dukkha*). Still, we always have the power to change how we relate to the world and ourselves.

I was raised to think of this possibility—the hope of breaking old patterns through practice—in terms of *discipline*, a concept that's central to Buddhism. Western teachers of Buddhism, though, often shy away from the word—and even the concept— for reasons that deserve some attention.

Modern American Buddhism first reached these shores in the late '60s and early '70s, part of the youth rebellion against the conservative family values of the 1950s. The teachers who first brought various Buddhist traditions to the US, like Chögyam Trungpa (Tibetan), Shunryū Suzuki (Zen), Joseph Goldstein, Jack Kornfield, and Sharon Salzberg (Theravadan Vipassana), and Thich Nhat Hanh (Vietnamese Thiên) found their dharma talks and meditation sessions overrun with young people seeking liberation, not only from *dukkha* but from everything. To them, *discipline* may have conjured up the sound of the punitive crack of Dad's belt on their behinds. It may have evoked the training of soldiers in the Vietnam War they were trying to end through protest. But as so often happens in revolutions, some babies got thrown out with the bathwater. Everything is vulnerable to corruption. If discipline in that time had devolved into meaningless ritual, then it was in need of reform, not eradication.

Here, Buddhist scripture has valuable guidance to offer. The Eightfold Path is a flexible system. It contains a set of tools you can apply to the problem of living. The Buddha explicitly encourages his disciples to use what seems useful, analyze the results, and adjust as needed. This is self-discipline based on self-knowledge and trust, not blind obedience to a punishing authority.

All living things seek homeostasis. I always imagined homeostasis as a state of easy, natural balance and equilibrium—systems humming along and maintaining themselves effortlessly. But as the neuroscientist Antonio Damasio explains in *The Strange Order of Things*, maintaining homeostasis demands constant, vigilant effort against entropy and decay. Resisting the natural tendency toward chaos takes a lot of energy. So living systems have evolved various strategies for finding and acquiring that energy. For bacteria, this may mean absorbing nutrients through the cell wall and even—as Damasio points out—cooperating with other bacteria to more efficiently capture a nearby food source. He sees in the "social" behavior of single-celled organisms and of insects like bees and ants a kind of prototype for human civilization—spontaneously arising structures with the same fundamental goal: organization toward homeostasis.

This organization is a form of discipline. We can't ask ants and bees about their feelings. Until some enterprising scientist designs a clever experiment we'll tend to assume they're content with their lives of nonstop productivity. But we know that humans and other complex beings have needs beyond survival and energy storage. So our efforts toward survival-based homeostasis can bring in all kinds of problems along with their benefits.

For example, agriculture gave us longer lives and a population boom, but it also led to serfdom, slavery, and (through industrialization) to our current climate crisis. Nationalization is an effective way of organizing group identity and mobilizing a people, but it also seems to produce war and dictators, both of which produce a lot of misery. In an individual life the homeostatic drive aims at security for yourself and your family. But fear can easily send it into overdrive, producing greed, hatred, violence, and self-harm.

What was it like to be our parents when Meri and I were kids? Why did the discipline we learned from them come with so little compassion, so little of anything we could recognize as love? I can only patch bits and pieces together from my memories of what happened, how it felt at the time, and what they've told me since.

Lives are made of events, of context, of feelings, of perspective—a million complex factors, always in flux. And we never have access to all of it at once. A story is a paved road through this wilderness. A convenient fiction. Meri was always quick with a story. She judged swiftly and decisively, and rarely seemed troubled by extenuating circumstances. I, on the other hand, can get so lost in trying to understand the whole picture that I no longer know what to feel or believe.

Still, I ought to start with some context.

Mom's dad, my grandpa Jim Manis, was the American-born son of immigrants from Messina, Italy. Just after the Great Depression, with his father out of work, his income as an "aeroplane mechanic" (as recorded in the 1940 census) went a long way toward supporting his parents and his brother, Philip. He went on to become a self-taught aeronautical engineer, designing one of the first-ever drone helicopters for the US Navy in the 1970s. Even by the 1940s he was such an expert aeronaut that the navy kept him in the US to train fighter pilots, dashing his dreams of flying missions into enemy territory, where he might have gotten himself killed when my mom was still a baby and before her three sisters were born.

Jim died when I was eleven or twelve. I remember him as robust and barrel-chested (we share the same stocky, medium build), sitting in his tan armchair, laughing with a glass of Scotch in his hand. He called me "kiddo" and taught me how to cook home fries—soft in the middle, extra crispy on the outside. I remember his wife, my grandma Beatrice, as the embodiment of what I now know as *mettā*—all warmth and welcome and deep, deep hugs—a sun that seemed to shine only for me.

But she and Jim had four children, and when Mom was a kid, life wasn't easy. I once asked her why she always got me monogrammed things at Christmas—like stationery and pens. To me, monograms were incredibly stuffy and uncool. "When we were kids," she said, "everything was a hand-me-down. Nothing was ever new. Nothing ever fit. And I hated that. I wanted you and Meri to have things that were all your own."

Italian-American families in those days didn't raise their children by committee. When something was demanded or forbidden, there were no lengthy conversations or explanations. None of the endless negotiations we now have with my son, who at twelve has developed the verbal wizardry of a star trial attorney. Back in the day, apparently, my marshmallow of a grandma and my jolly old grandpa were total hard-asses. The rules in the Manis house were many and strict. Complete obedience was expected. And infractions were met with the crack of Jim's belt.

Old-school, authoritarian parenting is expedient. It was likely a survivalist tactic developed in response to the hard and dangerous lives our ancestors lived, and it's passed down through the generations as emotional and physical trauma. The body remembers. The trouble with this kind of discipline is that it's extrinsic—enforced from the outside through fear of the parent. When the child grows up and these habits are internalized, the self-discipline that results is reflexive rather than reflective, good enough for survival and material competition, but ill-suited to the project of building a happy, self-directed life.

For most of our childhood, maybe all of it, my mom was not happy. Her strict upbringing, coupled with her temperament, had turned her into a relentless perfectionist. On the inside, she suffered from levels of anxiety that today would be considered clinical, but the perfectionism meant that she confided in no one other than my dad, who most of the time, in one way or another, was away on business.

That left Mom in charge of us. Without much outside support or self-compassion to rely on, she tried to discipline us more or less as her parents had disciplined her, minus the belt. But the culture had changed. We were the *Mister Rogers* generation, taught in school and by the media that we were special, that our feelings mattered, and that we could be whoever we wanted to be. Authoritarian, perfectionist parenting and 1980s child-centered America were a combustible mix, and for Mom's well-being (and ours), a recipe for disaster.

It gets worse. Over the years, there were lawsuits from my parents' business partners. A double-mortgage on our house at a time when the company was on the brink of collapse. And then my sister's cancer. Through all of this, trained not to show vulnerability to her children, Mom tried to maintain an illusion of normalcy, with the result that our lives became anything but normal.

Just as all suffering is on the continuum of trauma, screaming is on the continuum of violence. There was a lot of screaming. And there was relentless, withering emotional cruelty and emotional neglect.

On the plus side, Meri and I both learned to work hard and to take our work seriously—not to procrastinate, make half-hearted efforts, or blame other people for results that were within our control. We learned to set high expectations for ourselves. These are habits that served us both well in so many areas of our lives. But the discipline came at a cost. We both absorbed Mom's anger and her hypercritical inner voice. We both struggled—as I still struggle—to trust other people and to treat ourselves with kindness rather than contempt.

Meri, more stubborn and willful than I was, tended to externalize everything. When the early traumas did, inevitably, resurface, she directed them outward toward her husband, back at my parents, and toward strangers in the form of harsh opinions and bitter attacks. In me, most of the anger and shame turned inward. I became insecure and self-loathing. And my attempts at self-discipline often elided into self-harm.

In various scriptures and retellings, the story of the Buddha always goes something like this. Named Siddhārtha Gautama, he is the privileged, cosseted son of a king or regional nobleman. In young adulthood he goes out for a carriage ride and sees, for the first time, three terrible things: old age, sickness, and death. Learning from his chaperone that these states of being are universal and inescapable, he's devastated. He resolves to leave home (some versions omit the part about abandoning his wife and child to do so, some don't) and becomes a wandering ascetic in search of freedom from all this suffering. For a few years he trains under a series of well-respected yogis, mastering their systems one by one.

Most of these teachers err on the side of fanaticism, or what I think of as "tyrannical self-control"—fasting for days or freezing alone in a cave or otherwise tormenting themselves in hopes of extinguishing desire and attachment. After the childhood memory of simple joy, Siddhārtha decides this is all a bit much—that a healthy body and mental clarity are necessary to the work of spiritual growth. He resolves to eat. Not too much, nothing too fancy, but regularly and enough. He decides to approach the whole project of spiritual growth with self-compassion and experimental curiosity rather than rigid perfectionism. He sits down under a tree, recalls that joyful childhood memory—that *mettā citta*—and gets to work.

This approach to self-discipline, called *majjhimāpaṭipadā* in Pali, is usually translated into English as "the middle way." Like Damasio's entropy, it relies on effort and energy, but it also strives for balance. It's compared in the scriptures to the proper tuning of a guitar—too loose and it's out of tune, too tight and the string may snap. It's a long game: self-discipline, the healing of trauma, and spiritual growth, one best approached with self-love. Fanaticism is a brutal, unsustainable shortcut. In its impatience to solve one problem, it produces a hundred more.

I have this much in common with the Buddha: the site of my early, most wrongheaded experiments in self-discipline was always the body. For the most part, these experiments were attempts to practice the discipline I'd been taught, or reactions to the trauma it caused in me.

One day in the fall of ninth grade I sat in the lounge of the student snack bar at St. Albans—the ivy-covered all-boys' private school I attended from seventh to twelfth grade—on a break before a French test I hadn't studied for and was certain to fail. Unbeknownst to my parents, I was failing all my classes that semester and had sunk to "into a deep depression—a confusing cluster of feelings I didn't have language for.

I was complaining to a classmate, trying to convince him to punch my hand and break my wrist so I wouldn't have to take the test. He was about to do it—or try to do it—but I chickened out at the last minute. He made some offhand crack about how fat I was getting (from all the Twix bars I'd been self-medicating with lately), and headed off to class.

For Mom in those days, obesity was a sign of moral corruption. That day in Sam's Bar, I was wearing the "husky" pants she'd bought me on a burning-shame-filled trip to Montgomery Mall, my belly spilling over the waistband. I was accustomed by then to tuning the worst of her out, but my classmate's comment was the last straw. I quit the Twix, learned how to make myself vomit after meals, and started doing three hundred sit-ups a night. In the midst of that depression, struggling to regain some form of control, I adopted a Spartan regimen of self-denial and self-mortification.

Nothing changed at school. I failed most of my classes that quarter. As far as I knew, nothing like this had happened in our family, ever, and I couldn't even begin to imagine the horrors that would ensue when my parents found out. So I checked the mailbox obsessively every day after school, intercepted my report card when it came, and hid it in my sock drawer under the Halloween candy (untouched since that day in the school snack bar). I convinced my folks that there was an administrative delay—some kind of problem with the school's printer.

So on top of being a failure and a report card thief, I was now also a liar. The chaos of my terror-ridden mind had to be brought to order somehow. So I developed another physical discipline: cutting my forearm with a pocketknife every night in the bathtub. I can still see some of the fine white scars that used to spell out the word *Watchmen*—the title of the gritty, brilliant Alan Moore comic everyone was reading that winter.

On a cold New York winter in 1994, the year I graduated college, I decided one morning that for the foreseeable future I would eat only bagels. Whole poppy or sesame seed bagels. No cream cheese or butter. One in the morning on the way to the PATH train to commute to my barista job at the now-long-defunct Coyote Coffee Company in the Prudential Building in Newark, New Jersey, and one bagel on the way back home at night. Sometimes, if I was truly starving, two.

This wasn't about diet or money. New York was cheaper in the '90s and I earned enough to eat decent meals and pay my rent. The bagel regimen was an ascetic practice—a reflexive act of self-discipline. I was twenty-one years old, fresh off a terrible breakup, in my worst depression since ninth grade, and expected to start making a living. Cast out—as I felt—into the cold, pre-dawn New York winter by my 5 a.m. alarm clock, I reverted to the discipline I'd learned as a kid: if something is hard, make yourself harder by making everything harder on yourself.

Self-discipline meant controlling what I could—food, my body—through the simple act of refusal. It turned my anger at the situation inward, punishing me for the confusion and discomfort of this new working life. It was both a hunger strike and a brutal attempt to toughen myself up for adulthood. Trapped in a tight space, I tightened it further, rather than looking for a smarter way through.

These reflexive attempts at self-discipline were trauma-driven. They served no purpose, offered me no benefits in the search for homeostasis. What felt like self-control was usually, in fact, self-harm. In the end, everything has to be mourned. If you heap more suffering and trauma on top of what life gives you, you're just piling up a massive debt you owe to yourself.

Meri didn't survive our childhood unscathed, but her anger and her stubbornness may have shielded her from the worst of it. I, on the other hand, took all these lessons to heart. I saw harsh, extrinsic discipline as an essential survival skill, one I might be too sensitive or weak by nature ever to possess. While Meri could shrug it off and carve her own path, for me it became larger than life, something I either had to rebel against or force down my own throat. So my young adulthood was a roller coaster of extremes, a series of prison breaks and attempts to crawl back inside, where at least the meals were regular.

It's a Friday as I write this, and my twelve-year-old son has been struggling all week with insomnia so terrible that it's kept him out of school. And my self-discipline as a writer has come into harsh conflict with my responsibility to be a loving parent.

At 2:30 this morning, I hissed at him for waking me because I needed to write today. Exhausted and frustrated, reflexively passing on the trauma Mom reflexively passed on to me, I screamed: "You have no right to do this to me!" His face turned red and he started to cry. "I haven't slept at all!" he protested. "I'm dying inside!"

I'm dying inside. That got through to me. Something in me softened. I hugged him and helped him resettle on the couch, where he slept. I'm grateful, even now, to whatever internal fortitude helped him find those words in the face of my terrible rage. If you don't heal your own trauma, you'll pass it on and give others the job of healing it for you. Pushing back as I was never able to do at his age, my son taught me something about the difference between self-discipline and selfishness, breaking my heart a little bit in the process. The weight of healing my unresolved pain is one he shouldn't have to bear.

The structures that organize our lives are always at risk of turning into straightjackets. In the face of chaos and change, we need to hold them lightly and with a sense of humor. Like genetic reproduction—that ancient, cellular discipline—they need to be firm, yet flexible. DNA transcribes itself with a balance of consistency and error that keeps us adaptable in an unpredictable world. That's how we survive and grow over evolutionary time.

A single lifetime's no different. Self-discipline, as I understand it now, is the opposite of self-harm. Where it applies self-denial, it does so with compassion, toward some beneficial purpose. I can forgo the pleasure of a massive cheeseburger at lunch in order to feel clearheaded for an afternoon interview. I can cut back on alcohol or quit it altogether if my drinking habits are hurting my relationships or draining my motivation to do things I value more, like writing a book.

It can also take the form of positive commitment: of showing up to write at a scheduled time and place because experience tells you that the part of you that would rather stay in bed isn't doing you any favors.

But healthy, mature self-discipline is always a work in progress. Sometimes inspiration is best achieved by breaking your own routine. There's space for experimentation, spontaneous risks, mistakes, and revision. "Flexible commitment" might seem like a paradox. If so, it's the central paradox of life—the need for order and organization in an ever-changing world.

At difficult moments, when our equilibrium is at risk or completely lost, self-love and compassion are especially necessary. It's not necessary to blindly perpetuate the cycle of intergenerational fucking-up that Philip Larkin describes in his poem "This Be The Verse":

> They fuck you up, your mum and dad.
> They may not mean to, but they do.
> They fill you with the faults they had
> And add some extra, just for you.
>
> But they were fucked up in their turn
> By fools in old-style hats and coats,
> Who half the time were soppy-stern
> And half at one another's throats.

It's not okay to shrug it off on the grounds that we had it worse as kids. When trauma drives us to harm ourselves and our loved ones, we can take responsibility for learning how to end it. We owe it to ourselves, our children, and our ancestors who may not have had the time or the right tools to figure these things out.

Animal Entanglement

RONALD GOTS

Jason and Meri play with dirt.

Dear Meri,

Might as well admit it. I'm writing this book about you, about us, and sometimes I'm not even sure that I knew you at all. Sometimes when I try to conjure up your voice, I only hear my own.

First, we were kids, so entangled and on top of one another that it was impossible to tell where you ended and I began. I picture us in the game room, aged eleven and seven perhaps, playing sibling power games—binding one another to the columns in the room with a jump rope, throwing darts into the wall around each other's bodies like old-school carnies, or rolling pool balls as hard as we could across the table at one another's knuckles, trying to yank away our hands at the very last moment.

Weird, ambiguous, instinctive times. I remember good times, too, as we got older—shared laughs over Garfield, Bloom County, Saturday Night Live, *and* The Far Side. *Building forts in one another's bedroom and stocking them with every imaginable snack and our '80s "portable" black-and-white TV that must have weighed thirty pounds, minimum. Almost getting killed when a gumball machine slipped off my desk where it was holding a bedsheet in place. Building igloos and tunnels through snowfalls so deep they seem like fairy tales now. More than any words we ever said, I remember the feeling of our bodies grappling with one another—fighting, hugging, jostling for space in the back seat of the car on road trips to our grandparents' houses for the holidays. I can remember that early, unquestioned, sometimes suffocating closeness.*

Then in middle and high school I was so wrapped up in my own identity that I barely noticed you. Unsure of myself, I tried on a succession of selves, each with its own ready-made costume: fringed hippie jacket, magenta Goth hair... In each scene I tried to be a part of, inclusion meant playing it cool, which meant ignoring everything that wasn't cool—and that usually included you, my little sister.

Not that you ever seemed to mind much. You were strong and secure—busy with Girl Scouts, horseback riding, and your own, well-adjusted best friends. And with battling and surviving cancer, of course. I missed that almost entirely. For all of our sakes, Mom and Dad sent me away for the summer during the worst of it. I was too cool for hospitals, anyway.

In my early years of college, we met again as if for the first time—two independent, very different adults with a common past to sift through. You were smart, funny, bold, and eccentric, and we had so much to catch up on. We took a road trip across the country and drank beer together like grown-ups, got close and conspiratorial about the shared history no one else knew. Each of us realized for the first time that the other was our one, true ally, our only living link to what had happened back then from a child's perspective. And what a precious thing that was.

Then you married and our lives diverged again. You worshipped your husband—to all appearances, a man as self-involved and damaged as they come—in a way I couldn't fully understand. Together, you moved to California, thousands of miles away. Then your life fell apart but you couldn't yet see it, and so, for a long time, neither could I. That central fact—of your life's derailment, your inability to face it, and the life you built to keep it at bay—kept you as distant from me for most of the last decade of your life as you may have been from yourself.

But siblings can never be strangers. That early, animal entanglement runs deep. So the somatic memory of your presence—and the pain of your absence—are like underground rivers running through my life. Sometimes I lost you. Sometimes you lost yourself. And at a different level we always knew each other more deeply than anything else.

I'm writing this book to find you again. I don't know how much of your voice will make it into these pages. As I've admitted, I'm an unreliable narrator and my memory is shoddy at best. And to the extent that I knew you, I knew only the self that surfaced whenever we were together. But I loved you, even when we were strangers. I loved you and I always will, with blood trust and hope and animal need.

In other words, I love you as I love myself.

Jason and Meri lounging with Snoopy.

RONALD GOTS

A Girl and a Boy

One wall of my bedroom was covered in cork, the other three in navy blue corduroy wallpaper. So nobody stumbling into it that fall of 1984 could have the slightest doubt that this room belonged to a boy. I stood on the brown-and-mustard-yellow-plaid carpet, the door closed (locking the door was forbidden, otherwise it definitely would have been locked), staring at the wall behind my bed. Every visible inch of it was covered with pictures of Michael Jackson. From *Tiger Beat* magazine, there was a carefully torn-out shot from the "Beat It" video, featuring the chain-mail-shouldered, zipper-covered jacket I would never own as it cost $550 at Wilsons Leather at the mall. There was domestic, casual Michael, hanging out at Neverland Ranch in jeans with his chimp, Bubbles. And with pride of place at the center was a massive, horizontal blowup of *Thriller*'s album cover featuring a dewy-eyed, reclining Michael, resplendent in his white suit and his glistening Jheri curls. *Please*, I prayed—to God and to Michael—*let me wake up tomorrow morning to find that I'm not Jason Gots anymore. Let me become Michael Jackson.*

I was a month away from ten years old when *Thriller* dropped. By the fall of seventh grade, my interest in Michael had become something between a religion and an identity disorder. With my Fisher boom box playing "Billie Jean" on endless repeat, I spent hours in front of that wall trying to replicate Michael's dance moves from the Grammys. Perfectionist that he was—as I knew him to be from all those fanzines—it would never be enough. Like religious faith, the impossible ideal kept me humble and it kept me going.

While trying to master the moonwalk, I greased my penny loafers with vegetable oil, so they'd slide on our hardwood living room floor. Nota bene to any aspiring young moonwalkers out there: it doesn't work. Vegetable oil's too viscous. It just messes up the floor.

Mom was an energetic accomplice to this alternative lifestyle. Sewing on hundreds, maybe thousands of sequins by hand, she painstakingly created a replica of Michael's iconic glove. It was for the wrong hand (left, not right) and it wasn't covered with Swarovski crystals, like the real one, but it was better than nothing. She helped me put together a replica of a lemon yellow outfit Michael once wore, with a vest and a hand-sewn, golden sash. Although the "Beat It" jacket was out of the question, she bought me the *Thriller* jacket with the dramatic V lapels. I wore it everywhere, proudly, though it made me secretly uneasy because it had come from the women's department, and the zipper was on the wrong side.

In retrospect, Mom's support for all this was surprisingly enthusiastic. I can't imagine Michael was the role model she'd have chosen for her only son. My parents weren't fundamentalists, but this was the '80s, and gender expectations in suburban Maryland were pretty conservative. Boys were supposed to be into sports, not spinning around in circles, praying to a pop singer, and wearing clothes with sparkly epaulets.

Michael was sexually ambiguous long before ideas of gender fluidity were remotely mainstream, and he was famously eccentric—living in a Disney castle and possibly literally believing himself to be Peter Pan. My dad did his best to ignore the

HUMANITY IS TRYING

RONALD GOTS

Jason in Michael Jackson gear. Mom in supporting costume.

whole thing, hoping it was just a phase. Mom must have been moved to pity by my adolescent desperation to be something, anything, other than myself.

But why Michael?

Between a brother and sister, in that time and place at least, questions about what it meant to be a boy or a girl were a constant, insistent subtext. None of us had the language or the conceptual framework to think about masculinity and femininity

85

as a spectrum of tendencies or preferences, separate from biological sex.

Some of my earliest memories of Meri are of arguments with Mom about her hatred of skirts, dresses, brushing her hair, and the color pink. Meri's earliest true love was horses, and her horsey style was rough and ready. No nonsense. At ten, you could imagine her on the porch of her someday ranch, chewing tobacco and warning off intruders with a shotgun. Years before we heard of punk music, we knew Sid Vicious as a cautionary tale about the fate of Meri's hair if she kept refusing Mom's brush. Where Mom heard about Sid Vicious is anyone's guess.

In adolescence, Meri showed little interest in (and sometimes open hostility toward) perfume and makeup. Any hopes Mom might have harbored of bonding with her over clothes shopping or beautification were repeatedly and emphatically dashed.

I started out more or less the same way. Early childhood photos show me knee-deep in a mud pit or climbing on a jungle gym, glistening with sweat. I can still feel the sensation of Mom's tweezers as they picked gravel out of my bloody knees the hundredth time I hurtled down our steep driveway on a plastic tricycle and wiped out in the scree of Cindy Lane, below. But when school sports started up in earnest, my sister's path and mine diverged.

On any field, I was a disaster. I remember hanging out (once and only once) at the house of a classmate who, in fifth grade, already had thick, black hair covering his legs and a corporate sponsorship as a tennis player. I remember getting tripped hard by this same boy a week or so later on the school soccer field: the special, sporty anguish of emerald green grass rushing up to meet your shins and nose. Sports, then and forever after for me, meant blinding sunshine and shame.

As a schoolkid Dad had been strong and tall for his age (whereas, thanks to Grandpa Jim, I was short and stumpy). Street games like stickball left him with warm feelings about teamwork

RONALD GOTS

Jason after baseball practice.

and running around with a crew of toughs with cigarettes rolled up in their sleeves, while Boy Scouts taught him that real men knew how to survive in the woods with arrows, knots, and fire. Also, to be fair, with a lot of botany—he still knows the name of every tree he sees. As an American boy of his generation, his childhood heroes included he-men and survivalists like Tarzan, Robinson Crusoe, and John Wayne.

My dad grew up to become a sensitive and gentle man. But everything fathers and sons typically bonded over in the years of my childhood—the Super Bowl, for example—reduced me to sniveling. In the hope that some sport would finally make a boy of me, I was dumped experimentally on to one extracurricular team after another: wrestling, soccer, and ultimately—as a last-ditch compromise—flag football. Even when coaches wisely neutralized me, putting me in positions where all I had to do was stand there, I was miserable.

Emotions start in the body. Then, if left unchecked, they proliferate in the mind. The sports-feelings always started as a dull ache in my solar plexus. This would escalate into shortness of breath, cold sweat, and a bone-deep sense of shame. I was about to make a fool of myself. I did not belong here. Everyone was bigger, stronger, tougher, and better than me.

More than one study has led scientists to posit the existence of a "fear pheromone" that others can smell and that makes fear contagious. If fear's contagious, then boys on a sports field are antibodies—primed to attack and extinguish it before it infects them, too. My teammates read the signals I was giving off. And they agreed with me: I definitely didn't belong there.

Meri picked up the slack here a bit. She got more worked up than I ever could about the Redskins' epic rivalry with the Dallas Cowboys. In addition to competitive riding, dressage, and horseback gymnastics, she played basketball enthusiastically on a county team. Some of this was temperamental—she liked competition and always ran headlong at life, even if it meant getting knocked around a bit. I hated competition. I hated pain. I had (and still have) no desire to do battle with or win against any opponent. In this way, I'm a lot like my mother.

What's trickier to tease out is the gender subtext—how we competed or compensated for one another in terms of boyishness and girlishness—masculinity and femininity—so that balance could be maintained and our parents' (often unconscious) expectations met, even if in the wrong body.

Along with her dislike of games, I shared Mom's love of literature and, from middle school on, fussed much more than Meri ever did over clothing, body image, and hair. When Madonna's

Like a Virgin album came out, I covered my arms in the fluo-rescent, rubbery "jelly" bracelets she wore in her MTV videos. I spent hours staring into mirrors, torn between my impatience for the arrival of pubic hair and the desire (learned from Mi-chael) to stay young and pixieish forever.

By sixth grade, I knew I was definitely attracted to girls. On Valentine's Day in our classroom, I analyzed the handwriting on the six or seven cards I got from girls like some philologist trying to decipher a lost dialect of Akkadian. The style: flirta-tiously bubble-written, or angular and perfunctory? The ink: Bic or precious metallic paint pen? Scented or non? The *i*'s: plain or dotted with hearts?

By Valentine's Day, the guy with the sports sponsorship and the hairy legs had already "gone out" with three of the most popular girls in the class. As I knew from Anthony Michael Hall movies, this probably meant an introductory phone call from the girl's friend saying she "liked" you, followed by a phone call or two with the girl herself, followed by holding hands once at a movie, followed by a tearful telephone breakup.

Oh, what I would have given even for that introductory phone call! But I barely had the courage to send a harmlessly generic valentine to Allison or Tyrell, the girls I liked, let alone talk to them. I was short, goofy, and hopeless at sports. In the movies, the only way that kid ever got noticed was if he was a video game champion, using his powers to defeat the Russian government.

Michael Jackson—my alter ego—was for weekends only.

Michael didn't have to worry about his masculinity. He didn't need sports or hairy legs to be cool. He could literally defy grav-ity with his moonwalk! Surrounded as he was by millions of adoring fans and ever-present music—oh, the music!—he was invincible and above it all. Unlike anyone else in the world, he had built his own isolation bubble—a magical castle and amuse-ment park where he was free to be entirely himself.

Taking Michael as my personal savior might not have impressed the girls in my class (had they known about it), but it promised me protection from fear, loneliness, and insecurity—ironic when you consider that fear, loneliness, and insecurity were probably a very big part of Michael's short life.

In seventh grade I transferred to St. Albans School for Boys, an ivy-covered, all-boys' private school on the grounds of the National Cathedral, founded toward the end of the nineteenth century for the boys of the Cathedral Choir. By 1984, it was well established as a kind of American Eton or Harrow—a venerable training ground for the scions of the DC elite who would run some future industry from a wood-paneled office. It was Harvard to the Yale of Sidwell Friends, the more liberal Quaker school up the road that Obama's daughters would one day attend.

The cathedral—one of a very few things I remember fondly about the place—took over a hundred years to build, the work passing from father to son down three generations of craftsmen. When I graduated high school in 1990, it still wasn't finished. That year a friend, a choir boy with whom I sometimes smoked pot in the cathedral gardens (once, memorably, rolled in an onionskin page of T.S. Eliot's *The Wasteland* torn out of the *Norton Anthology of Poetry*), took me through a secret entrance up a spiral staircase to the catwalk between the unfinished towers, for a breathtaking view from the highest point in Washington, DC.

The cathedral's smooth, vaulting buttresses, the pungent purples and periwinkles of its massive stained glass windows, even the ecumenical, edifying speeches we sometimes shuffled in to hear still live inside me as a sense of spaciousness and hope in a dark time. In memory, St. Albans School for Boys squats nearby like one of the cathedral's leering gargoyles, blotting out the sun with its leathery wings.

I brought Michael with me to the new school like a secret identity, itching for any opportunity to unveil him. I wasn't born yesterday, though. There was real danger here. Like the English boys' boarding schools on which it was modeled, St. Albans had an unspoken, brutal social hierarchy within which bullying, homophobia, and gang aggression were the most reliable pathways to high status. Low status boys were subjected to relentless psychological and physical abuse.

At St. Albans in 1984, "gay" was a catchall term for anything (or anyone) a higher status boy despised. You could be called "gay" for listening to the wrong kind of music, talking (as I did) with a lisp, or having the wrong brand of backpack. This was homophobia, of course, tuned so high that it created a kind of magical force field—a spell to ward off the unimaginable possibility of anyone's actually being gay by projecting metaphorical "gayness" everywhere. Wanting to become Michael Jackson, as it turned out, was a serious violation of the taboo.

By late October I was somehow sufficiently emboldened to come to school dressed as Michael for Halloween. Halloween costumes mean different things to different people. Sometimes they're an opportunity to become something fantastically, playfully far-removed from your ordinary self. Sometimes they're just a sight gag. I think it was immediately obvious to everyone that I had no sense of humor at all about my costume—that I was, in fact, wearing my soul on my sleeve.

That alone would have been enough to set the sharks circling. But Michael's svelte physique, his gentle falsetto, and all that dancing put St. Albans' fanatical 1984 gaydar on extra high alert. The moment I unveiled my sash and glove, the name-calling began. My innermost self, the deepest and most sacred part of my being, was on display. And everyone hated it. Then came lunchtime, and things got even worse.

Our dark wood-paneled lunchroom, lined with gloomy paintings of past headmasters and notable alumni, was called the "refectory." In groups of eight or ten, students sat around wooden tables, each run by a senior despot who forced lowerclassmen to bus the dirty dishes to the kitchen.

After lunch, there was a costume contest. I don't remember which costumes won first and second place. Alf the wisecracking sitcom alien, probably, and Marty McFly from *Back to the Future* in a cardboard DeLorean. But I sure do remember what happened next: "And now," said the Latin teacher into the PA, "with the costume we least want to see ever again...Jason Gots as Michael Jackson!"

In the made-for-TV movie, the sound designer would fade out the jeering of the five hundred plus boys and cue the deafening lub-lub of my heartbeat and the high whine of tinnitus. I'd stumble—as I did—dazed out of the lunchroom, my cheeks flushed red, knowing nothing but hot shame.

I don't remember much after that, including telling my parents the story. But I must have been visibly crushed, and they must somehow have wrung it out of me because the next day after lunch I was summoned once again up to the microphone, this time to accept a public apology and a gift: a puzzle of Michael Jackson wearing that lemon yellow outfit. As anyone who has ever been thirteen knows, this was worse than getting the award in the first place.

That public shaming might be my strongest early memory of community. The hunger to belong to something bigger than yourself and the feeling that most of you isn't welcome there. In so many communities I've known since then, similar principles operate: belonging means concealing something, adapting to unspoken norms, jostling with others for proximity to power and status within the group. As hungry as I ever was for human connection, I struggled for years to find any community where the trade-offs seemed worth it.

St. Albans was also my introduction to the community of

men. And the message was clear: my brand of masculinity—whatever it was—wasn't welcome there.

In bell hooks's *The Will to Change: Men, Masculinity, and Love*, the visionary feminist argues that men, being human, have a deep, innate capacity to love. But patriarchy—the system that trains men to wield power and dominate at home and out in the world—also teaches us to be ashamed of our emotions and suppress that capacity. Instead of learning to give and accept love, we're taught to wield violence in its various forms: verbal fury, physical aggression, and silent disapproval among them.

As a seventh grader looking for a role model, I think I intuitively related to Michael's creative energy and his grace. He offered me the freedom to be different. The immediate, intensive threat-response at St. Albans supports hooks's observation that boys' peer groups do much of the work of instilling and enforcing patriarchal norms. St. Albans couldn't turn me into a macho man, but it taught me—at least for the next couple years—to be ashamed of (and keep quiet about) my differences. On the cusp of adolescence, patriarchal training did its job of making me less emotionally open, more afraid to be vulnerable around other men.

I was learning similar lessons at home. In many households, hooks argues, women—because of their direct power over children and more direct contact with them—do the heavy lifting of passing on patriarchal values of violence to the next generation. It happens, she says, mainly through "verbal abuse and shaming," which are harder to track (and therefore more historically invisible) than physical violence.

In our household, for all the reasons I've shared and others I'll probably never know, Mom embodied and enforced these patriarchal ideals. Her violence most often took the form of emotional abuse, making it easy to deny and hard to document. For the most part, Dad passively endorsed it with his silence. If they could have done otherwise, I know they would have, but these are the facts. This was the context in which Meri and I first learned what it meant to be a girl and a boy, a woman and a man.

One Christmas in the mid '90s, Meri and I sat in her childhood bedroom, beers in our hands, talking. She was gushing about her new college boyfriend—the man who would later become her husband. "He's brilliant," she said, "A polymath. He knows six or seven languages! And more importantly, he's got a spine." Unlike her high school boyfriend, who I'd liked a lot, this new man knew how to "keep her in check."

Everything about this felt wrong. The violence and anger in Meri, that legacy of trauma, wasn't something a man was supposed to come along and control. With the help of friends, therapists if necessary, and loving partners (not domineering masters), she was supposed to face her demons and, through knowing, disarm them. Health and happiness ought to mean more freedom, not less. But instead of questioning the patriarchal violence we'd inherited, she'd come to the conclusion that "real men" existed to keep women like her from turning into monsters.

Every man in the shadow of patriarchy knows that around some corner is another, faster draw—and a bullet with his name on it. He knows that life's tough and a real man has to be cooler, more badass, or more brilliant than the next guy to get by. Not only is this destructive, but like all ideals, it's impossible to live up to. In its grip every man, no matter how outwardly successful, feels, at his core, inadequate and ashamed. And whether that shame turns outward or inward, it's poison.

At this point I wonder whether it's even helpful to aim for categorical definitions of masculinity or femininity. Even the fluid Jungian archetypes Robert Bly and other leaders of men's and women's movements reach for always risk essentialism: the feminine as intuitive, accepting, emotional, and nurturing, the masculine as protective, forceful, rational, and providing. Do we still even need them? Instead of worrying about how to categorize our instincts, shouldn't we stand up in a thousand different ways for people's right to feel what they feel, to love and to be loved, and to challenge the structures and practices that reproduce violence?

Meri and I didn't know how to talk about any of this, at least not with each other. It was too deep, too personal, too potentially explosive. Formed in the crucible of family, our beliefs about men and women, masculinity and femininity were all tangled up with our judgments of one another.

After the end of her long, painful marriage to a man who knew how to "keep her in check" but not how to love her or love himself, I wonder whether she came to any different conclusions. I wonder if she ever missed the kindness and decency of her "spineless" first love. I'd like her to know what a loving and generous young man my son is becoming. To hear how he navigates the sometimes brutal, mostly male worlds of online gaming with grace, courage, and a sense of humor. To see how I'm still working on becoming the kind of man I want him to be.

Taking Refuge

Dear John,

Golden-haired child of Albion! In memory you're as shining and rarified as one of Tolkien's high elves, sailing in the silver ships across the sea to Valinor, never to be seen in this diminished world again. You're Mercutio, spinning wild and feckless tales of Queen Mab, herself a spinner of tales. Stories within stories, perpetual, so it's impossible to tell where one ends and another one begins. With you, John, live youth, possibility, cartwheels on the tightrope across the abyss.

Drama camp at Balliol College, Oxford, then a week in Edinburgh. At the festival we ran from place to place, surviving on a six-pack of bread rolls (and a farewell treat of fish and chips wrapped in newspaper) because you'd spent all your remaining Oxford cash on a giant stuffed bear for a girl who claimed (and who you believed) to be an "empath." She could hold a hand once, it was said, and read the person's whole heart.

We saw Macbeth with that Scottish company that poured buckets of blood into a white plastic-bag-lined orchestra pit. Saw a Twelfth Night so alive it could have played to a rapt and fully comprehending crowd of kindergarteners. Stood on the high, stony hills and looked down across the lichen-covered edifices of the ancient city.

Motion is what I remember best. We were always in motion. Running through Edinburgh's hilly streets, breathless and laughing, to catch a midnight Emo Philips comedy gig. Then later that year, in the win-

ter of our last year of high school, running in the darkness in some part of DC we weren't supposed to be in, ever—your deciding to hop the fence into a construction site to scale a giant crane. Driving dangerously fast to school in our friend's Mustang convertible, your hair flying in the wind, "Ride of the Valkyries" blasting from the speakers at top volume and all of us feeling so free, so clever, so unlike all those other teenagers driving fast in other cars everywhere, ever since teenagers were first allowed to drive.

In one of the two physical photo albums I have, I've got a series of pictures your mother gave me. One is of John the Dancer—your torso transformed into a rippling trapezoid by ten hours a day of obsessive training that led to your dropping out of Berkeley, dancing away from the venerable academic legacy of your famous Czech historian father, following in the djinn-like, flaming footsteps of your hero, Nijinsky.

This next photo leaps back further in time to you as Mercutio in our high school production of Romeo and Juliet: your eyes flashing, chin upturned, rapier aloft—the role that turned you into a sex symbol at our sister school and (briefly) shook our friendship. How I envied you the attention of the girls who gathered around in the lobby after school. How I envied you the glorious role by contrast to my tiny part as Gregory (or Sampson?): "Do you bite your thumb at us, sir?"

"I do bite my thumb, sir!"

"But do you bite your thumb at us, sir?"

Mercutio the poet. The raw talent, too rare for this world, cut down in the street before his time.

That year, in your reflected glow, I felt squat and dumpy and dour. I envied the mercurial, trickster energy that got you the part—that dangerous, vivid quality I worried I lacked. We went to see Amadeus—that tragedy of genius and mediocrity—and I sat there thinking: Is John the Mozart to my Salieri?

But that was a story of hate. And between you and me, there was so much love. So after a couple months of tension, the floodgates burst. We talked it all through and we cried, and I learned that this is what it means to love a friend: it's how you bring into your life those qualities you lack. Or don't (yet) know how to access.

97

Jason and John backstage, in costume for Romeo and Juliet *at St. Albans School.*

★ ★ ★

All friendships begin with a secret. Ours was the power of language. What I remember first is Shakespeare's sonnets. And John Donne. And how suddenly one day in an English class we took together, the language unspooled like one of those fractal animations people watch on LSD, revealing infinity. I understood that words were transparent things. Fragile containers with histories and meanings jostling around inside them. Words moved through time, accruing memories, but like us they were amnesiac, capriciously sloughing off skins that no longer served, hanging on to others for no apparent reason. And they were ours to conjure with. We could make magic.

Years later, all grown-up and in a different city, I talked to the philosopher of mind Daniel Dennett about the "magic trick" of consciousness. He told me that ever since he was a kid, he's been figuring out how magic tricks work. Knowing the secret doesn't diminish his sense of wonder, he said—it adds to it. People are always accusing him of grubby materialism for focusing on what he calls "the meat": trying to understand consciousness as an emergent property of structures in the brain. Consciousness is as personal as it gets, and some people don't like the idea that it's a penetrable illusion.

I'm susceptible to this kind of sentiment. Always in love with the mystery. But based on what we learned in that English class, I know that Dennett is right. Understanding the mechanics of pentameter and metaphor made Shakespeare's magic all the more powerful. And it gave us the courage to pick up the wand and the top hat ourselves.

I started by writing a few clumsy sonnets, my first serious poetry since "I sold my soul to rock and roll" an a cappella song my ten-year-old self is probably still singing on a dusty Betamax cassette in a box somewhere. Then you and I started working on an epic Lovecraftian poem, written in tetrameter and divided into verses we called "spasms." I still remember a spasm of yours (though none of mine):

> *Darkness fell, fey forms descending*
> *A shriek awoke, night's fabric rending*
> *A keening cry, commanding, sending*
> *To find the psyche near to bending.*

Jesus, what I'd give to read that poem in its entirety now! There were hundreds of spasms. A stack of illustrated pages that no one ever read. That was the beauty of this project—it was ours alone, it was ridiculous, and it could go on forever.

Your house was maybe a ten-minute drive from mine, but it became an oasis—a refuge from the suffocating atmosphere that hung over my home. I'm an adult now with a family of my own and I no longer blame anyone for this. Well, I try not to. Everybody was overworked and underslept, battling demons both overt and invisible, ill-equipped to seek or accept the help we each needed. There were sweet spots now and then. Like when we went out every Thursday night for Roy Rogers, just my mom, Meri, and me, and competed to discover the largest ever French fry (I did! It was a foot and a half long!). But on Cindy Lane there was mostly a pall over everything—of fear, shame, frustration, and guilt— erupting now and then into terrible fury.

Your house, on the other hand, was forest inside and out. Full of giant, thriving, broad-leaved plants—trees, really. In every sense, it was easier to breathe there. Your mom in my memory was a wise, gentle soul. She trusted you and gave you space, looking on with admiration as you flowered. There was strategic nourishment, too. She took us, for example, to all thirty hours of Wagner's Ring Cycle at the Kennedy Center. Great gardeners know when to subtly intervene.

Your house was an outgrowth of the forest it sat in, in Glen Echo, Maryland. Wood, plants, glass, and your bedroom off the front entrance, at a tasteful remove from where your mom and younger sister slept. In senior year you had girls sleeping over now and then, with your mom's permission. The one time (that same year) I furtively had sex with a girlfriend at home and my mother found out she came flying at me the next morning, hissing and spitting out words like "filthy" and "disgusting" and "animal." I remember cowering in the corner of the laundry room like the animal she said I was, humiliated and weeping.

But at your house there were no such horrors. I remember studying Roman history in your bedroom, laughing about "Q. Fabius Maximus, Cunctator"—whose surname meant "the delayer" because he screwed up so badly against Hannibal in the Second Punic War. I remember imagining ourselves as the arbiters elegentiae of ancient Rome, whose job it was to walk around Rome deciding what was "in" and what was "out," aesthetically speaking: "Statue of Anubis in the town square? Lose it!"

"Bowl haircuts? Yes—a thousand times, yes!"

These sessions were the hints of a secret life of yours to which I didn't have much access—a life in which you'd studied history for fun from early childhood, memorizing the lineages of English royalty all the way back to those proto-kings scrabbling around on the rocky heaths, sitting on their rough-hewn, mossy thrones of stone. You were such an Anglophile—so obsessed with dead royals and Shakespeare and Tolkien and

C.S. Lewis that I assumed you had English ancestry on your mother's side (which you didn't). Out of love for you, I became one, too. Still am, I suppose.

Then came William Blake. You introduced me to the song "Jerusalem," based on his poem.

I will not cease from Mental Fight
Nor shall my sword sleep in my hand:
Till we have built Jerusalem,
In Englands green & pleasant Land

Whenever I hear it, I think of you, and it still moves me to tears—I sit there crying like a fool at this triumphal religious anthem of a fallen empire neither of our ancestors ever set foot in.

You had a copy of Blake's Songs of Innocence and Experience *and some of his prophetic writings. Sprawled out on your bed reading them and poring over the illustrations, I felt the first stirrings of something like a personal philosophy.*

William Blake was a poet, visual artist, and what today we might call a spiritual visionary. He's considered part of the Romantic movement in English art—a reactionary response to the horrors of eighteenth-century industrialization. Like Dickens, he heard the stories of children suffocating in coal mines and saw the black chimneys belching out their smoke and thought the Western world was on a steam engine headed straight for hell.

As a teenager in love with art and increasingly at war with my businessman father, I saw in Blake's philosophy a vindication of everything I loved. Everything I thought my parents couldn't understand.

Blake's twelve "prophetic books"—from *Tiriel* in 1789 to *Jerusalem: The Emanation of the Giant Albion* in 1820 consist of thousands of pages of dense, poetic, illuminated scripture. They elaborate his own personal mythology and touch on historical events of his time. Urizen, a recurring figure in these books, is a kind of god of reason, pictured in a famous Blake illustration as a bearded old man holding an architect's square—a tool for drawing right angles. As a lawgiver, a maker of rules, Urizen is cousin to the God of the Old Testament.

Like all of Blake's mythological figures, Urizen plays many roles throughout the prophetic writings. Reading selectively (the books are incredibly long and dense, sometimes reading like the ravings of a schizophrenic) I understood Urizen as a demonic figure—the opposite of Los, Blake's god of imagination. Like the Industrial Revolution, Urizen set about organizing and imprisoning the world. He had ripped humanity out of relationship with the natural world and bound us to factories and cities.

In my adolescent imagination, Urizen represented the force of order and explanation that tried to suffocate beauty. Urizen was St. Albans' cruel rigor (five hours of homework a night!) and my parents' seemingly grim and unrewarding work lives. By extension (and by association with my dad), Urizen was the cold, utilitarian nature of math and science and business as I (barely) understood them, all of which were tools for carving up Nature into pieces that were clear, comprehensible, and dead.

Los, by contrast, represented the energy of creative discovery. It was the feeling of my friendship with John—open-ended, limitless in its possibilities.

Blake ultimately decided that Urizen and Los were two parts of a god that had split into four. Elements that had once balanced each other out, now estranged and at war. Set loose, Urizen had rebelled like Milton's Satan in *Paradise Lost*, producing horrors like coal mines and factories. But reason and imagination had once been necessary parts of a whole.

In his 1959 Rede Lecture at Cambridge University, the writer and thinker C. P. Snow talked about what he called "the two cultures"—a dangerous intellectual split in the Western world between science and the literary arts.

Literary intellectuals at one pole—at the other scientists, and as the most representative, the physical scientists. Between the two a gulf of mutual incomprehension—sometimes (particularly among the young) hostility and dislike, but most of all lack of understanding. They have a curious distorted image of each other. Their attitudes are so different that, even on the level of emotion, they can't find much common ground.

Snow sees this shift as relatively new in his time and extremely dangerous. He's particularly critical of the arrogance of the literary intellectuals, who:

...give a pitying chuckle at the news of scientists who have never read a major work of English literature. They dismiss them as ignorant specialists. Yet their own ignorance and their own specialisation is just as startling. A good many times I have been present at gatherings of people who, by the standards of the traditional culture, are thought highly educated and who have with considerable gusto been expressing their incredulity at the illiteracy of scientists. Once or twice I have been provoked and have asked the company how many of them could describe the second law of thermodynamics. The response was cold: it was also negative. Yet I was asking something which is about the scientific equivalent of "Have you read a work of Shakespeare's?"

...So the great edifice of modern physics goes up, and the majority of the cleverest people in the Western world have about as much insight into it as their neolithic ancestors would have had.

The clashing point of two subjects, two disciplines, two cultures—of two galaxies, so far as that goes—ought to produce creative chances. In the history of mental activity that has been where some of the breakthroughs came. The chances are there now. But they are there, as it were, in a vacuum, because those in the two cultures can't talk to each other.

At sixteen, I took sides in that cultural split, declaring my loyalty to art and making an enemy of everything else, everything I associated with my dad. In the sanctuary of John's home I found an empowering alternative to self-pity. In Blake's Romanticism I found a sense of pride in myself and independence from my family. But by casting myself as Los to Dad's Urizen, I was turning my own ignorance of science, math, and money into virtues. Deciding that art and the imagination were the only things in the world of value, I fell into a cultural binary. All these years later, I'm still climbing out.

To be fair, Reagan's America (much like the America of today) was in need of correctives toward the imagination and the heart. Entrepreneurial zeal might have pulled the economy out of its Carter-era doldrums, but selfishness and naked ambition now ruled the day. My teenage brain was at war with an imbalance that existed not only in my family but everywhere in the culture—a plague of materialism driven by finance, which was powered by technology: the offspring of science and industry.

People were living longer and arguably, as Snow asserted in 1959, better than in agricultural societies:

It is all very well for us, sitting pretty, to think that material standards of living don't matter all that much. It is all very well for one, as a personal choice, to reject industrialisation—do a modern Walden, if you like, and if you go without much food, see most of your children die in infancy, despise the comforts of literacy, accept twenty years off your own life, then I respect you for the strength of your aesthetic revulsion. But I don't respect you in the slightest if, even passively, you try to impose the same choice on others who are not free to choose. In fact, we know what their choice would be. For, with singular unanimity, in any country where they have had the chance, the poor have walked off the land into the factories as fast as the factories could take them.

Fair enough. But thirty years on from Snow's speech, from my vantage point in the suburbs of DC, I wasn't seeing much around me in the way of hope or meaningful life. Everywhere I turned, Urizen seemed to be working overtime, building his "dark, satanic mills." Ironically this wasn't long after medical science had saved Meri from cancer, and technology her leg, and as a result she had come to very different conclusions. For her, reason and science were a shining beacon out of the darkness of ignorance.

John's love gave me some space to imagine a different world. Art offered a way out of my own personal darkness. Both beckoned me sweetly, unconditionally. So naturally, I followed.

The Church
of the Page

In her 2019 book *The Lost Art of Scripture*, theologian Karen Armstrong defines *scripture* as words and ritual working in harmony to transform the individual and, in the process, create community. From the earliest Vedic writings of India—prayers to Agni the god of fire—to the extensive Midrashic and Talmudic commentaries of Judaism on the Torah, scripture as Armstrong sees it is a living thing. In the act of singing it, sharing it, adding to it, and interpreting it, a community discovers and perpetually reinvents itself.

Armstrong is deeply critical of any orthodoxy that treats its sacred texts as dead, unapproachable things whose one, true interpretation belongs only in the hands of its priestly caste. She argues that scripture left inert on the page isn't scripture at all, any more than notes on a page are music.

But when ritual brings scripture to life, personal and cultural transformation can happen through the experience of *kenosis*—a feeling of transcending the confines of self, the limitations of ego.

In Buddhist thought, the ego is the source of all human suffering. *Dukkha* comes from clinging to impermanent things, which begins with clinging to the self. From early childhood, we are driven biologically and psychologically to seek out the things our bodies want, ignore the things they don't care about, and avoid the things that bother or threaten them. In a recursive loop, these attachments continually reinforce the ego—our sense of the reality of self. The whole of Buddhist practice can be seen as a curriculum for moving away from ego and toward a permanent state of kenosis, which Buddhism calls Nirvana. Whether or not you buy that enlightenment is achievable, the curriculum is clearly structured (in ancient texts like the *Sattipatthana Sutta*) to lead the practitioner progressively toward a view of self (and all things) as interdependent, contingent, and impermanent—no more real in their separateness than a wave in the ocean.

At first this struck me as a very cold and inhumane perspective to aspire to. How could you live in the world thinking of everything, yourself included, as an illusion? But for the Buddha, kenosis doesn't lead to indifference—it leads to compassion. As the story goes, upon achieving enlightenment, freed from the ego's narrow concerns, he sees at a glance the suffering of all sentient beings, caught between reality and illusion, struggling in the chains of selfishness and greed. He's moved by our pain and our desire for freedom. Instead of vanishing into nothingness, he returns to the world to teach.

Kenosis has been described and facilitated a thousand different ways throughout history by the faithful of sects and practices ranging from Sufi whirling dervishes to young people at rock concerts. Accounts of the peak experiences of religious visionaries, artists and art lovers, users of psychedelics, hikers in the mountains, scuba divers, and more have so much in common that science has begun to take an interest. At the Center for Psychedelic and Consciousness Research at Johns Hopkins University, Dr. Roland Griffiths and his colleagues are currently studying these spiritual experiences of ego transcendence—whether in-duced by prayer or by psychedelics like psilocybin—and find-ing that they produce similar (and significant) benefits to mental health.

Kenosis is almost always accompanied by a sense of awe and connection to a larger whole: the rest of humanity, the atoms in the chair in front of you, Brahma, the "sacred geometry" of the universe—the specific imagery matters less than the sense of non-duality from everything you normally think of as "not-you." A state of trust, acceptance, and connectedness, kenosis is the antidote to meanness of spirit.

People have done and continue to do terrible things in the name of every religion, as they do in the name of democracy, family, a better tomorrow, business, and so much more. Fol-lowing Armstrong's logic, the worst offenders are invariably the most orthodox, from the Theravadan Buddhists of Myanmar to the Islamic State, to the Christians of the Inquisition, the Crusades, the Salem Witch Trials, and homophobic hate cam-paigns. But kenosis, wherever it appears, is a force for positive change in the world.

In the ancient and the modern world, poetry, music, phys-ical movement, and psychedelics like ayahuasca, psilocybin, psilocin, muscarine-containing mushrooms, and the mescaline-containing cactuses have all been known as catalysts for kenosis.

In ancient Greece, at festivals in honor of Dionysus (Roman: Bacchus), the god of wine, alcohol was used as a spiritual solvent, dissolving the boundaries between his followers and their god. As music producer and ethnomusicologist Christopher C. King explains in his book *Lament from Epirus: An Odyssey into Europe's Oldest Surviving Folk Music*, remote mountain communities in Greece today still continue this tradition at all-night festivals where music and drink blur the boundaries between performer and audience, self and other, self and the natural world.

Encountering Meri again at that first ayahuasca retreat was an instance of kenosis. I lay down guilt, doubt, and shame and—with the help of the medicine—relaxed into the sense of her presence. For an hour or two I was no longer the brother who hadn't managed to save her or who couldn't love her enough to mourn her fully. My attention was no longer a closed-circuit TV, turned inward—it was open and connected to my sister, and through her to everything else. Like a baby floating in its amniotic sac, I was nobody, and I belonged.

But the first experience of kenosis I can remember happened to me much earlier, in high school. It was in a ninth grade English class where we were studying poems by three long-dead English writers: John Donne, Robert Herrick, and William Shakespeare.

I guess my brain was wired to love language and it must have been the right developmental moment to make the leap, but my teacher did two things that helped transform these words on a page into scripture. First, she had us read each poem aloud—slowly and more than once. Second, she showed us how these writers used wordplay and metaphor to create cunning, multi-dimensional structures. If you read them with the right kind of attention, they unfolded like one of those giant, alien flowers from *The Day of the Triffids*, a classic sci-fi movie my dad once made me watch, and—just like those alien flowers—swallowed you whole.

I remember going line by line through Shakespeare's sonnets, practicing this new form of exegetical magic. On a first reading, I understood nothing. Some of the music might have caught my ear: *"Rough winds do shake the darling buds of May."* Nice. But the meaning lay so tightly coiled in the poem that the mind slid right off the shiny surfaces. *Words, words, words.* The second reading was trickier. The mind stood at military attention: *What is the theme? What is the subtext? What, exactly, is this poem* about? The poet and writer Robert Macfarlane told me that many of his literature students at Cambridge, brilliant as they are, arrive as freshmen armed with this kind of critical apparatus, eager to flay a poem alive but unable to allow the poem to do the same to them.

The trick to the second reading lies in what the Zen Buddhist master Kōshō Uchiyama called "opening the hand of thought." This reading is a leap of faith, and like all true faith, it's born of experience. The growing awe of language John and I shared was part of that experience and the teacher's scaffolding gave us the rest. We took her at her word that there were hidden dimensions of beauty in this writing, and that they couldn't be pried out of it under torture.

So on the second reading we aimed for a state I would now call *meditative*, resting what Buddhism calls "bare attention" on each word, each line, and allowing the meaning to blossom forth. With this kind of "right mindfulness," consciousness goes to work on itself, gradually unraveling its own confusion.

In childhood, imaginative play is second nature. "Losing yourself" in a game of tag or a fantasy story is an everyday experience. I would argue that kenosis is truly possible only after what the great child psychologist Jean Piaget called the "concrete operational" phase of development, that period from roughly seven to eleven years old when we're fascinated with reality, justice, and the physical world. During this phase kids leave behind what Piaget saw as the strong egocentrism of early childhood. But in the process they paradoxically become more self-conscious—more aware of the differences between themselves and everything else. By twelve, when many kids are entering middle school, they are often too rigid in this thinking to slip easily into and out of fantasy worlds. Friendships don't just happen—they have to be negotiated. Kenosis is the spiritual act of crossing that gulf in reverse—returning to a state of unselfconscious innocence.

It's one thing to be subject to magic, another to understand how it's done, and still another to find its power enhanced, not diminished, by that knowledge. In those years language took hold of John and me in a different way than it ever had before, and we took hold of it. And as with everything else that's ever moved me, I couldn't shut up about it.

Not everyone was interested. In many people—my dad among them—poetry and literature didn't produce much kenosis. They were important in theory but much less important in fact than the evening news or what time to set the alarm clock for work in the morning.

That's the tricky thing about kenosis. If you can't resist the explanatory, evangelical urge, the ego comes roaring right back, stronger than ever. While annoying everybody you meet with your conversion story, you will learn that people have other interests and priorities that don't remotely include John Donne. Faced with their indifference or pushback, you will feel like one of the biblical prophets out in the wilderness, crying, "Repent! Repent!" You'll wonder what's wrong with these people. Why they can't see transcendence when it's staring them right in the face. You will come to the conclusion that only you and a select group of seers possess the true knowledge and that everybody else is an idiot.

This is terribly sad, of course. Because in doing so you will have taken that sense of universal connectedness and turned it into plate armor for the ego. A walled garden with no doors or windows.

Basketball, math, entrepreneurship—all of these were more or less closed books to me. In all of them kenosis was possible, just not for me. So I pledged my soul to the Church of Art and decided that everything else was a total waste of time.

I wanted to climb to the top of the (as yet unfinished) National Cathedral and sing these poems out to the world. I wanted everyone to stop dead in their tracks and listen. And I wanted some of that magic for myself. My first girlfriend politely accepted a string of sonnets she had inspired: horrible doggerel in the early John Donne mode of "we're all going to die one day, so let's sleep together now." Luckily for both of us, the poems were incomprehensible.

Kenosis is like falling in love. Nothing in the world exists besides the source of that extraordinary experience. This is especially true of young kenosis. As with love, it takes years to learn that you're not automatically worthy of the gift. It comes with responsibilities. It demands patience, humility, empathy, hard work. And if you want to nurture and sustain it in a world that's pulling you in a thousand different directions, you need to understand the physics of those forces. In other words, you have to grow up.

The Bells

Dear Meri,

I've been talking to some of your old friends. One told me about a night you both spent sleeping on the roof of her family's second home in Austria. This was the summer after the operation and the chemo, when you were both thirteen years old. The bold roof-camping idea (which was yours, of course) shocked her well-mannered family at first. They were open-minded people, but this was extraordinary. You argued respectfully and persuasively, citing the health benefits of fresh air, the educational benefits of studying the night sky, and in the end they had to give in. They were all crazy about you, she said. Putty in your hands.

Your friend remembers gratefully the exhilaration of that new, lofty rooftop perspective, of the freedom you gave her to do the unthinkable. "Meri owned her space in the world," she said, "like, wherever she was, she belonged there."

The cancer had changed you, she said. You came close to dying. And no matter how much support one might get from family, friends, or doctors, death is something we all have to face alone. Maybe after an experience like that you learn to keep your own counsel. Maybe you don't look outside yourself, so much, for answers to the biggest questions. As far back as I can remember, you never shied away from speaking your mind, never got paralyzed, as I did, contemplating other people's feelings or intentions. Surviving cancer, maybe, just made you even more like yourself.

Another friend, from college, remembers your loyalty. More than once in the middle of the night a classmate called in desperate circumstances… police trouble, a broken-down car in the middle of nowhere…and off you ran to rescue them. Though you never had kids of your own, you were mother to many a lost child. People came to expect this—to rely on it. People of whom (I often thought) you couldn't expect the same in return. I remember the flip side of this loyalty, too; God help anyone who got on the wrong side of you. Your judgment was fair, for the most part, but it was swift and it was total.

"You know what your problem is? You're so money, and you don't even know it." You said this to me once when we were both young adults. I didn't recognize the movie quote, but I rolled my eyes at the idiom: I'm so "money"? Where did you even pick that up? Why would any-one want to be money? But I also understood exactly what you meant. I spent so many years looking to the outside world for validation or its opposite—confirmation of my own fears of worthlessness.

Any fears of worthlessness, any self-doubt, you kept to yourself for as long as you could. You spat in the face of anything that threatened to slow you down. That college friend visited you one winter in Bethesda. Your leg was in a full cast from a recent adjustment to the prosthesis, but you insisted on driving into DC to show him the cathedral. In high school, you'd been a bell ringer there, heaving with all your might on the thickness of rope, testing your body weight against the tonnage of brass. Turning force and determination into music.

The Church of the Stage

In ninth grade I was drafted into a school play: a production of Luigi Pirandello's *Six Characters in Search of an Author*. My character was mute—a troubled boy who shoots himself at the end. The senior who recruited me for the role later told me I'd been chosen because (a) I looked "bug-eyed and weird," and (b) the kid who was supposed to play the part had to drop out because his mom wasn't comfortable with the suicide.

I sat, stood, and lay there dead through every rehearsal, mutely enraptured as Pirandello's poetry filled the theater and my schoolmates became different people—ghosts from a time long before any of us was born. As we entered tech week, the week before opening night, the costumes, the makeup, and the lighting through colored plastic "gels" had the strange effect of making everything more real and more imaginary at once.

Theater was scripture in Karen Armstrong's sense because—unlike poetry—it brought our school together. After sports, Drama was the best-funded department at St. Albans, which gave us Broadway-grade rotating stages, a full-time costume department, and professional lights. A theater production at the school was a big event, drawing students, faculty, alumni, and people from around DC's Northwest.

The ritual of the play—these same words repeated nightly with the same sequences of lighting and sound—was a whole world you could lose yourself in while at the same time watching it unfold, always with one side-eye on the audience.

The Dionysia, ancient Greek festivals for Dionysus, were the origins of theater in the West. In Euripides's *The Bacchae*—a story I first encountered in a video of the transcendent and terrifying 1969 Richard Schechner production *Dionysus in '69*, the kind of brilliantly reckless psychodrama only the late '60s could have come up with, complete with nude actors and random audience members rolling around and groping one another—delight crosses the invisible borderline into delirium as women, gone bestial under the god's spell, tear the king, Pentheus, limb from limb. This sums up neatly the chaotic, impassioned spirit of Dionysus and his art.

From the beginning, the ecstatic heights theater could reach and the transformations it could effect in people were held within (and made possible by) the container of ritual. This strange balance is somehow essential to kenosis—this simultaneous immersion in and awareness of the experience. There is always a fourth wall. The Buddhist practice of *sati*, or mindfulness, relies on the same creative tension. Observing your own unfolding experience, you gain liberating insight. Or to put it another way, the container is the discipline that makes freedom possible.

Sophomore year I was cast as another kid who says very little, then dies: Macduff's son in *Macbeth*. Hearing Shakespeare's words brought to life each night, joking backstage with the cast and crew, I felt I had found my true home. This was poetry in action, sounds as spells, and for the first time in my life, a real community. There was some competition for parts, of course, but once the play was cast, you were family. Theater people were an eclectic bunch, many of us misfits everywhere else. We were talkative, awkward, overenergetic, drawn to the fantastical and the absurd, and we were grateful, one and all, for having found one another.

Then John and I met Francine Tacker ("Frankie"), a veteran of repertory theater and television (*Dallas*, *The Paper Chase*) who directed musicals and plays at St. Albans. The only adult in my life who seemed to see me clearly, Frankie cast me as the bumbling gangster Moonface Martin in *Anything Goes*, and taught me to tap dance. Captivated, as she later told me, by our friendship, she took John and me under her wing and totally changed the direction of our lives.

Frankie was everything my homelife was not. She was glamourous and bursting with vivid joy. Loving, kind, and stunningly beautiful, she swept into our lives like Mary Poppins, making the fantastical real. At a time when I was suffocating under the weight of grim responsibility, she confirmed the value of fun and beauty, the possibility of magic in the world.

Frankie was a Dionysian oracle, a high priestess of the Church of Art, and we were her acolytes. She convinced us that art was the key to escaping the ordinary, and that more than anything else (except possibly for love), it was worth pursuing with blind, single-minded passion. She offered us both the vision of a better life and a concrete discipline for making it happen.

The vision came first, though. Frankie showed us Zeffirelli's film of *Romeo and Juliet*. Like so many adolescents before me, I fell in love with Olivia Hussey as Juliet. In imagination I traded places with Romeo and through him entered the world of the play. This was a world of high stakes—where lifelong happiness or death could hinge on a turn of phrase. Most of all—by contrast to the mall and homework and church every Sunday—it was utterly, intensely alive.

Frankie took us to see the glorious, restored *Lawrence of Ara-*

bia at the Uptown Theater, DC's last remaining grand movie palace (now, sadly, closed). John and I were captivated and went on to rent every movie we could find starring Peter O'Toole, many of them costarring his real-life drinking buddy Richard Burton. In some ways Burton and O'Toole offered a vision of what John and I might one day become, and consecrated our differences. Burton's stocky body, bookishness, and moody, introspective temperament reminded me of myself. O'Toole's thousand-yard cerulean stare and his ethereal lightness of being were John, writ large.

In junior year, Frankie pulled off the magic trick of convincing my parents to let me study acting in an Oxford summer program with members of the Royal Shakespeare Company. John's mom needed no such convincing. For months at St. Albans John and I trained intensively, watching the whole of the BBC's *Playing Shakespeare* series—a master class in classical acting starring Jane Lapotaire, Judi Dench, Ian McKellen, and more—and trying to apply its lessons to our monologue work. Then we went to New York, where we stayed with former students of Frankie's, to audition. After we were accepted, we spent the summer on the college lawns and streets of Oxford, where we learned as much about cider, hashish, and girls as we did about acting. Jane Lapotaire, my teacher there, taught me one lesson sufficient to fuel a lifetime of practice: presence and connection are everything. The words and the details of character come after.

Frankie knew all about the business side of art, but she kept those lessons to herself. At the peak of her career, disillusioned with the industry, she had fled Hollywood and come east to DC. She joined a closed religious community, devoting her life to the sect of the Indian guru Meher Baba. She had learned about "Sufism"—as Meher Baba called his teachings, though they had little in common with the Islamic mysticism from which they got their name—from The Who's lead singer, Pete

JOANN SMYTH

Jason gone Goth at Oxford, age sixteen. When he first came to Shakespeare class like this, the instructor, actor Peter Jeffrey, quipped, "So, what have we come as today?"

Townshend, a neighbor of Frankie's when she had briefly lived in England. When we knew her, she was still a practicing Sufi. This wasn't the kind of thing you could talk about openly at St. Albans in the '80s without risking termination. But somehow Frankie ended up sharing it with John, who—at a critical moment—shared it with me.

Like Islamic Sufism, Meher Baba's is a mystical religion of

self-realization through love and devotion to God. It also borrows elements of its complex metaphysics from Hinduism and Buddhism. In it, Frankie had found a meaningful life path—an alternative to what she'd come to see as the hollow materialism of the film and TV business.

So the teachings of the Church of Art she passed along to us were orthodox, pure and unmuddied by the grubby realities of making a living in theater or film. The focus was on transcendence and the training it took to achieve it.

From the moment I started gushing about poetry and theater, my father tried to warn me about the challenges of making a living as an artist. It was fine as a hobby, but too risky as a career. What about dinner theater on the weekends? Mom Mom had raised him to love museums and visual art. History of Art had been one of his favorite classes back in college. But so much of his life as a businessman and a father—his real life—was focused on how to make money. When we weren't arguing, we stared at one another from across the divide of the Two Cultures, each shaking his head in disbelief at the other's ignorance.

Money matters affect everyone, of course. But our big suburban house, the Lexus he drove, our private schools, our summer vacations—the whole apparatus of the life he'd built cost a staggering amount of money to maintain. In his world, professions like medicine and law made sense. Being an actor did not.

Meanwhile, everything in the popular culture reinforced my position in the drama we were playing out: every movie, TV show, and pop song insisted that life was about finding and following your passion, and that anyone who called your dreams impractical or unrealistic was an enemy or an obstacle to overcome.

In our senior year, after *Romeo and Juliet*, Frankie produced Peter Shaffer's *Equus*—an independent project costarring me and John and backed by the religion department. It was mandatory viewing for the whole school. I played the troubled and bug-eyed (though very much non-mute) Alan Strang, who develops a personal, psychosexual religion around horses. Like the Church of Art, Alan's passion is misunderstood by the everyday world. It demands total, obsessive devotion and promises transcendence in return. I threw myself into the role so completely that I couldn't tell where Alan ended and Jason began.

John played Dysart, the psychiatrist Alan's sent to after blinding a whole stable of horses with a dagger in a religious fit of ecstasy. The play is about the fine line between kenosis and madness. Between everyday living and the dream of something greater. It hinges on the question of whether a life of pure passion is possible, and at what cost. As the representative of science and reason, Dysart struggles with the job of restoring Alan to normalcy. How can Dysart in good conscience rob this boy of something he himself has always longed for, but has never known: the ecstasy of being fully alive?

In the small world of St. Albans and its sister school NCS—which Meri attended—the play was a massive success. All the praise I got from teachers and classmates confirmed what I already believed—that the theater had chosen me. That the Muse had swept me up in her arms and would banish forever all those feelings of insignificance, awkwardness, and shame.

Around the same time I was accepted into NYU's Tisch School of the Arts, and because its program left space for non-acting classes and therefore the possibility of "something to fall back on," my folks reluctantly agreed to send me there.

Part 2

Bicoastal

Dear John,

Why don't I remember that first separation, when you went off to UC Berkeley and I went to NYU? You were home and safety to me. Our friendship was a terrarium in which I took root, dared to grow some bold and exploratory branches. How I needed you—the warmth of your smile, the light of your intellect, your readiness for any adventure! I was quick with a joke, I put on a brave face, but my thoughts were always turned inward, rooting around in the dark for the source of some indefinable pain. Your love drew me out into the light of the world. How could I so easily have let that go?

Even before you followed Meher Baba, you struck me (and others) as a holy child, someone not quite of this world. Before you began your physical and spiritual transformation into a dancer, your academic accomplishments were staggering: cum laude at St. Albans, a National Merit Scholarship Finalist, a Brown University award for literary achievements and one from the Folger Shakespeare Library. The year we graduated, you were one of a handful of students in the country with perfect SATs. We never talked about any of this—a mercy on your part, because it might have come between us. Outside of English and drama, I struggled to stay afloat at St. Albans. I was lucky to graduate, never mind win-

ning any awards. You were so aware of what our friendship meant, so protective of that irreplaceable thing.

I always felt I had so little to give you. Scrabbling around in the dirt of my own fears and grievances, I felt so ashamed of the smallness of my heart compared to yours. As the circle of your spirit expanded and you made new friends through dance, I was terrified you'd leave me behind.

Some fears are too great to bear, so when we went off to college I think there was no grand goodbye, no acknowledgment of closure or change. I must have latched on to the momentum of New York for dear life and tried desperately not to look back.

I know that you loved me, too. Libby, the love of your life and the one who held you as it ran out, says I kept you grounded, kept you from spinning off into infinity like Nijinsky in that poem you wrote. Like your older sister, who lost her mind and took her own life.

Libby says (this makes me laugh) that with my biker jacket, Sex Pistols CDs, and inner darkness, I taught you something about how to be "cool." How to translate your genius from Old English into something sexier, more contemporary. For all our differences, our souls recognized something in one another—a love of language and beauty, some special flavor of curiosity. I might not have been able to memorize the entire English royal lineage back to Egbert or learn as much as you did of Elvish high script, but together we celebrated what moved us and decided what made life worth living. And as sex and romance entered our lives, we tried to help each other understand the nature of love.

So unceremoniously, off we went—you to the home of American optimism, sunny Northern California, and me to the gritty, aggressively real streets of New York. I was in a Lou Reed fever dream, looking for poetry in the glitter of glass chips in the sidewalk, and you, as always, were elsewhere, in search of something divine, indivisible, infinite.

Curiouser and Curiouser

Freshman year, I lived in Hayden Hall, a dormitory on the east side of Washington Square Park. My roommate Ed, from Freehold, New Jersey, sported a blazer, hair gel, and Calvin Klein cologne, all of which I instantly judged as square and "cheesy." Like Bob Dylan, Jimi Hendrix, and so many others before me, I was an artist newly arrived in the greatest city in the world to discover myself and make my mark. At first glance Ed was St. Albans material—everything I was leaving behind. Worse, he was premed: aspiring to be like my parents. Meeting my dad, he was articulate and deferential, an impressively mature young man with a deep voice and a firm handshake. Dad helped me drop my stuff off in the dorm room, took us both out for dinner, bought us a six-pack of Grolsch beer, and left us to start our new life.

From the moment I arrived in New York City, everything was supercharged with meaning. St. Mark's Place in the East Village—already a pale shadow of its glory days as a hangout for the Velvet Underground and Patti Smith and Richard Hell—

was nonetheless a place where you could buy fifty varieties of Doc Martens in one store (Trash and Vaudeville), stop into a deli for rolling papers, and feel yourself walking in the footsteps of those rock 'n' roll giants.

Wandering up Sixth Avenue, I'd find a random playing card or the poem "Annabel Lee" ripped out of a Poe compendium and study it like a tarot reader or a Talmudic scholar, searching for hidden meaning: *The queen of diamonds. Dignity. The sorrow of responsibility. This is adulthood. I'm a grown-up now...*

Walking around in a Byronic haze was only part of my new life. There was also the frenzy of freshman orientation—a series of pep rallies with purple balloons. There was the excitement of freshman classes: in History of Dramatic Literature with Todd London, I read Shaw, Chekhov, Ionesco, and Beckett and saw how—after the horrors of the first World War—the theater followed (and led) the modern imagination away from orderly realism into the symbolic, the stylized, the surreal.

There was the novelty of the beer Ed and I could now miraculously acquire without ID from any deli. Beer I started opening with my teeth—because this was the kind of carefree chap I now believed myself to be—until a piece of one of my molars broke off and I gave up the practice. Square or not, Ed quickly became a friend. And like Nantucket and John's house, college became a place of refuge, somewhere I could experiment, explore, and belong.

Theater training happened three days a week in what Tisch called "studios." Some were acting schools in the city, like the Lee Strasberg Institute, home of method acting. Others, like the "experimental studio" were run in-house by NYU. Circle in the Square—a professional school attached to a theater in Midtown—seemed to offer the most well-rounded training in movement, voice, and naturalistic acting, so I decided to start there.

First year acting training at Circle had less to do with scenes and monologues than with a kind of whole-body therapy, an exploration of the depths of self. Through yoga, voice exercises, and imaginative games you came face-to-face with old habits of mind and body. The teacher's job was to help you see them and stretch past them, increasing your emotional and physical range. This was preparation for the real work of an actor: embodying the full spectrum of human experience.

I found a lot of this work painful and difficult, but I took it seriously. I had come to college full of defensive postures, self-protective strategies that separated me from myself and others. I understood the value of trying to break down these walls. Playing theater games like the mirror exercise in which you try to mirror a partner's movements without any planning or verbal communication, I saw how self-enclosed I was, how afraid of emotional and physical connection. Struggling with yoga postures in our movement class, I felt how much tension and fear I carried in my body.

One teacher asked us to lie on the floor and envision a blue circle of light scanning us slowly from head to toe. In this meditation—the first I'd ever done—I noticed the irritable nitpicking of my critical mind as it worried about what shade the light should be and whether or not I had properly understood what she meant by "scanning." While students around me broke down in tears and reported breakthroughs, I got a first glimpse of the cunning masonry of my own inner walls.

All of my breakthroughs happened outside of the studio. Face-to-face in our dorm room, Ed and I began experimenting with psychedelics—LSD and mescaline. I don't know who proposed it first, but for both of us this had nothing to do with partying or "tripping out" to cool visuals. It was a sacred ritual to be done under safe and controlled conditions. Most Friday nights we became what the previous generation of psychedelic explorers had called "psychonauts," on a mission to discover deeper layers of self, reality, and consciousness. For eight to twelve hours at a stretch we talked intensely about the thoughts, feelings, and memories that arose, arriving at new insights about our families, ourselves, and the fabric of reality.

In those days the public internet, with its subreddits and dark web and chat rooms that could steer you to reliable sources of quality psychedelics, did not yet exist. So scoring was hit-or-miss. Fake LSD—little squares of paper bearing designs like the Grateful Dead's dancing bear—was indistinguishable from the real thing until about forty-five minutes after you took it. We tried Washington Square, then Sheep Meadow on the east side of Central Park, near Strawberry Fields and the Dakota apartment building (where pioneering psychonaut John Lennon was shot dead in 1980). Washington Square was hit-or-miss. Sheep Meadow was mostly hit. We bought LSD and tiny yellow mescaline pills and psilocybe cubensis mushrooms. And one time, some salad mushrooms, still wrapped in butcher paper from the deli where the guy bought them after I'd handed him my fifty bucks.

Our trips had nothing to do with butterflies and moonbeams and fairy tales. For me, there were no visual hallucinations beyond a slight distortion of perspective: hands looked bigger than they were, flat walls bowed slightly outward, and everything, if you looked at it long enough, seemed to breathe gently in and out. If anything, these visuals felt like a distraction from the real work of conversation, connection, and sinking ever deeper into being itself.

According to everything I'd learned growing up in 1980s America, sinking of any kind was not a good thing. Even sitting still was suspect. In his powerful book *This Life*, philosopher Martin Hägglund holds, with Marx, that value under capitalism transforms the time of our lives into a commodity to be bought, sold, and squeezed for every last drop of productivity, robbing us of the freedom to value that time in and of itself, or as a means to whatever ends we might value in the absence of the profit motive. Raising our children with love, for example, or building a more equitable society. Or sitting in a park. Or exploring the nature of reality on LSD.

What psychedelics did for me—in the collegiate bubble of safety my parents' work in the marketplace had paid for—was to show me what it felt like to value my existence for its own sake.

I can't overstate the power of this insight. In childhood, if we're loved and living in a place of relative safety, we're not expected to prove our worth through performance. We don't have to defend ourselves against charges that who we are or what we want to be isn't useful enough or of sufficient economic value to others. That sense of intrinsic confidence and self-worth are the foundation for valuing other people as something other than a means to an end. In the adult world, in the marketplace, everything conspires to undermine this certainty.

It isn't the conversations I remember, or even the narrative arcs of the trips (which do, always, have surprisingly compelling and coherent narrative arcs.) It's the surrender of forward momentum and how that opened up space for being. Forced by these molecules to turn off our storytelling brains, Ed and I were flooded with gratitude and awe at the interconnectedness of all things. It was a new doorway into kenosis.

The other effect of these medicines was to show me the walls I'd glimpsed in acting class and help me break them down. Many times I found myself weeping, suddenly struck with some painful insight into my own past behavior, my attitudes, and my biases. I felt this as a process of mourning, metabolizing stuck bits of self, and healing old wounds. During the trip and afterward, it helped me flow with the present, instead of haunting forever these sites of past trauma.

To be sure, there was a *Flowers for Algernon* quality to the way the blinders could slip surreptitiously back on in the days and weeks after these experiences. I'd go home for winter break and watch myself reliving all the old scripts, mortified at my mealy-mouthed attempts to explain my new vision of reality to a skeptical mom and dad over dinner: "I mean, it's just like...people are all in their own little worlds all the time and they don't, like, really see what's going on, you know?" And I'd reasonably wonder whether it had all been a pipe dream. If you couldn't articulate these deep truths, if you couldn't inhabit them as fully at your parents' dinner table as in your dorm room, how true or deep could they actually be?

It wasn't the drugs' fault; being true to yourself is so much easier in a place of refuge than in a space where everything about you is contested. And where it matters most, explanation so often falls short.

I once asked Joseph Goldstein, a great Buddhist teacher who deserves a lion's share of the credit for bringing what is now called "mindfulness" to the West in the early '70s, what he thought about psychedelics. Having taken some himself in the '60s, he conceded that these substances offer a glimpse of the deeper truths meditation teaches. In his understanding, they "add energy to the system," whereas the purpose of Buddhist practice is to learn to generate that energy yourself, which he understood as preferable. I asked him whether he considered Buddhist scripture an outside substance that adds energy to the system. He laughed, but didn't answer the question.

On this one point I have to disagree with Goldstein, whose teachings have given me so much. I don't think it matters where the energy comes from. Over time I've come to see Buddhist practice and psychedelics as mutually reinforcing tools, working through different mechanisms toward the same ends.

The history of psychedelic use in indigenous cultures with no written records is a matter of debate among anthropologists. But there is strong archeological evidence—in the form of paintings and stone artifacts—that humans all over the world have been using psychedelic plants, cactuses, and mushrooms for thousands of years. Among indigenous tribes throughout the Americas today they are used for medicinal and religious purposes—to heal sickness, to cast out bad spirits—as well as for personal development, as in rites of passage to adulthood or mental preparation for a hunt. While every culture evolves over time, it is likely that these modern-day ceremonies preserve some of the ancient features and purposes of these traditions. In other words, our species has a long and ongoing relationship with these substances as medicines for the body, mind, and spirit.

In modern Western cultures, where body, mind, and spirit have tended to be divided from one another and considered separately, first by the Catholic Church in Medieval Europe and then further by philosophy, medicine, psychology, and psychiatry, the history is very different. There's evidence that Greek mystery cults like those that performed the Eleusinian Mysteries—though the details of these secret rituals are lost to history—may have used psychedelic substances like ergot (a fungus that grows on rye) to induce trancelike states. Viewed as demonic, these cults were persecuted mostly out of existence by the Christian Roman Empire after the fourth century. Something similar happened when Spanish conquistadors encountered the ceremonial use of mescaline-containing cactuses in South America and mushrooms in what is now Mexico: the newcomers denounced these traditional medicines as tools of the devil and outlawed their use.

The chemist Albert Hofmann's accidental discovery of LSD in 1938 reintroduced psychedelics to the modern Western world. Until the mid-1960s, the drug was the subject of widespread psychological research, with promising results for treating anxiety, depression, obsessive-compulsive disorder, alcoholism, and other conditions. But by 1966, a conservative cultural backlash against these substances had grown to the point that Nevada, then California, then the rest of the US declared LSD a Schedule I substance with "high potential for abuse" and without any "currently accepted medical use in treatment," making its possession and sale illegal. In 1968, the Federal Food and Drug Act was amended to prohibit the possession of psilocybin and psilocin, the psychoactive components of magic mushrooms.

Clearly, prohibition didn't stop people from using psychedelics openly in the late '60s. But it meant that scientific research on their potential benefits came to a screeching halt. These drugs were relegated to countercultural status and became the subject of political propaganda by Nixon and other conservative politicians seeking to associate them with "dangerous," "radical" elements of the left, including Black Americans marching for racial equity and young people protesting the Vietnam War. No longer considered potential medicines, psychedelics came to be seen by mainstream culture as a threat to industry, family, and the American Way.

The late '60s saw an explosion in psychedelic use among young people. It's reflexive at this point to ridicule Timothy Leary's transformation from respected Harvard prof into LSD Pied Piper, exhorting college kids to *turn on, tune in, and drop out.* But in the absence of any scientific guidance or cultural tradition to guide their efforts, the hippie generation followed the leaders it could find and engaged in a mass, uncontrolled experiment with these powerful substances.

The results were sometimes unfortunate. The Buddha famously warned his disciples not to become too attached to him. Like a boat that carries you across a river or a finger that points at the moon, he said, his teachings were the path to enlightenment, not the destination. Once they'd served their purpose, you were supposed to let them go. But the '60s psychedelic movement was "young kenosis." Many became too intoxicated—figuratively and literally—with the drugs themselves.

Some assumed that tripping all the time or on ever-increasing doses would, on its own, transform them and society permanently for the better. Some assumed that if they personally embodied the freedom of consciousness they'd tasted, the world would rearrange itself accordingly—as in the fake but compelling Gandhi quote: "be the change you want to see in the world."

These experiments opened "doors of perception"—a William Blake phrase borrowed as a book title by psychedelic pioneer Aldous Huxley—with the potential to benefit humanity. They unleashed the rock revolution led by Jimmy Hendrix, Parliament, The Beatles, the Grateful Dead, and Pink Floyd, among others. They fueled new visions of social justice, ecology, and collective living. And they inspired many young seekers to travel East in search of Buddhist and Hindu spiritual guidance, which they brought back with them to the West.

But there were also a lot of casualties. Psychedelics are risky for people vulnerable to schizophrenia or personality disorders like bipolar. Indigenous ceremonial use and current psychological testing suggests that they're best taken in a mindset and setting of safety, comfort, and positive intent—elements that might or might not exist at a random party or the Woodstock festival. While psychedelic-induced deaths are extremely rare, there were "bad trips" (sometimes made much worse by the arrival of an ambulance and police), psychotic breaks, the murder of pregnant actress Sharon Tate by Charles Manson's cult "family," and other horror stories of LSD use gone wrong. As Danny the philosophical drug dealer puts it in the film *Withnail and I*, set in 1969: "They're selling hippie wigs in Woolworths, man. The greatest generation in the history of mankind is over…and we have failed to paint it black."

The fallout from late '60s idealism—as hippies gave way to yuppies in the Reagan '80s—reinforced a notion that what these substances offer is fantasy. Escapism. A foolish daydream world antithetical to grown-up responsibility. That hasn't been my experience at all. Grown-up responsibility is about self-awareness. It's about connection to others. In the absence of awareness and connection our survival efforts—our attempts at homeostasis—

cause harm and perpetuate intergenerational trauma. In my experience, psychedelic medicines can make us wiser, more skillful stewards of our lives, families, and communities.

Happily, modern psychological science is starting to agree. Since 2009 there has been a renaissance of research with psychedelics and controlled psychoactive substances like MDMA (ecstasy) and ketamine. Laboratories at Johns Hopkins, NYU, and other major universities are doing active clinical trials, continuing the research into the potential benefits of these medicines for treating anxiety, depression, and trauma. A week before this writing, Stanford announced its own forthcoming psychedelic research department.

These laboratories are producing valuable data on dosage, effects, and the duration of the benefits of these chemicals. In the not-too-distant future, there will be legal psychedelic therapeutic retreats in the United States. Given the millions of Americans currently taking Lexapro, Prozac, and other antidepressants, and given what I know of psychedelics, we may be on the cusp of a revolution in Western consciousness and the treatment of mental illness. Along with the growing scientific understanding of the "mind-body connection" at play in autoimmune diseases and psychopathologies, this may be a powerful corrective to the mind-body-spirit split that has brought us so much trouble along with so much of our knowledge. The two cultures, bridged. Los and Urizen, reunited at last.

Simultaneously there are grassroots efforts underway to decriminalize psychedelics in America. In May 2019, the city of Denver, Colorado, voted to do just that, followed by Ann Arbor, Michigan, Oakland, California, Washington, DC, and Cambridge, Massachusetts. This trend is likely to continue. One can only hope that we've learned some of the lessons of the '60s so that these new freedoms don't lead to another political backlash that threatens scientific research all over again. "Ayahuasca tourism" from America and Europe to Peru and other parts of Latin America is a growing phenomenon, with mixed effects on indigenous cultures—on the one hand, new streams of income and global connection and on the other threats to their traditions and cultural integrity.

With rapid changes coming from multiple directions, these medicines are once again poised to become mainstream. If managed wisely, I believe they have the power to transform Western culture for the better, healing some of our deepest wounds. Given the cultural divisions and existential threats we currently face, I think we need this healing more urgently now than ever.

Freshman year I read both of Lewis Carroll's *Alice* books a few times through. One of my favorite moments, in *Alice's Adventures in Wonderland*, is the heroine's first encounter with the Cheshire Cat. The illustration, by John Tenniel, of Alice standing at the foot of the tree looking up at the giant, grinning apparition haunted my imagination for almost thirty years until this past summer, in Istanbul, I had it tattooed in meticulous detail on my upper arm.

Alice: Would you tell me, please, which way I ought to go from here?

The Cheshire Cat: That depends a good deal on where you want to get to.

Alice: I don't much care where.

The Cheshire Cat: Then it doesn't much matter which way you go.

Alice:... So long as I get somewhere.

The Cheshire Cat: Oh, you're sure to do that, if only you walk long enough.

A gifted logician and mathematician, Carroll pokes fun at the self-importance of the rational mind. As a scientific thinker, he's well aware of the great discoveries of the Age of Enlightenment. As a poet and an artist, he's wary of its relentless solutionism and the threats of industrialization to the human spirit.

Appearing and disappearing at will, the Cat repeatedly shows up to disrupt any story Alice can construct to make sense of this upside-down place, tripping up her determination to "get to the bottom" of whatever's going on here. Like a psychedelic, he's an anti-explainer, drawing her deeper into the mysteries of the world. Sinking into its strangeness, Alice gains knowledge about herself. She gains strength, agency, and the creative flexibility she ultimately needs to defeat the Queen of Hearts.

It's an understandable error, but an error nonetheless, to confuse openness and receptivity with passivity. Sitting in Hayden Hall with Ed, psychedelics opened my mind and heart to new levels of reality. They taught me new, skillful means of engaging in the world.

I had arrived in New York shrink-wrapped in the story of the misunderstood artist whose triumph on the stage would prove my dad wrong about me. Almost immediately, the story began to shift. I hadn't gained much maturity when it came to practical matters, but unexpected doorways into new forms of love, philosophical inquiry, and self-expression opened up and I stepped eagerly through them.

In doing so, I was already leaving acting behind. But old stories rarely die without a fight.

The Church of Harold and Maude

Maude: Let's play something together.
Harold: I don't play anything.
Maude: Dear me...everybody should be able to make a little music!
That's the cosmic dance...

—From *Harold and Maude* (1971)

I don't know how I first heard about Hal Ashby's 1971 movie *Harold and Maude.* But it's no exaggeration to say that it became holy scripture for me that freshman year. I watched it at least a hundred times and insisted that Meri and every other person I knew sit down and watch it with me. I memorized the script and mumbled the words along with the actors. I bought the CD *Footsteps in the Dark*—of Cat Stevens's songs from the film, and listened to it constantly. The ideas of the movie fit like synaptic endings into my psychedelics-expanded neural network and became guiding principles for my life.

Half of the film is a black comedy about twenty-year-old Harold's relationship with his mother. It's not clear where her money comes from, but she's the kind of socialite you might find at any museum fundraiser, her head wrapped in an Hermès scarf. They live together in a forbiddingly grand mansion in the Bay Area of Northern California, and the first time we meet Harold, he is floating facedown in their swimming pool, dead.

Only he isn't dead. He's a performance artist. Staging elaborate "suicides" is Harold's form of rebellion. It's how he lets his mom know he's unhappy with their boring, mainstream, suburban life. For his birthday, Mom gives him a Jaguar XKE with a bow on it. With an arc welder and an airbrush, he turns it into a hearse. Mom has a dating service send over a nice young woman and as she chirps about her exciting job as a file clerk at Harrison Feed and Grain ("We supply, for example, most of the egg farmers in Petaluma...so you can imagine!"), Harold calmly sets himself on fire.

Like Dustin Hoffman's character in *The Graduate*, Harold is on the brink of his adult life but directionless. Or rather, all of his creative energy is wasted in a recursive loop. His mom will never change, and none of the elaborate psychodramas he performs for her makes him any happier. In response to the predictable but empty forward momentum of the life he was born into, the only thing he knows how to do is resist. He can't yet imagine a better alternative.

Then he meets Maude. She's just shy of her eightieth birthday and, like Harold, enjoys attending strangers' funerals as a hobby. But while Harold's interest is morbid, Maude shows up dressed all in white and carrying a bright yellow umbrella, in celebration of the cycle of life. After winking at him through one such funeral, Maude offers Harold a ride in a car she has just casually stolen. Then his life begins to change.

Maude is a Holocaust survivor—a crucial detail that's easily missed. Somewhere in the middle of the film Ashby lets the camera play across her forearm just long enough to reveal the concentration camp numbers tattooed there. Having endured those horrors and outlived two husbands she's become what I now think of as a kind of Taoist—determined to live life fully, playfully, and joyfully, dancing with the ebb and flow of inevitable change. Like my sister, another survivor, she's unwilling to let anything stand in her way.

With Maude, for the first time in the movie, we see Harold smiling and laughing. When she hooks him up to a contraption she's made that tells stories through smell, we see him reconnecting to feeling and delighting in beauty for its own sake. For the first time in years (or possibly ever), Harold is fully alive.

Like many audience members when the film was released, Harold's mom is shocked when he announces that he's fallen in love with Maude. The priest she sends him to for counseling can barely stammer out his disgust at the thought of Maude's "...withered flesh...sagging breasts...and flabby buttocks..." But the point here isn't the unlikely love story between a young man and an old lady. It's that love is love, plain and simple, whether or not the world is ready for it.

But Harold's education isn't over. On her eightieth birthday, he fills her house with sunflowers and serves a romantic dinner with champagne. "And after dinner," he says, placing a ring box on the table, "one more surprise...which I hope will make you very happy."

"Oh I am happy, Harold," says Maude. "Ecstatically happy. I couldn't imagine a lovelier farewell."

Maude has taken pills to end her own life. As a horrified Harold rushes her to the emergency room in an ambulance, we learn that this has been her intention for years. Eighty is "a good round number." Maude has lived fully and is ready to move on. "Don't you understand!" screams Harold through his tears, "I love you! I love you!"

"That's wonderful, Harold," says Maude. "Go—and love some more."

Love life fully and without attachment. Accept the joy and

the sadness alike with courage. These messages echoed everything I was learning on psychedelics and in acting class. But the film had another crucial message for me, too.

At one point Harold opens a freestanding wardrobe in Maude's house. It's crammed full of musical instruments.

Maude: Let's play something together.
Harold: I don't play anything.
Maude: Dear me…everybody should be able to make a little music! That's the cosmic dance…

So Harold picks out an old banjo and starts plucking away, tunelessly but joyfully.

At the end of the movie, after Maude dies, we hear the fierce rhythm guitar and gut-wrenching vocals of Cat Stevens's song "Trouble" as Harold drives his Jaguar/hearse at top speed up a winding mountain road: *"Trouble…oh trouble set me free… I have seen your face and it's too much, too much for me…"*

Having reached the top, the car goes flying off a cliff. We wonder for a second whether Harold has done it for real this time. Then the camera pans slowly back to the rolling hills behind the cliff's edge. There's Harold, plucking his banjo as he dances a slow jig away. He's practicing the melody to Cat Stevens's "If You Want to Sing Out, Sing Out":

…if you want to be free, be free
'Cause there's a million things to be…

The film, like the song, leaves us with the message that we are the authors of our own stories. Rather than resisting the flow of life's changes or being drowned in the tide, we have the choice, always, to sing or dance along with them.

Dance is a useful metaphor for active engagement in an impermanent world. Tapping into the flow of nature (the Tao of Taoism, the Dharma of Buddhism) doesn't mean dissolving into nothingness. It means letting go of the cookie-cutter stories that define the ego. In smashing the hearse, Harold is also smashing the role of suicide artist and letting go of his anger at his mom. He's releasing himself to enter the world, get entangled with other lives, and become some of the "million things" he might become.

That Christmas of freshman year, I asked for a guitar. I bought a book of Cat Stevens songs and learned a few open chords: D, then C, then A, then G. With these, I could play and sing some songs from the movie: "If You Want to Sing Out," "The Wind," and "Where Do the Children Play?"

Zen Buddhism talks about "beginner's mind." It's a mindset of openness and simplicity—a friendly curiosity that's willing to take risks and make mistakes. Beginner's mind comes naturally to us in childhood. As adults we face serious challenges. These are best met with openness and imagination, but the weight of responsibility can shut down our ability to access beginner's mind. It can frighten us out of our willingness to be vulnerable. In order to simplify things, we may default to a jaded pragmatism that offers one-size-fits-all solutions. This is a natural response to overwhelming difficulty. But the child is always alive somewhere inside of us. Though we may have silenced it for decades, we can always invite it out to play.

I was eighteen years old and my musical training had stopped after two years of clarinet lessons in middle school. But because of *Harold and Maude*, I suddenly felt free to write songs. I cared less whether they were "good" in some objective sense than whether they felt honest and true. Cat Stevens was my mentor here: many of his songs were structurally very simple but the words, his voice, and the passion of his playing had the power to break your heart.

Since high school I had been filling notebooks with thoughts and poems but writing lyrics felt different. It drew on every-thing I'd learned about meter, rhyme, and wordplay, but instead of overwrought imitations of Shakespeare or Sylvia Plath these songs were attempts at the honest expression of what I was feel-ing and learning in my life. Unlike acting, they lived outside the story that had brought me to New York. They were free of the pressures of my parents' money and expectations, and of my own fears about whether or not I was talented enough to "make it" as an actor. As scene work and monologues entered our studio curriculum, pretending to be other people felt more and more remote to me. I felt awkward and disembodied on-stage. But songwriting was everything I'd wanted from art in the first place.

I filled my free time with this new kind of work. This was a discipline I could embrace as my own. The song itself dictated the process, demanding engagement until it was finished. I'd

Jason in NYU's Hayden Hall dormitory, learning guitar.

find myself working out verses in the shower or on the way to class. There was no nonsense about schedules or organization. However loose or rigorous, the structure of each song and the process of writing it unfolded organically. You started with a couple of chords or a phrase but you were drawn on by some mysterious force, discovering the song in the act of creating it. Maude was right. This was the cosmic dance.

Meanwhile, out at Berkeley, John was learning a different dance, a different discipline. Training in ballet and modern techniques, he saw his body changing and felt his heart drifting away from academia. While I wrote lyrics, he poured all his energy into the work of learning to express the truth beyond words. John knew the price of leaving college—it would mean estrangement from his father, a renowned history professor—but the call grew more and more insistent. When the semester ended, he answered it, dropping out of Berkeley to dance full-time.

John becomes a dancer.

LISA MASTNY

I'll Never Fall in Love with You

The first time I fell in love was at a dance that brought together the boys of Camp Sea Gull—*The Seafaring Camp of the South*—and the girls of Camp Seafarer—*Tagline Unknown*. I don't remember anything about the girl except that she was taller than me, had a Southern accent, and smelled like strawberries. Sea Gull and Seafarer were monthlong, sleepaway YMCA summer camps in Arapahoe, North Carolina, with an astonishing array of activities: for the first half of each day I would roam the massive grounds barefoot, clutching my green "Land" book and picking excruciating burrs out of my feet, doing activities like riflery to master skills that would enable me to earn ranks (in the book) like "marksman" that would unlock privileges like shooting a bigger gun. Afternoons were devoted to "Sea." I was too anxious to sail, but that didn't stop me from repeatedly taking out a tiny Sunfish boat only to freeze in terror thirty yards from shore, unable to find any wind or remember how to look for it. Showing off my sailing skills in Nantucket one summer after camp ended, I got myself and my mom stranded "in stays" barely in sight of shore, screaming "help!" until a Hobie Cat came to rescue us.

But let's stick with love for a bit. Meeting for the first time on the dance floor, the girl and I danced for hours to Madonna's "Into the Groove," Rockwell's "Somebody's Watching Me," and other hits of the day. Slow dancing with my nose at the level of her shoulder, I prayed that magical embrace would never end. It did end, of course, along with summer camp (this was the end-of-camp dance, after all). The girl went back to some exotic place like Alabama and I went home to Bethesda.

But she left me her address. Immediately upon returning home, I began deluging her with multipage letters about the intense sincerity of my love and my plans for our future life together. Her replies were sweet and friendly, at first. But as the onslaught continued, she became increasingly creeped out. Finally she wrote to tell me that her parents thought I was crazy and that I should never try to contact her again. It was an unsettling awakening—to learn that the object of my love was a person, not an object, and also that she was afraid of me.

The thing about romantic love is that we're so rarely honest with ourselves or one another about our motives. Love operates on several levels at once, many of them inaccessible to consciousness. On the surface, there's the person: we fall in love with details that add up to a story—her spidery handwriting. The depression she struggled with in the past. The scratchy sound of her voice. And we fall in love with the less definable energy of her presence. It is literally true that we've never met anyone quite like her before.

And then there's sex. I was not raised in a "sex positive" home, and while Judy Blume books and sex ed in school had taught me the basics, my own sexuality was this vague and murky mystery, as disjointed as dreams. In adolescence, I had no coherent language with which to think or talk about it. I was too shy and atypically masculine to run with a snickering crew of boys, tossing around terms like "sixty-nine" or "blow job." And even if you do have the language—even for the likes of Henry Miller, Anaïs Nin, or Prince, a lifetime of exploration and/or therapy barely scratches the surface. We all struggle to make sense of the body's strange logic and idiosyncrasies. Of why it wants what it wants. Separate from whatever stories couples might tell themselves about how they met and why their love was fated to be, sex takes its own tectonic course.

And then there's the level of psychological need. Sitting in my mental armchair, observing myself on the imaginary couch, I see a pattern stretching all the way back to Camp Sea Gull and continuing well into adulthood: I meet a girl (or woman) through some activity or peer group. The relationship starts organically, sparing me the awkwardness and terror of having to ask her out (something I have never once done in my life). I fall in love quickly and completely. At first there's this sense of having finally found "the missing piece" (as in Shel Silverstein's wise picture book of that name). For a month or so, I am whole—free of the insecurity, doubt, and deep, generalized longing that have always plagued me. I'm probably a fun partner, too—full of songs and poetry, adventure and merriment. But gradually the doubts start to creep back in, gnawing at the edges of my consciousness. Soon the pressure becomes too intense, so I start to talk about the anxiety in hopes of absolution. Then the well-meaning woman becomes my confessor, trying to absorb all this darkness and reassure me that things are okay, until my need and my negativity finally become too much to bear. At some point the relationship ends, confirming what I'd feared to begin with: that there's no love in the world deep enough to cure this pain.

Hard as my conscious self might try to be a loving and generous partner, this wounded self is infinitely selfish and demanding. An insatiable black hole of need.

This pattern of male behavior in heterosexual relationships is well-documented in feminist writing. Understandably, plenty of women are well and truly fed up with doing this kind of "emotional labor" for men who are too out of touch with our own feelings to seek the help we need elsewhere. bell hooks takes a more comprehensive and compassionate view. She holds men accountable for the devastation they often cause in women's lives. But she also traces the ways patriarchal masculinity circumscribes our relationship with our own feelings, conditioning us to perform invulnerability in the world, leaving many of us with nowhere to turn except our partners.

In his book *I Don't Want to Talk about It*, family therapist Terrence Real (a favorite author of bell hooks) takes this a step further, making the case that many men suffer from hidden depression caused by our attempts to conform to masculine ideals. Being an emotional vampire is bad enough. But for those unfortunate men who can't even manage to share their feelings with a partner, this depression often leads to alcoholism, violence, and/or suicide.

My baggage from childhood included this insatiable black hole and the belief that it was a shameful secret, a fundamental character flaw for which I was to blame. Beneath the surface story and the sexual dance of every relationship, this psychological dynamic ran like a dangerous and invisible riptide. And of course, each partner came bearing some baggage of her own.

I met Lisa in October of freshman year at NYU. She looked like a young Carol Kane—a giant mane of frizzy Ashkenazi hair, soulful eyes, and a wry, intelligent smile. I remember noticing her a few times in the Hayden Hall cafeteria and then being introduced by a mutual friend, probably at one of those spontaneous gatherings that was always springing up in one dorm room or another.

Lisa's voice was earthy—somewhere between Lauren Bacall's and Marge Simpson's—and her manner was calm and grounded.

To the boy I was at eighteen, she gave the impression of some-one older and wiser than her years. There was a mysterious background sadness, too—nothing she would allow to cloud the conversation or demand anybody's attention, but ever pres-ent. It was like the sadness of Paris or Istanbul, inextricable from her beauty, and maybe it intrigued me because it echoed my own. She rolled her own cigarettes—a habit that struck me as exotic—and, like me and everybody else I knew, she smoked a lot of weed. Lisa passed the *Harold and Maude* test. We watched it with Ed and she loved the music, the ideas…it was obvious she was a kindred spirit. Soon I was spending all my free time in her room smoking, talking, and listening to music. Once when her roommate was out, we ended up in bed together. I remember how remarkably easy and natural it all felt. It was as if I'd known Lisa my whole life.

But she was emphatic: "I'll never fall in love with you," she announced early on in this thing she didn't want to call a rela-tionship. There were things she couldn't talk about. Past disap-pointments and possibly betrayals. This was new territory for me. In every past relationship (with the exception of that one at Camp Sea Gull) I'd been free to tumble headlong, sonnets and all, but Lisa was telling me to put on the brakes. To accept this for what it was without any strings attached. To cement the point, she lent me a copy of Robert A. Heinlein's *Stranger in a Strange Land*, a hybrid of science fiction and New Age spiritual-ity in which polyamory is presented as an evolved human state. *Okay*, I thought. *Lisa's way more mature than I am. I don't know what I've gotten myself into, but there's no turning back now.*

Meanwhile, out in California, John was falling in love, too. In one of his dance classes, he'd met a girl named Libby. She was a talented mathematician and dancer, and stunningly beautiful—a wood-elf, savvy in practical magic, paired with John's high elv-ish ethereality. On her father's side, Libby was descended from Spanish-Mexican royalty, her family name still powerful in the city of Mérida in the Yucatán Peninsula. Two weeks after they met, John decided this was the girl he would marry.

Like Lisa, Libby was open to other partners and exploration for both of them outside of the relationship. She believed that if the love was as real as it seemed, it would last without artificial constraints. And John was polyamorous by nature. Long before he adopted Frankie's Sufism, he was constitutionally unable to understand why you wouldn't simply follow the heart wherever, whenever, and to whomever it led.

I was monogamous, but not for ideological reasons. Growing up, my parents' marriage never seemed particularly great to me: he was distant and she was yelling half the time—at us or at him, when he couldn't manage to escape somewhere. Apart from the double suicide, of course, Romeo and Juliet always seemed like a better model: a self-enclosed universe of two stars orbiting one another, held in place at an intimate distance by the gravity of their mutual admiration.

Out in California, John and Libby gave their sexuality free rein, seeing it as separate from the force of love that bound them together. Not that this was without its challenges. At one point, John expressed his curiosity about a man he'd met, a fellow dancer. With Libby's blessing, the two men spent a passionate night together. Afterward, terrified that John might realize he was gay and end their relationship, Libby cried for two days straight.

On a long-distance call (expensive in those days), John told me how different and liberating it had felt to explore this other side of himself. He didn't mention Libby's tears. I imagined him and Libby as elevated beings, wise and unconditionally loving, free of petty attachment. By contrast, I felt like a lowly, craven creature, binding Lisa with Urizen-like chains of jealousy. Why couldn't I be braver? Freer? More secure?

I'd dutifully read the Heinlein, but one side effect of the black hole of need was paranoia and jealousy. I was not wired to handle an open relationship, and I told Lisa so. "That's fine," she said. "We don't have to sleep with other people." So we became a happy couple with this primal guilt lurking somewhere in the background of my consciousness—the idea that I wasn't strong enough (*man* enough, maybe) to handle the woman Lisa actually was. The fear that I might be the type of "spineless man" my sister so despised.

Ironically, in my position Meri would have had no such doubts. For her, open relationships were a lame joke from the '70s. Sometimes she could be quite a Puritan—judgmental of girls who wore tight skirts and low-cut tops, disgusted by the undiscriminating randomness of male sexuality. But Meri wore her prudishness (as she wore everything) with disarming confidence. On her, it somehow looked like liberation.

For the time being, Lisa and I just ignored these warning signs. Our lives just fit so comfortably together. By the end of the spring of freshman year, we were spending all of our free time together, listening to Cat Stevens and Van Morrison, picnicking in Central Park with friends, and building a kind of sanctuary that felt grown-up and secure. We took acid together outdoors in Sheep Meadow and for the first time I sat there marveling silently at nature rather than dredging up the demons of the past or exploring the hidden recesses of my soul. For the first time ever, I was content; with Lisa, it was enough just to *be*.

In the summer, she moved into a duplex apartment on Morton Street in the West Village with her black cat, Max. I helped her shop for a futon and a decorative blanket with a medieval sun on it, and for the first time I got a taste of what it must feel like to make a home and a life with someone. Then I flew out to California to visit John.

Road Trip, Bethesda to Houma

A few months earlier—winter break, freshman year, December 1990—we're in John's mom's sky blue Honda Civic hatchback, heading south. There's no CD player—instead we insert one of those plastic, fake-cassette adapters into the tape deck. It connects with a wire to a portable Panasonic CD player. We're listening to Talking Heads' *Little Creatures*. A peppy pop song about a woman who just is, a woman moving in sync with the world.

We're heading southwest on I-81. In the early '90s, there's no American Freedom like the road trip. No single experience that more definitively embodies the United States' daydream of itself. Of course westward is the true vector. To go south is to head backward in time, toward a past we Northerners would rather forget. Westward lies that most American trick of all—amnesia: you hit the open road, heading optimistically toward the future, and you never look back.

The Civic is a stick shift. Manual transmission. I've never driven one before but John gave me quick lessons in some school parking lot one Sunday before we left. I hate having to think about shifting gears. I can't get the timing right on the clutch so the transmission always makes a horrible grinding noise and I'm certain it's about to fall out any minute, with a sickening *clunk* on the asphalt. The anxiety reminds me of sailing at Camp Sea Gull.

This is some grown-up shit. John and I are sharing the driving all the way from Maryland to (just outside) New Orleans, Louisiana, and back. For some reason we've decided it must be nonstop each way, so we'll trade off as needed on the seventeen-hour journey.

We're headed to Houma, Louisiana, about an hour from New Orleans. It's the childhood home of Libby, with a bayou right in the backyard. We'll visit New Orleans for the first time ever—hear some good music, eat some crawfish and beignets. Most important to me, we'll be together, best friends in situ (as opposed to in memory, three thousand miles apart). We've brought along Umberto Eco's just-published *Foucault's Pendulum* and committed to reading it aloud to one another on the way. Aside from music and conversation, the background to our journey will be the labyrinthine schemes of Knights Templar and Rosicrucians. History porn, basically, full of esoteric Kabbalistic symbols and ancient conspiracies, just philosophical and well written enough to feel like we're learning something important. It's Dan Brown for lit snobs.

Through Virginia, 81 is open and expansive. The lollipop-green forest still looms barely tamed on either side, a reminder of a time when the woods were everything and Iroquois ran soundlessly through them in pursuit of the deer that now menace white suburbanites' costly landscaping. Into Tennessee the road is wide, the sky is Superman-blue, and the primal chaos of the forest stays in its lane, submissive under the downward thrusts of the industrial Northeast.

It's been months since we spent any real time together, so we're talking about college and all the ways our lives have changed.

John is now deadly serious about dance, obsessed with Nijinsky and Martha Graham. Like Meri, he is disarmingly sure of himself; he has found his calling.

John has transferred his loyalties from Burton, O'Toole, McKellen, and Stewart—our high school acting heroes—to these new avatars of single-minded artistic devotion. Although I don't know the words for it yet, he's developed what Buddhism would call "right discipline," practicing with integrity, diligently and well. When he isn't dancing or busy with Libby, he's watching videos of classic performances or reading about the history of dance.

And here we go again... I'm a little bit threatened by all this. Between the psychedelics, the freedom of New York, and this new, easygoing kind of love I've found with Lisa, I'm anything but single-minded these days. From my Cheshire Cat perch in my Hayden Hall dorm room I'm a benevolent panopticon, open to the world and soaking everything in. Back there, this wide-eyed openness feels so right. Next to ultradisciplined John, though, I feel like a dilettante at best and a traitor at worst to all the ideals of our high school brotherhood. A heretic to the Church of Art.

I shrug off these poisonous thoughts. This is my best friend. He's taking me to meet the love of his life. Next to their elven beauty and magic, Lisa and I might be homely hobbits, but while the elves are fleeing to Valinor, the hobbits are busy saving Middle Earth.

We hand-crank the windows open and the unseasonably warm winter air ruffles our hair, John's cut short (for dance aerodynamics?) and mine finally liberated to grow into a muppety, Jimmy Page–like mop. We put on The Who's "Baba O'Riley," and John explains that it's about Meher Baba. About spiritual love as the only hope in a "teenage wasteland."

Then I'm daydreaming about senior year of high school. A spontaneous sleepover John and I had at my house one night when my parents were away. Earlier in the day, my high school girlfriend had told me she was attracted to John, shaking me to the core.

By that point John and I were like brothers, so I shared what she'd told me, confessing how wretched I felt and how terrified I was of losing her. In response, he told me about Meher Baba and his spiritual belief in a higher love. Earthly love and desire were illusions, pale echoes of the spirit's desire to reunite with God. I had never encountered ideas like these before—as we talked through the night, I felt my heart unclenching. In what sense was my girlfriend "mine"? What could this jealousy mean in the face of the interconnectedness of all things? Who was I to "keep" her if she wanted to leave? Surely there was love enough in the universe to go around.

In the morning, not having slept at all, I called her and said without hesitation or bitterness, "If you want to date John, go ahead. It's okay with me." I meant it. They had my blessing.

A few days later, they kissed and decided there wasn't any chemistry. She and I ended up back together and I'd forgotten about it completely until this moment on this narrowing highway through nowhere.

On a westward journey across the continent the land and the sky open up, becoming immeasurably vast. You and your car become tiny by contrast, and there's an exhilarating freedom as you disappear into the spreading landscape. If the tree-choked East is the story-bound ego, the open road is kenosis.

Heading south is different. Deeper into Alabama the road narrows to one lane in each direction. The forests change, too, becoming lusher and more tropical, wearing menacing beards of Spanish moss. They loom overhead like Ents—those tree-creatures in *The Lord of the Rings*. They look like they're ready to swallow us whole.

In freshman lit, I've been reading Carson McCullers and

Flannery O'Connor. For me, these forests are now haunted by the blood-soaked sacrament and the ghosts of the antebellum South. But even without the Gothic literary filter, the sense of enclosure is scary.

We speed along in our boxy metal cocoon. John is driving and I'm reading Eco's dense prose, using the tricks I've learned in voice class to take natural pauses for breath and keep the sound rich and open. I'm savoring each syllable, relishing this opportunity to keep John spellbound, drawing him deeper into the story. I wish that time would dilate, that the driving would go on forever, that John would never go back to his life three thousand miles away from New York.

In Houma, Libby greets me like family, with a surprisingly strong and deep embrace. Her face, like John's, is light and openness itself, and it's immediately obvious that they belong together. What would it take for me to achieve this kind of grace? This easy hope—or *faith*, rather—that the world is full of signs, that you can read them correctly, and the great work of life is to devote all your energy to following where they lead?

We eat at a crawfish restaurant in the middle of the bayou. The waitress brings us three pounds each of fire-engine-red, spice-encrusted boiled crawfish heaped atop some potatoes in a paper bowl. Libby demonstrates how to eat them: you twist off the tail (like lobster), peel it open (like shrimp), and eat the meat. Then, if you're a native, you squeeze the carapace and suck out the juice and the innards. Then you stick your finger in the head and rotate it slowly, drawing it out covered in flavorsome orange-yellow "fat." This all sounds pretty gross on the page, but it's one of the most delicious, sensuous meals I've ever experienced. Rich, slightly sweet and sour, pungent with celery seed, cayenne, and garlic. And it costs us like four dollars apiece.

Over the next few days Libby and her dad—some kind of dubiously connected man-about-town in the New Orleans way, where politics and business and alcohol mix freely and it's tough to tell where one ends and the next begins—roll out the red carpet. We drink Sazeracs in magenta booths in some fine old hole known only to locals. In a dark, wooden room we listen to the Preservation Hall Jazz Band and drink the obligatory hurricanes on Bourbon Street, making fun of the hurricane-drunk businessmen stumbling past us. At 4 a.m. we wolf down beignets with chicory coffee at Café du Monde. It seems like every bar we wander into, no matter how empty or run-down it may be, has its own genius live musician. In one otherwise totally deserted place there's a "one-man band": a Black guy in his midsixties with an instrument I've never seen before—some kind of electric wind-keyboard he blows into while fingering the keys—and a kick-drum, playing a fantastical hybrid folk-jazz-blues seemingly of his own invention. The music draws us together, Libby, John, and me. The hurricanes don't hurt, either.

I become fixated on the idea of getting a set of tarot cards and learning how to read them, so Libby finds us a voodoo tourist shop where I pick up that classic deck in the yellow box and a book about tarot. I flip through the cards in wonderment: The Devil. The Ace of Cups. The Hanging Man. Powerful, arche-typal imagery. Raw story-stuff without any author to sequence it. The only author here is Fortune, or Fate.

Back at Libby's house, she reads my fortune. Maybe this is something everyone who grows up in Houma can do. She places the cards facedown on the table in a ritualized order. One for the past, one for the present, and one for the future. Another card, off to the side, represents the theme of the reading as a whole. When she turns it faceup, it's the Knight of Swords.

Libby explains: "This card means adventure. Your life won't always be easy, but it will never be boring."

After the giddy, touristy first few days, John and Libby pretty much live in her bedroom. They're newly in love, after all, and there's plenty of novelty and delight left in exploring how their bodies fit together.

Alone in my room, I study the tarot cards. I practice doing my own readings. It's one of those "negative capabilities," as Keats describes the genius of Shakespeare: the ability to grasp something loosely enough to allow it to flower forth under your attention. It's a lot like the way John and I learned to read poetry. You don't have to worry about whether the reading is "right." You rest your awareness on the cards and let the story assemble itself.

A week after arriving, we leave Houma at nightfall. For some reason we've decided to drive through the night. I'm at the wheel. There's something darkly romantic about hearing *Foucault's Pendulum* as we make the reverse nocturnal trip through history, speeding away from all the old Southern ghosts toward the well-regulated, sensible present.

John reads for an hour, maybe. Then he falls asleep and it starts to rain. I'm driving on a one-lane highway with few or no streetlamps, due north out of Houma and suddenly it's raining like it's the end of the world. *Deluge* would not be an over-the-top choice of word here.

Also, the Civic hydroplanes if you go over sixty miles an hour on wet streets, meaning it glides like a Zamboni on ice, drifting left into oncoming traffic or right toward the demon-haunted woods. The only other vehicles on the road are massive tractor trailers. They loom up behind me, their headlamps blinding in the rearview mirror. If there's no oncoming traffic, they pass, then swerve in front of me, blinding me again with the spray of water in their wake. If they can't pass, they tailgate and lean on the horn, pissed that I'm maintaining exactly fifty-nine miles per hour. I am terrified. I'm hunched over the wheel, knuckles white, certain of our imminent death. Just beyond the fringe of trees to my right is a yawning abyss out of Lovecraft—a forest-chasm in which our car, when I do finally skid out of control, will be lost forever. Like Poe's "Imp of the Perverse," the chasm calls out to me. How easy it would be, just as I relinquish consciousness each night for sleep, to let go of the wheel and this terror along with it—to succumb to the sweet, inevitable darkness....

Fiddling with CDs is too complicated and dangerous, so I switch on the radio. Down there, wherever we are, it's nothing but country music and fire-and-brimstone preachers. Even bad company is better than none, though, so I tune in to some Book of Revelations imagery about beasts with multiple heads and oceans turning to blood. It's enough to keep me focused. Enough to keep us alive until morning.

Morning comes and we're in Nashville. We're not supposed to be in Nashville. Nashville is about eight hours away from where we're supposed to be. As the sun rises, Nashville's gleaming metropolis sprawls out beneath us and it slowly dawns on me that I've made a terrible mistake. Then my head bumps the steering wheel and I jolt back awake, mercifully still in my lane. I pull over, climb into the back seat, and John takes over the driving.

I read him the part about the pendulum. For centuries, it has been in perpetual motion. It is anchored in a ceiling two hundred feet high. Gently, its ellipses echo those of the heavenly spheres. It's in *unio mystica* with them, mysteriously bound to them as are all things and beings, one to another, part of some incomprehensible whole. John and I are bound to one another. Wherever we go in this world, whomever we love, whatever we commit to or don't, we are and will always be brothers. Cradled gently in this certainty, I close my eyes and I give in to sleep.

Jason Has to Get a Job

In June 1991, at the end of freshman year, I flew out to Northern California to spend the whole summer with John. I must have convinced my folks to buy the plane ticket, but somehow we skipped the conversation about how long I was planning to stay and who would be paying for my food and entertainment. Also, John failed to mention (or I failed to hear) that he'd be gone pretty much all the time, dancing. I arrived in the afternoon on a weekday, figured out the BART train from San Francisco Airport to Oakland, and made my way to a house with blue siding he was renting with a couple other college kids.

John wasn't home. He'd told me the door would be open and I should let myself in, which I did, calling out, "Anybody home? It's John's friend Jason from New York!" A woman's voice called back from the bathroom: "Come here!" But it was the bathroom. And the door was closed. "Come *there*?" I asked nervously. "Yep!" she chirped. So I did.

John's housemate, a fellow Berkeley student, stepped out of the shower completely naked, a wide, totally unselfconscious grin on her face. "Welcome to California!" she said, calmly wrapping a towel around herself. "Oh, by the way—" she added, pointing to the toilet "—yellow is mellow. Brown, flush it down. We're in a drought." Droughts. Casually naked strangers. I definitely wasn't in New York anymore.

The roommate showed me to a sunny little guest room at the front of the house, and I settled in a bit. I pulled out my guitar and stumbled through a Van Morrison tune I'd been trying to learn—"Sweet Thing," from the album *Astral Weeks*. To this day, when I'm alone far from home, playing and singing immediately reanchor me in my body, short-circuiting the inevitable urge to flee. *Okay*, I thought, scanning the room. *This is all right, then. Let's see what this California thing is all about.*

There was a knock on the guest room door. I had a self-conscious moment wondering whether it was culturally okay to shut your bedroom door in California in the middle of the afternoon, or whether that was considered unfriendly. Standing there with a mild smile on his round, pleasant face was Bill, John's other roommate, also a freshman at Berkeley. He'd grown up in Northern California, but with his laconic manner and wry sense of humor, Bill immediately felt like home to me. We sat together cross-legged on the floor and started talking about beat poetry—a subject Bill was intensely passionate about. I played him a couple Cat Stevens tunes. This summer was getting off to a great start.

John got home late—around 10 p.m.—and as we talked I understood that his every waking hour was devoted either to dance or to Libby. Every weekday, he trained from early in the morning until nighttime, then typically slept over at her house. We'd have plenty of time to hang out on the weekends, but that would be about it. I wondered for a second whether I should be offended that he'd let me come all the way out here just to sit in a guest room for two months, then decided to let it drop. This was John, after all. His motives were pure. He'd wanted to see me but was too ethereal to sort through the logistics.

The next morning, I called home. My dad answered. I told him about the BART train and how surprising it was that Oakland didn't look anything like I'd imagined it from gangsta rap. I gushed about Bill and the intensity of John's devotion to dance. There was a pause. "How long are you planning on staying there?" he asked. "What are you going to do with yourself?"

With John off dancing, I had no plans beyond writing thoughts in my notebook, reading, and playing guitar. Dad had other plans. "We're not just going to send you money while you sit out there all summer doing nothing. If you were taking summer classes it would be one thing, but if you're just planning on hanging around, you need to get a job."

I had no idea how to get a job. The only job I'd ever had before was one my mom had gotten for me senior year of high school, shelving books after school at the mall bookstore under a small, tidy, high-strung manager named Jerry. And that job had lasted about two weeks. So the next morning I took the BART into Berkeley and started wandering around.

Some of the many useful things I didn't know at the time included:

1) What a résumé was.

2) That before looking for a job, it's a good idea to imagine what kind of jobs you might enjoy doing and be well suited to.

3) That the best way to look for a job is not to walk around nervously wondering where a job might be.

I was ignorant, but determined. After several hours of wandering, I came across a promising sign on an electric pole: JOBS, it said. Followed by a phone number.

The next day at eleven o'clock I showed up to a nondescript white room in a small office building in Berkeley. A group of similarly hapless people of all ages sat on sagging couches as a long-haired guy with a clipboard gave us the game plan. We were now working for CALPIRG—a nonprofit environmental group that had recently had extraordinary success in cleaning up an "estuary," whatever that might be. Our job was to convince people to give us money so CALPIRG could clean up more things. We were to stay upbeat, on-message, and unwilling to take "no" for an answer.

I knew nothing about the environment. My mom hated bugs, so we'd never even gone hiking or camping. And my parents' business kept them squarely on the conservative side of environmental politics. Activism in general, and environmental activism in particular, was not in my blood.

They piled us into a van and dropped me off alone in some suburb of San Francisco with a map and some literature. I knew from the first that this had been a bad idea. I just didn't have the stuff, on any level, to become a CALPIRG success story. Scared of people? Check. Totally ignorant about the Earth? Check. Deeply embarrassed ever to ask anybody for money for any reason? Also, check.

But I wanted to stay in California, and this job was the price of entry. So I screwed my courage to the sticking place and marched up to the first house on my list. In front of it was a pickup truck with two bumper stickers: a confederate flag and another that announced: "This vehicle insured by Smith & Wesson."

Knocking on the screen porch door, I woke up a seriously unkempt biker dude with red eyes, a beard like the husband in Roald Dahl's *The Twits*, and a Harley-Davidson sleeveless T, hairy belly spilling out from underneath.

"Hi!" I said. "I'm with CALPIRG! We're the group that cleaned up the something-or-other estuary…"

He locked my eyes in a wavery gaze, and announced: "I been knocked down, turned around, don't know which end is up." I was sorry to hear that, I said. So he opened up about his struggles with alcoholism. He'd been on the wagon, but had fallen off again, and his life was a shambles now. He was living with his aunt and wasn't any good to anyone anymore.

I listened anxiously, aware of the time. The imaginary CALPIRG coach on my shoulder kept whispering that this was a dead end. It was time to cut my losses and resume canvassing. But I just stayed there, listening, nodding intently as he told his story. It's the one bit of good I was able to do that day.

Forty-five minutes later, I managed to extricate myself and approached a second house. As I entered the driveway, a car pulled in. A man got out dressed in what I would now call "business casual." This looked more promising. Even if he wasn't interested in donating, there probably wouldn't be a bleary-eyed, heart-wrenching confession.

"Hi!" I said. "I'm Jason. I'm with CALPIRG. We're the group that—"

The guy put a reassuring arm around my shoulder. It was surprising, but not totally unwelcome.

"Jason?" he said cheerily.

"Yes?"

"Fuck off."

In tears, I called home from a pay phone. Mom was sympathetic. Maybe CALPIRG just wasn't the right fit? Still, no job, no summer in California. So the next day, Friday, I was back to my trusty job-finding strategy; I took the train into San Francisco and walked around looking at windows and telephone poles. After just a few hours of this, I was hired at a Pizza Hut.

The manager handed me the thick employee handbook and asked me to report at 7 a.m., Monday morning.

On Saturday, John and I drove into San Francisco and walked around Haight-Ashbury looking for acid. I had been preaching the gospel of LSD for months, and this would be John's first experience. That night we sat on the floor of his living room as the drugs kicked in, talking about the importance of finding your "calling."

If I taught an Acid 101 class today, one of the first lessons would be: "While tripping, do not have your Pizza Hut employee manual close at hand." Unfortunately, it was right there next to me on a side table. I flipped it open to a random page and read: "Male employees shall have hair no longer than one-quarter inch below the collar."

There was a backstory here. Hair length had been the whole focus of the war for independence from my mom senior year of high school. For half a year, we'd been in a stalemate, my hair stuck in a horrible, midlength Lou Reed no-man's-land. As it had for the proud hippie pioneers before me, my big, bushy college hair represented the freedom to live my life the way I wanted to. It was no accident that the employee manual had opened to this page. See? This was what the working world did to people! This was what Harold and Maude were fighting against. Soullessness. Conformity. A living death.

I picked up a dollar bill from the coffee table. John and I studied the pyramid on the back, topped by the all-seeing eye of God, which turned the conversation to Freemasonry, the Illuminati, and all those secret societies Umberto Eco wrote about in *Foucault's Pendulum*. We wondered aloud how many of these shadow histories were hiding in plain view, embedded in currency, architecture, and language itself.

But I was still stuck on jobs, money, and finding one's calling. I grabbed a pen and a scrap of paper and drew a dollar sign, changing the *S* into the serpent climbing the tree in the Garden of Eden. There it was, plain as day! Money was the root of all evil. How could I have failed to see this hidden symbolism before?

Even with the help of LSD, the day's work at CALPIRG and the shocking revelation of Pizza Hut's grooming standards hadn't led to a moment's reflection on how to find a better job or outgrow my own sense of entitlement. They had proven what I thought I already knew—that the necessity of working for a living was the enemy of art and beauty. The best thing to do, I decided then and there, was to run as fast as I could in the opposite direction, back to the refuge of books and romance. I would leave California, go home to Lisa, and enroll in some summer classes. The next day, having triumphed over evil and alive with a new sense of hope, I wrote her a song, the second one I'd ever written:

The Lisa Song [excerpt]

Chocolate-sueded Lisa rolls her olive cat's eyes
When my jaded tongue slips and begins to criticize
She digs her cowboy-booted feet into receding ground
Because every friend she's ever loved has let her down

You ask me what is going on with you two
Well, Li and I know even less than you pretend to
But I love you... Oh, Lisa...

She's rolling cigarettes cross-legged in her canvas chair
And from the bed I see her smiling under all that hair
And when she finally says "I love you," which she has to qualify
Well, I don't think I can blame her, because so do I

She says "I'll never fall in love with you"
I say "Li, you don't have to"
And the skies above Sheep Meadow are blue
For you, Lisa...

A Marriage of Convenience

Apparently there's a common pitfall for advanced meditators wherein they have an intense experience while meditating and become convinced that they've achieved enlightenment. It might be an out-of-body sensation, or it might be a moment of ecstatic joy. Or something less dramatic; maybe meditation just "goes well" for a while. Sitting is easy and comfortable, the sensations are pleasant, there is a pervasive sense of calm and well-being and the meditator thinks: *Aha! I've finally got it. Now I am a proper meditator. The struggle is over.*

What often happens next is that the practice becomes difficult again, as it naturally will from time to time. Physical aches and pains, distracted thoughts, sleepiness...and because of the earlier story of how well everything was finally going, the meditator is now beset with doubt and self-judgment. From a redemption narrative, it has turned into the story of a Fall.

In one sense we're good at adapting to these twists and turns; when the story changes, we just restructure the narrative. The meditator becomes convinced that her practice is a failure. That she will never achieve enlightenment. She wonders why the hell she ever bothered in the first place.

So I left Oakland, flew back to New York, and moved in with Lisa for the rest of the summer at 56 Morton Street in the West Village. For some reason Columbia University let me enroll in two graduate-level classes: one on James Joyce's *Ulysses* that changed my life, and one on the philosopher Wittgenstein, of which I understood exactly nothing.

But life was perfect. The West Village had an architectural uplift and European elegance that felt somehow more grown-up than Washington Square. Here I was, living with my soul mate in an actual, rented apartment. The ground floor duplex had gleaming hardwood floors, two bathrooms, one window that looked out on Morton Street and another that looked into an airshaft, and a spiral staircase down to Lisa's basement bedroom. Lisa—a vegetarian and a serious cook who would later become a professional chef—was cooking her way through all the recipes in Mollie Katzen's *Moosewood Cookbook* series and devouring the food and travel writing of MFK Fisher. I was writing songs, reading great literature, and pretending to read great philosophy. We were two autonomous beings on our own paths, hand in hand by choice. Unlike Pizza Hut, *this* was adulthood, and everything about it felt right.

Only it wasn't yet entirely our apartment. Lisa had a roommate, an aggressively sex-positive girl with a flapper haircut who years later became a dominatrix. Back then, she dominated every conversation—about home decorating or cats or the weather—with graphic accounts of her own sex life, as if daring anyone to express the slightest discomfort. She was out of town for the summer, and the apartment was too tight a squeeze for three, so when fall came and she returned, I moved back into Hayden Hall with Ed.

You know those nightmares where you find yourself back in

middle or elementary school and the horror slowly dawns on you that you're going to have to go through those years all over again? Having tasted something like married life, I felt lost in the dorm, desperate to get back to that state of cozy domesticity. Ed and I were still close, but he was gone all the time—either at class or at the library. His academic life had suddenly gotten very intense, full of grueling, premed science courses. Uncertain about acting, I was taking classes in Chaucer, Eastern religions, Jewish mysticism, and—influenced by a mystical poetry-loving friend of mine—Arabic.

Even my use of psychedelics now reflected this sense of being unmoored, adrift: I'd go with a random group of acquaintances up to the statue of Alice in Wonderland around Seventy-Fifth Street in Central Park, take acid, walk the seventy-five blocks south to Hayden Hall, and sit alone in my dorm room, my mind reeling. The city lights sparkled magically, but the insights were vague and often tortured.

In November, Lisa told me that her roommate was moving out at the end of the semester. She'd love for me to move in if I wanted to, but NYU housing contracts were yearlong. So we went together to the housing office and asked what it would take to break my contract. "Well, you could always get married," the admin person joked, "but that's about it."

We could get married.

To Lisa, marriage was just a piece of paper. Love was love, regardless of vows or legal declarations. She saw no problem with the idea of getting married just to break a housing contract. To me, the housing admin's wisecrack was a neon sign from the universe cutting through the fog of the past couple months, pointing the way to my future with Lisa. So one day on Morton Street, I dropped to one knee and proposed. I can't even remember if there was a ring.

Unbeknownst to our parents, we got married at city hall in Manhattan on January 8, 1992. Neither of us felt close to our parents in those days, believed in traditional weddings, or considered it any of their business. John—in town for New Year's—was our combination best man and witness. This was just a lucky accident of timing, but John—never judgmental of love in any form—was happy to lend his signature and his blessing. I have a photograph of the three of us against a nondescript government wall in front of a tiny, abject print of a Klee painting. I'm in the middle smiling wanly, with blue prescription glasses, a black suit, and one arm around each of them, looking a bit like Michael Hutchence from INXS. Lisa's in a flower-print dress and leggings with her eyes closed, her posture suggesting that she'd rather skip the wedding photo or somehow disappear into the blank wall. John's in jeans and a biker jacket with a Watchmen pin (smiley face, bloodstain), leaning on my shoulder and beaming.

So, wedding certificate in hand, I broke my housing contract and moved into Morton Street with Lisa for the spring semester. Like a meditator seduced by his own practice, I was sure that this was the end of painful uncertainty, the long-awaited start of my one, true life.

At pivotal moments of breakdown or breakthrough, it's always tough to resist the tendency to tie the story up in a neat bow. To make some grand declaration and tattoo it on your forehead. With all the uncertainty in life, what a relief it is when something is clear at last! But we only ever have so much control. We're vulnerable to future events and bound by our pasts in ways that are impossible to account for. I guess the moral of the story is: be careful with forehead tattoos.

Trickster Breaks the Story

In his book *Trickster Makes This World*, cultural critic Lewis Hyde considers the mythological figure of the trickster. Loki in Norse mythology. Anansi the Spider from Ghana. The Serpent in the Garden. Puck in Shakespeare's *A Midsummer Night's Dream*. Wherever it appears, says Hyde, the trickster's role is to cross thresholds. To break boundaries. Literally and figuratively, to transgress.

Sometimes the trickster is a messenger between worlds, like wingèd Mercury—the only being who can pass between Hades and the realm of the gods. Often, though, its job is to divert the narrative—to take the story in a totally unexpected direction. This can be good fun for the reader but a source of unbearable confusion and suffering for the characters, as in *A Midsummer Night's Dream*, when Puck causes four young people to fall in love, each with someone who cannot love them in return. And after reading a few Norse myths, it comes as no surprise when the gods tie Loki to a rock with the entrails of his children, while poison drips into his eyes for all eternity.

The trickster is a nuisance, but it's there for a reason. Among other things, it exposes the narrative expectations we all take for granted. It sticks a pin in the balloon of any pretentions that we're on the road to the Big Answer. In this sense, of course, Death is the ultimate trickster. In a monologue John acted powerfully in high school, Shakespeare's Richard II kneels in the sand and says:

> *For God's sake, let us sit upon the ground*
> *And tell sad stories of the death of kings:*
> *How some have been deposed; some slain in war;*
> *Some haunted by the ghosts they have deposed;*
> *Some poison'd by their wives; some sleeping kill'd;*
> *All murder'd: for within the hollow crown*
> *That rounds the mortal temples of a king*
> *Keeps Death his court and there the antic sits,*
> *Scoffing his state and grinning at his pomp,*
> *Allowing him a breath, a little scene,*
> *To monarchize, be fear'd and kill with looks,*
> *Infusing him with self and vain conceit,*
> *As if this flesh which walls about our life*
> *Were brass impregnable, and humour'd thus*
> *Comes at the last and with a little pin*
> *Bores through his castle wall, and farewell king!*

There the antic sits. Ever present and lurking somewhere at the back of our consciousness, the trickster Death waits to unravel whatever neat story we might be telling ourselves.

2:30 a.m., October 21, 1992

Lisa and I are sleeping in her bedroom on Morton Street when the phone rings. It's a landline—there are no cell phones yet—and it's *loud*. Lisa picks up, then hands it to me.

"It's Bill, from California."

Bill? Do I know a Bill? Oh yeah, John's roommate...beat poetry... What time is it? What could this be at 2:30 a.m.?

Bill's voice is breaking. It could be the connection. "Jason..." he says "...I'm so sorry to tell you this... John is dead. He died half an hour ago."

Over the following days and weeks, more details emerged. John had been with Libby in Berkeley, leaving a late-night dance rehearsal on campus and heading toward the BART train home. At the intersection of Milvia Street and Channing Way, a boy two weeks shy of his sixteenth birthday approached them with a gun.

I'm looking at the exact location right now for the first time—a 360° view on Google Maps. On one corner there's a baseball field, on another a palm tree, and down Channing Way in one direction in the far distance, there's a mountain. There's a guy on a bike and another guy walking his dog. Aside from the palm tree and the mountain, this could be any quiet, residential neighborhood in any city in America. There's nothing to indicate the enormity of what happened here.

As Libby remembers it, John had recently lost a wallet and had just finished replacing all his credit cards and IDs. So when the kid demanded he hand over his brand-new wallet, John's reaction was something like, "Hey, can we please not do this?" For half a minute, John tried reasoning with him. "Look. I've only got five dollars on me. This isn't necessary. You could just walk away—"

Reason didn't work. There were multiple gunshots and John crumpled to the ground in Libby's arms.

Trauma happens when we're faced with horror and powerless to prevent it. Its most recognizable effect is a kind of paralysis—without healing, some part of us stays stuck forever in that moment.

As I listened to Bill on the phone, everything froze. *John is dead.* That was the singular fact of the world, a Zen koan that I would have to sit down, shut up, and contemplate for a lifetime if necessary to discern even the tiniest glimmer of its meaning.

Today, I can't stop looking at Google Maps. I don't want to close the browser. Which corner was it? Where were they standing, exactly? What were he and Libby chatting about in the moments before it happened? I keep rotating the view because as long as I do so, John is a little bit alive again.

A couple weeks after Bill called, I took an Amtrak to Union Station, then transferred to the DC Metro, whose vaulting tunnels inspired the sets for that production of Wagner's Ring that John and I once saw. I spent the whole trip writing in a notebook, working on a eulogy that I've long since lost. I'm sure the draft was a crime scene of spidery scrawls, false starts, asterisks— a map of the inward convolutions of mind and heart. Whatever it was, it wasn't enough. A fitting memorial to John would be something on the order of *Hamlet* or Mozart's *Requiem*, something it wasn't remotely within my power to create.

But I delivered it—in a broken voice the next day at the National Cathedral, at a memorial service about which I remember nothing else. They would have talked about John's talent. His potential. How the world had been robbed of a beautiful soul with a brilliant future. When anyone dies young it's hard to avoid putting them on a pedestal or painting in a halo. Brilliant, beautiful, and talented as John was, in his case it was even harder. But where in this tragic cliché, this shorthand for memory, is the actual person I knew?

As I write this now, all these years later, I'm thinking about the ways we try to stanch the wounds of death. All the fingers that reach in to plug the holes in the dam lest the river break through and wash us away. Turning the dead into angels is one way. Trying to move on and forget them is another. At the wake, several well-meaning strangers suggested I *compartmentalize* the loss and lose myself in schoolwork instead.

John's mom, Kitty, was the only one who really understood. A small, soft-spoken scholar of history and the arts, she radiated intelligence and a deep kindness born of sorrow. Kitty had already lost one child (John's older sister) to suicide—which John had mentioned to me only once, when it happened, and never spoken of again. Now John, her shining boy, was gone, too.

Kitty and I had never really spoken. She'd always been this calm, silent guardian of the space in which our friendship blossomed. At the wake, she took both of my hands in hers and held my gaze with her impossibly blue eyes—John's eyes—and made me promise not to let anybody tell me what to feel, or how much, or for how long. She gave me two keepsakes: John's complete Arden Shakespeare and his blue cashmere overcoat, which I wrapped around me like a cloak of invisibility. It still smelled like him.

I begged my parents to let me leave college for a year. Maybe

John during college at UC Berkeley.

even to buy me a plane ticket to India so I could wander around in mourning and hopefully stumble into some spiritual wisdom. Whatever *compartmentalizing* was, I wanted the opposite. Rather than returning to the narrow track of registering for new classes and accumulating credits toward graduation, I wanted to let the wound breathe, give my body to the river, let it take me in any direction.

This idea made no sense to my folks. If I left college, they worried, especially under these circumstances, I might never return. So back I went on the train with Lisa to New York, NYU, and our homelife together.

When someone dies we need time, space, and help to mourn them fully. We need rituals and cultural practices to support us through the long and messy process. But so much of American culture is based on productivity and forward momentum. *Let us sit upon the ground and tell sad stories of the deaths of kings?* No thanks. Can we talk about something more positive?

I was stuck between worlds—shuffling back and forth to classes wrapped in John's overcoat, trying to keep him alive in my heart without bumming anybody out too much. At home, I drank and poured my feelings out to Lisa. "I can't anymore!" she finally screamed. "I just need for you to stop!"

I knew nothing at the time about the psychology of trauma, but Lisa had come to college carrying more than she could bear. In her senior year of high school in Pittsburgh, a boy she'd been close to had murdered her best friend with no apparent motive. "I was wearing my *Clockwork Orange* shirt," he later said. "When I wear that shirt, I always do bad things." Lisa was the one who had introduced them.

There wasn't much in the way of therapy or support for Lisa at the time of the murder. She just had to pick up the pieces of her life and move on. Early in our relationship she had told me this story the way people with unprocessed trauma often do, as a series of facts with no emotional weight. *Wow... I must have said...my God...* and then promptly forgotten about it.

In retrospect, I understand her mysterious distances throughout our relationship. I understand why the harder I pushed her to talk about her feelings, the further she withdrew. And why, after a month of absorbing my inconsolable grief, she just couldn't take it anymore.

Nobody could take it. I don't know what I might have found in India or wherever the mourning led me, but there was no place in my New York life for this river of sorrow. So I did what I could: I wrote John a song. I journaled about him. Then I buried the river underground and tried to move on. But underground rivers always resurface somewhere.

I used to think mourning was a process of letting go. Of active forgetting. Now I think it's the opposite. To mourn fully is to let the feelings of love and loss work their way through you, burrowing deep into your cellular memory. Like life itself, it's unpredictable. The best we can do is make space and let it run its course.

Before Lisa and I met, the trickster Death had given her life story a devastating twist. Lacking the space and support she needed to heal from the trauma, she survived the only way she knew how—by guarding herself against the pain of further loss. John's death did something similar to me. It drove me inward, away from Lisa, and at the same time deadened my connection to myself. I made new friends after that, and even fell in love, but like the character Mr. Duffy in James Joyce's short story "A Painful Case," I "lived a short distance from [my] body."

By early '93 I had decided that Lisa Lisa had been right all along: we should see other people. It was a Hail Mary. I hoped that opening the relationship might somehow save it, but it ended up having the opposite effect. In June we broke up and moved to separate apartments. Her Super Mario–mustachioed father helped me lug our bedroom furniture up from the basement floor of Morton Street, his little eyes glinting ironically at me the whole time.

Every good thing, the Buddhists say, has its "near enemy." The near enemy of discipline is rigidity. The near enemy of joy is self-satisfaction. It's the fishhook of attachment hidden in the tasty bit of hot dog. Near enemies offer tempting clarity, simplifying the messy stories of our lives, offering an exit ramp from a long, hard road. Lisa was my one, true love. John was on the cusp of a glorious career. Finally and forever, the world was about to make sense.

The trickster reminds us that we're not in control of the story. That any crown we might affect is hollow. There are so many reasons and so many ways we can fight, excuse, or otherwise deny that fact, but all of them divide us. To be whole is a process of coming gradually closer to acceptance.

In January 2018, Libby traveled to Varanasi in India, where the Buddha sat under the bodhi tree and refused to budge until he attained enlightenment. She took with her the bloodstained T-shirt John was wearing that night in Berkeley, covered in handwritten messages from me and other people who loved him. Along with a wreath of flowers, she let it drift away down the Ganges.

"The sea refuses no river/and this river is homeward flowing"

...sang Pete Townshend in a song John and I used to love. Who knows how far it traveled, but I like to imagine that shirt carried along on the current, making the thousand-mile journey to the Bay of Bengal. Broken down by bacterial enzymes, then nibbled at by fish, sustaining little bits of life all the way until its last remaining threads drifted out into the Indian Ocean.

COURTESY OF ST. ALBANS SCHOOL

John as Mercutio in Romeo and Juliet *at St. Albans School.*

The Church of Tom Waits

The percussion is like an army of skeletons, like the jerkily animated ones in *Jason and the Argonauts*, the old movie about the myth I was named for. They march by the thousands, beating out a tattoo with femurs on skulls hung on heavy iron chains around their collarbones. I'm marching, too, doggedly beating the pavement in Midtown to make a rush delivery to *Saturday Night Live*. It's June 1993, and I'm a walking messenger. The soundtrack is Tom Waits's album *Bone Machine*—the song is called "The Earth Died Screaming." On this record, the first I own of Tom's (bought in the once-glorious, now-vanished Tower Records on Broadway and West Fourth), it's almost as if he's channeling the Grim Reaper itself or Shakespeare's Death-as-court-jester: gleefully, noisily reminding us of the one hard fact we're all rushing around trying our best to forget. On the job that summer I'll listen to *Bone Machine* exclusively, obsessively, hundreds of times on repeat.

Everything happened in such quick succession. John's death. The breakup with Lisa (it would take almost a decade for us to finalize the divorce). A new round of arguments with my father about work and money. I was less than a year away from graduation and his anxieties about my ability to survive in the world had reached a peak. I dug my heels into the receding ground of the notion that art would eventually somehow save me, and he demanded that I go out right now and get a goddamn job. A sensible middle ground might have been an internship or a summer gig in theater or music or literary publishing—something remotely connected with my interests. Instead, like a hippie who couldn't escape the Vietnam draft, I finally said *fuck it*, gritted my teeth and marched off into the jungle.

In a hole-in-the-wall on East Ninth street, a couple blocks from my new apartment, surrounded by decades' worth of stacks of yellowing contracts and invoices, sat Jerry. Jerry could be anywhere from fifty to seventy years old—it was impossible to tell because he was so massively overweight, haphazardly shaven, and pale-greenish in hue from his regimen of never leaving this lightless office except to buy a bacon, egg, and cheese on a roll. On Jerry's desk (one assumed there must be a desk supporting this ziggurat of crap) there was a yellowing computer running DOS, a bottle of vodka, and a teetering tower of porn magazines with names like *Sweet Cheeks*. Next to Jerry sat Mike, smaller but similar in all other respects. Barney to his Fred Flintstone. Mike's job, as far as I could ever tell, was to listen appreciatively as Jerry waxed philosophical about the messenger trade, laugh at his jokes, and second his many strong opinions.

Every morning around 10:30 (Jerry was not an early riser), I walked from my apartment on Lafayette Street across from the Public Theater down St. Mark's Place to Second Avenue, up one block to Ninth, and turned right.

Just before Jerry's lair there was a shop that sold nothing but pigments. It was like nothing I'd ever seen before: buckets heaped high with dazzling, powdered color in its purest form. Burnt umber direct from Umbria, a blue that once had been coral or lapis lazuli. Often I'd stop and just linger in that shop, surrendering my consciousness to the power of these hues. A little bit of medicine, a little bit of poetry, then off to deal with Jerry again.

Well into the bottle by 11 a.m., Jerry explained his business to me. He did this often in the two months I worked for him. Back then, I was easily intimidated by big personalities, so I mostly just stood there, nodding anxiously.

Jerry: What you want is the rush jobs. I've been in this business a long time, so there's the regular customers. Long-time relationships. Big shots in entertainment: NBC, Late Night. You're an actor, right? You could meet some of these people. Just hand 'em your audition tape! Not right away, though. Establish a connection. Some of these relationships we got go back—what—twenty years?

Mike: That's right. Twenty years.

Jerry: Twenty years. A lot of these guys are close together in Midtown. Thirty Rock. Radio City. I'll try to give you the rush jobs. Good for you, good for me. You can hit more jobs in an hour and the rate's double. No guarantees. But I'll try. You like Johnny Carson?

Me: Sure. (I didn't, really)

Jerry: Used to be a regular. (dramatic pause)

Me: Wow.

Jerry: We know 'em all. Right, Mike?

Mike: That's right, Jerry!

Jerry: You stick with us. This could be good for you.

At some point, mercifully, the phone would ring. This was the first job of the day (looking back on it, I may have been Jerry's only messenger). I got the pickup and the delivery address along with a clipboard for signatures, hit Play on Tom's steampunk barn burner "Such a Scream," and headed for the subway.

Bone Machine, which won a 1992 Grammy for best alternative album, is all about death. It's Tom Waits's rawest, most elemental album and I'd argue it's his best. Shakespeare supposedly wrote *Hamlet*—another death-obsessed work of genius—in anguish over the death of his son, Hamnet, at the age of eleven. Tom Waits is famously cryptic and reclusive, so I don't know what happened in his life to bring *Bone Machine* into being, but the result was devastating.

Our heroes help us write the stories that help us survive (and sometimes the ones that destroy us). Starting that summer, in my own private imaginary, Tom Waits became an alternate father figure for me. *Bone Machine* vacillated between apocalyptic and romantic fatalism, between rage and world-weary cynicism. Still reeling from John's death and feeling utterly alone, so did I. In Tom's music, I saw a way to transmute those self-destructive emotions into something beautiful and imperfect and brave. As far back as *Nighthawks at the Diner*, an album he made when he was only twenty-five, Tom found poetry in broken, discarded people and things. He sounded broken and discarded himself, yet somehow sublime. I wanted some of that tattered grandeur for myself.

Tom's persona, especially on those older albums, was a gutter prophet soaked in booze. His most famous song from those days, off the 1976 album *Small Change*, was one of my least favorite—a self-parody about how the piano (not Tom) had been drinking. *Bone Machine* was full of Flannery O'Connor–esque imagery about whiskey, Jesus, and murder.

I absorbed my mentor's bad influences along with the good, believing that hard liquor was an essential piece of the puzzle. *Bone Machine* led me to its closest spiritual cousin, the Mississippi Delta Blues of the '20s and '30s. For Robert Johnson and Skip James and so many more of Tom's own heroes, whiskey was the embodiment of life's ambivalence—the reconciliation of life and death. It was lover, muse, and killer, all in one:

If the river was whiskey, and I was a diving duck/I'd dive to the bottom and never come up.

So after work and on the weekends, I started drinking Bushmills—an Irish whiskey Tom mentions on *Small Change*. It made the misery and solitude bearable, romantic even. As I sat in my small bedroom on Lafayette Street, listening to Tom's records or writing tunes of my own, the pain of John's death, the bitterness of the failed marriage, even the old insecurities of childhood temporarily vanished, replaced by a sweet, sad melody as old as song itself. A new kind of kenosis, this: one that—for a few hours, anyway—depersonalized my suffering, dissolving it in the sea of human sorrow.

Walking messenger shouldn't be a hard job for a young, more or less healthy person. Basically, you walk. Walking fast is encouraged, but no one expects you to run. As a particularly anxious young man, though, and one who usually had a terrible hangover, I had two major handicaps. First, this was before Google Maps and I had no sense of direction, even on Midtown Manhattan's perfectly regular grid. So I was constantly getting lost and having to call Jerry from a pay phone for help.

Second, I could never figure out where the messenger entrance was to any given building. Manhattan's unspoken but very real class segregation meant it was almost never through the front door. So pickup and drop-off were moments of near-total panic for me, always. Situational panic that quickly turned global. *Papañcha* is the Pali Buddhist term for the proliferation of thoughts—the way a feeling (like hunger, cold, or sexual desire) can rapidly breed fears and opinions. As I circled the block in confusion, my heart would race. I would break into a cold sweat. *Papañcha* would go into overdrive: *Moron. Not only are you so pathetic that this is the best job you can manage even to apply for in spite of a lifetime of privilege plus three years of college education, but you're totally incompetent at it. Christ!—you can't even be a decent walking messenger.*

On a good day, though, I got multiple rush jobs in close proximity to one another. The rush jobs paid extra, and proximity meant many more deliveries per hour. These were Jerry's regulars in Midtown, from Forty-Second Street to Rockefeller Center, a neighborhood I came to know well. Anxiety dispelled, I'd slip into its evil twin, grandiosity, speed walking to "Black Wings," a cinematic, hoofbeat-driven tale of a mythical, otherworldly stranger whose coat, some say, conceals a set of wings...

This was it! The *real life* my dad was always talking about. I was doing what a man was supposed to do: kicking ass and earning my keep. Actually, I was earning next to nothing. Barely enough to buy whiskey and ramen. At least the music was good....

Slow days meant a lot of waiting around near pay phones, reading. At The Strand Bookstore one day I picked up *The Autobiography of Gandhi: The Story of My Experiments with Truth.* Between calls from Jerry I would crouch against a wall and read, underlining every other sentence. For years I underlined and asterisked and highlighted books until one day I asked myself: *Has all of this ever helped you remember anything?* It hadn't. These days, I just take a few selective notes.

Gandhi's book touched a spiritual nerve that had been dormant since that all-night conversation with John in high school. This story of a man so committed to ethical growth and honesty that he dedicates his life to *ahimsa*—non-harming—and undergoes a transformation from British-trained barrister into a spiritual and political leader on a scale unprecedented in the modern world. I wasn't ready yet to give up Tom as my guru, but Gandhi's spirituality (his personal interpretation of Hinduism) planted the seed of a different dharma: self-mastery without self-destruction.

What I didn't know at the time was that a year earlier, right after *Bone Machine* was released, Tom went to AA and got sober. Apparently he's never had a drink since.

Liquor aside, *Bone Machine* is a search for truth no less sincere than Gandhi's. In song after song, Tom takes a cauterizing knife to self-delusion. "Who Are You This Time?" is a bitter love letter to an old ex:

> *How do your pistol and your Bible and your sleeping pills go?*
> *Are you still jumping out of windows in expensive clothes?*
> *Tell me, who are you this time?**

It's a love letter because the narrator has to write it. All these years later he burns with rage that she hasn't stopped running from herself. Her hypocrisy matters because it's his, too. It's the hypocrisy of the whole world—all our stupid human tricks to escape the fact of our inevitable death.

Across all of his albums, Tom strikes me as a man at home with his own frailty and mortality. *Bone Machine* feels like a primal howl of rage and sorrow at the loneliness of this position in a world hell-bent on amnesia and self-aggrandizement. It feels like Tom has reached a breaking point. Like life has left him no choice but to strap some C-4 to the tower of bullshit we're all so busy erecting.

---

* *Who Are You*
By Tom Waits, Kathleen Brennan
(c) 1992, Jalma Music (ASCAP)
Used By Permission. All Rights Reserved.

After John died, nothing in my life felt real. Everything was fragmented, meaningless, and abrupt. I couldn't take comfort anymore in Maude's wholesome, Eastern acceptance of the cycles of birth and death. In the world I lived in, death was an inconvenience. You were supposed to hurry up and get back to your life. I didn't realize it at the time, but I was furious with everyone—Lisa, my father, American society—for failing to bring life to a screeching halt in the face of John's death. Most of all, I was furious with myself for going along with it.

Tom knew what it felt like, I thought. *Bone Machine* wasn't mourning, exactly, but it was a daily memento mori. If it couldn't stop life's relentless march, at least it could set it to the rhythmic clattering of bones.

Road Trip, Bethesda to Santa Fe

In the spring of 1993, our parents had bought Meri a red Saturn sedan as a graduation present. Like her, it was both practical and ready for adventure. If the purpose of a bumper sticker is to capture the driver's spirit, then Meri's Saturn had the most perfect bumper sticker I've ever seen. *HUMANITY IS TRYING*, it said in plain, white letters. "It's a triple entendre," she explained: "'Humanity' means striving. Humanity is exhausting. Humanity's doing its best, even when its best isn't nearly good enough."

Meri applied to only one college, and she applied a year early. She was born decisive, but if she'd ever had any doubts at all about how to show up in the world, her middle school brush with death seemed to have burned them off. She knew her own mind, knew her judgment to be as strong as anyone else's she'd ever met. Life was a series of experiments—you took an educated guess and ran your tests. Why worry? Mistakes were to be expected—how else were you supposed to learn? And most often, the data confirmed what she already knew.

In those days, Meri seemed like a fully self-realized Maude to my anxious Harold.

Take songwriting, for example. By junior year of college I'd written ten or twelve songs. I poured everything I had into songwriting, sometimes devoting hours to refining a single line of lyrics. But aside from a few close friends and (when drunk) a few acquaintances at parties, I hadn't dared to play them for anyone. This was the '90s. There were open mics in coffee shops and bars all over New York. But the moment I imagined myself performing at one of them, I was overcome with doubt and terror, no longer able to feel the song from the inside.

In a safe and trusted space (or a drunken one, which offered the illusion of trust and safety), the songs felt true. They felt funny, smart, emotionally raw and powerful. But outside of that bubble all I could see were the weaknesses. My guitar playing? Pathetic. All those painstakingly crafted lyrics? Embarrassingly mediocre and confessional. On the rare occasion when I mustered up the courage to make a bold move—like the time a friend in acting class convinced me to play two songs on his NYU radio show—I'd come out of it shaking and numb, as if in some kind of shock, and promise myself to lay low for a good, long time to come.

Contrast Meri's can-do pragmatism with my Hamlet-like tendency to get lost in abstract analysis of every branching possibility, and then, periodically, to get so fed up with all this intellectualizing that I'd take some impulsive action, followed immediately by waves of doubt and remorse. But just as every virtue contains its own tragic flaw, every tragic flaw has some hidden virtue. I could be self-conscious and reflective to the point of paralysis, but at least I could question myself. Over time, that became more and more useful to me. And Meri's self-reliance—which could come at the cost of self-awareness—became more and more of a liability.

★ ★ ★

St. John's, the college Meri had picked, fit her perfectly. Founded in 1696, it's the third oldest college in the United States, with one campus in Annapolis, Maryland, and another—to which Meri was headed—in New Mexico. Its entire "great books program" was structured around the belief that curious minds don't need critical intermediaries—anointed authorities standing between them and the text, which, when you think about it, is a bit like what Luther did for Christianity, or Mohammed for Islam, in trying to remove the bureaucracy between the people and their God. In small seminars, students sat around a table and discussed Western classics, from the philosophy of ancient Greece to the *Principia Mathematica* of Newton.

Professors were called "tutors," rotated from class to class, and were rarely specialists in whatever subject they happened to be tutoring in. Rather than lecture, their role was to open the conversation with a provocative question and guide it gently, Socratically as it went along. As the students retraced, picked apart, and talked back to these texts directly, they reexperienced something of the twists and turns, the great experiments and errors of Western thought. In the process (so the school's classical liberal arts philosophy went) they learned how to think.

Meri already knew she wanted to be a doctor. But she was also her Mom Mom's granddaughter. Until she got an *education*, the technical nitty-gritty of anatomy and pathology could wait.

It's a muggy, storm-threatened day in Bethesda, August 1993, almost ten months after John's death. Meri and I pile her things into the Saturn. Straddling the gearshift, with pride of place, sits her stuffed Bill the Cat doll from the comic strip *Bloom County*, which we'd both loved since elementary school. Bill, a hard-living, wild-eyed rock-and-roller who's done more than one stint in rehab, is an avatar of chaos and resilience. He will be our mascot on the long road west.

But first, we're headed south. A shared love of Paul Simon's music and lyrics—especially on the albums *Graceland* and *Rhythm of the Saints*—has planted in our brains a vision of visiting Graceland, Elvis Presley's mansion in Memphis, Tennessee. Like most in our generation, Meri and I know Elvis only as the sad sideshow he became at the end—a bloated drug addict who reportedly liked deep-fried peanut butter and banana sandwiches and lived like a late Roman emperor. But if Paul considered a pilgrimage to Graceland worth our while, we were in, no questions asked.

On the way, we play the song on repeat. In it, Graceland becomes a symbol of healing and acceptance—a holy shrine with the power to wash the middle-aged narrator and his fellow pilgrims clean of marriages gone wrong and other sins. *"Maybe I'm obliged to defend every love, every ending, or maybe there's no obligations now. Maybe I've a reason to believe we all will be received in Graceland…"*

In Elvis's mansion, we tour the room with the priceless Italian silk-covered ceiling, then the "jungle room" carpeted in Astroturf, then the electric blue-and-yellow room at whose wall of TVs Elvis is said to have drunkenly, druggedly hurled many objects. At his grave in the garden we stand respectful of, yet baffled by all the women weeping, their Tammy Faye Bakker mascara running in branching rivulets down their cheeks. In the gift shop, I buy a trucker hat that says Elvisweek '93 and Meri gets a front license plate that says "Elvis: The Sun Never Sets on a Legend." For all the ironic posturing, though, we've driven almost nine hundred miles out of our way to get here. Unworthy as we are, Graceland has received us, too.

After Graceland, food is the greatest American roadside attraction. So we've brought along the most recent edition of *Roadfood*, a guide to eccentric American gastronomy, like the last remaining Woolworth's lunch counter still serving "Frito Pie" in a cut-open Frito bag.

Meri at the wheel of her Saturn, with Bill the Cat as copilot.

Not one place in that book has anything for a vegetarian like Meri. Frito Pie has ground beef in it. In the South, almost everything—even apple pie and collard greens—is made with some part of a pig. Meri subsists on biscuits, salad, and pancakes. But she's as excited as I am about hunting down all these kitschy, out-of-the-way relics of American culture. Another of Mom Mom's rules (one Maude would also have heartily endorsed): stick to your principles, but never let them stop you from living a full life.

I kept only a few photos from that trip. Here's Bill the Cat at Old Faithful in Yellowstone, looking bewildered on the wooden crosswalk that keeps tourists from falling through the crust of the Earth in that seismically volatile place. Meri's next to Bill in raggedy jean shorts she must have cut by hand and rainbow suspenders à la *Mork and Mindy* (another shared childhood favorite), hands on hips, elbows jutting definitively out—a very Meri pose. One wonder of nature confronting another.

Here's Bill again, staring at a farmhouse covered in giant

wooden signs that read Vegetables and Fat Sheep. Here's Meri, then me, perched on a suggestive Arizona sandstone boulder we dubbed "Butt Rock," looking backward at the camera in embarrassment over our massive stone ass cheeks. Here's the cartoonish, grinning sheriff with the double chin and aviator sunglasses who stopped us doing ninety-five somewhere in Utah, ticketed us, and then happily posed for a picture. And here, upon arrival in Santa Fe, is Meri in wraparound sunglasses and a black, Jesse James hat, leaning jauntily on her car door in the St. John's parking lot, gazing off in the direction of Atalaya Mountain.

All these little artifacts: the photos, the fragmented memories of objects and places. I can close my eyes and conjure up the hours of easy silence as we disappear into the vast Western plains and the ocean of sky. I remember sitting in a restaurant in Salt Lake City, the two of us creeped out by all the Mormon religiosity on display in that town and sure that the family at the next table (one adult male, three adult females, and a gaggle of children) must be polygamous.

What I can't get back, no matter how hard I try, is the words we spoke. I can't reconstruct the dialogue. Is it because two kids in a car, even when they're all grown-up and sitting in the front seats, are a single organism? Talking or silent or singing along with Paul Simon, no space between them big enough to fill up with questions about the miles and miles of space between them?

what Has Happened to Hamlet?

In Act II, Scene II of *Hamlet*, a traveling company of actors (called "players" in Shakespeare's time) arrives at Elsinore Castle, Prince Hamlet's home and the seat of power in Denmark. Hamlet loves actors, "for they are the abstract and brief chronical of the time"—the storytellers with the power to shape our memories of the age. They do this, as Hamlet says, by suiting "the action to the word, the word to the action." Unlike Hamlet since the start of the play, actors *act*. They don't sit around paralyzed by thought.

Hamlet comes by his paralysis honestly enough. In the beginning of the play he's visited by the ghost of his dead father, the former king of Denmark. Dad's ghost tells him that his uncle Claudius, in collusion with Hamlet's mother, Gertrude, murdered him to marry the widow and seize the crown. In modern terms, Hamlet is traumatized by the news. It's too much to process: the death of his father, the monstrous double betrayal, and the ghost's demand that Hamlet exact his bloody revenge. Bewildered and tortured, Hamlet has a full-blown existential crisis.

His erratic, antagonistic behavior drives his girlfriend Ophelia to suicide and convinces everyone he's going mad. He contemplates suicide himself, but decides he's too scared of the afterlife.

The inability to act—a figurative paralysis—is a common effect of trauma. PTSD patients are often overwhelmed by everyday decision-making. Stuck in whatever past horror they were powerless to prevent at the time, they're unable to take decisive action in the present. Hamlet's unable to act in both senses of the word—knowing what he knows, he can't play the part of the happy, dutiful prince—and overwhelmed with his own thoughts and emotions, he can't summon up the courage to do what needs to be done.

The arrival of the players is the first time we see Hamlet genuinely happy. At last! Here is someone (unlike himself) who knows how to take action. He asks the lead player to perform a speech from a tragedy about the Trojan War. The player tells the story of the death of King Priam and his widow Hecuba's grief, weeping as he tells it. And Hamlet is so moved by the acting that he can't resist a soliloquy of his own:

> *What's Hecuba to him or he to Hecuba*
> *That he should weep for her? What would he do*
> *Had he the motive and the cue for passion*
> *That I have? He would drown the stage with tears...*

Hamlet goes on and on, berating and mocking himself for his own cowardice. He calls himself a "dull and muddy-mettled rascal," "pigeon-livered," an "ass" who "must, like a whore, unpack my heart with words." In fact, inspired by the player, he's whipping himself into action. By the end of the speech, he's got the seed of his plan for revenge.

Hamlet has no good options. Paralysis is both an effect of his trauma and a reasonable response to the impossible situation he finds himself in. When he finally manages to take action, his revenge plot results in a bloodbath that includes his own death. Are Denmark and the world any better off than if he'd remained paralyzed?

In the fall of 1993 I started my senior year at NYU. Partly in homage to John, I switched into the Classical Studio, a small, newer division of the acting program that focused mainly on Shakespeare. Wrapped in John's blue overcoat, its collar turned up against September's winds, I silently committed to reading my way through the complete works in the Arden edition I'd inherited from him. It felt right—a homecoming to the literary haven we'd built together in high school.

In a class called Dramaturgy, the fifteen or twenty students in the studio cohort went line by line through scenes and speeches, breaking down Shakespeare's techniques for suiting "the action to the word, the word to the action." We saw how the rhythms of the language, the percussion of consonants, and the melody of vowels shifted as thought led to thought, emotion to action. Each line was full of hidden clues to the character's spirit and their movement through the world of the play.

Shakespeare's plays took over my imagination and anchored me with a sense of meaning and purpose I hadn't felt since John's death. I was as devoted a reader as Shakespeare could have wished for. But when it came to acting out his words in our classes and studio performances, I was as paralyzed as Hamlet.

Our acting teacher and the head of the program was Louis Scheeder. A former director with the Royal Shakespeare Company and the Folger Theatre in Washington, DC, he had the bemused, volatile, New York intensity of Harvey Keitel and was similarly sturdy and compact. I always think of Louis as a kind of basketball coach of Shakespeare. For him, all that mattered in this high-flown lyrical language were the verbs. *Whaddya doing? Whaddya want?*

Watching Louis direct a serious actor was an unforgettable experience: he would stand there on the sidelines, coiled and tense, exclaiming, "Yeah, that's right!" or "Go on—go get him!" He said very little, giving only the barest nudge at just the right moment to push the actor deeper into the character, into the scene.

From the beginning, our relationship was a disaster. When I practiced a monologue alone at home (just like when I sang my own songs without an audience) the actions and the words felt perfectly suited to one another. But when I got up in class to deliver the speech, I'd have a kind of out-of-body experience. Like Hamlet, I was too self-conscious, too distracted by irrelevant thoughts to act.

Performing a famous speech from *Richard III*, instead of feeling the hunchbacked king's disgust at his own crooked body, I'd get wrapped up in disgust at my own nasal voice, my ridiculous hands gesticulating wildly. Some actors might have found a way to use this disgust as a doorway back into the character, but my sympathetic nervous system was too engaged for that. As if from a distance, I'd hear myself speaking the lines by rote, without the slightest emotional connection to them. I'd stop midsentence and sputter that something was wrong, that I just wasn't feeling it today for some reason. I would "unpack my heart with words," hoping Louis could find a way to return me to Earth.

"Stop thinkin'! Ya thinkin' too much!" was about all I ever got from him.

For classwork, Louis steered me—brilliantly, I now realize—toward neurotic, self-conscious characters like Hamlet, Richard, or the creepy Iachimo in *Cymbeline*. Then, in the winter of 1993, he cast me as the anxious and incompetent Peter Quince in *A Midsummer Night's Dream*.

Quince is one of the "Mechanicals"—a group of laborers putting on some amateur theatrics (a play within the play within the play) about the very minor legend of Pyramus and Thisbe, would-be lovers separated by an uncooperative garden wall.

Quince is their director, and Shakespeare's gag is that the Mechanicals have no idea what they're doing. They're the comic relief of *A Midsummer Night's Dream*, but Shakespeare being Shakespeare, they're also humanity in microcosm: earnest, determined, pathetic, confused. *Humanity is trying.*

As the director, Quince is the quintessence of this human predicament: anxiously in charge of a production that has no prayer of being anything but awful. On paper, it was the right role for me at this moment in my life. Like Quince, I was a directionless, idealistic, romantic mess.

Midsummer was the biggest, most impressive production I'd ever been part of: an NYU Mainstage showcase with the full power of Tisch's deep pockets behind it, designed to attract donors and notable alumni. Opening night was December 11— my birthday.

For me, at least, it didn't go well.

The first thing I was supposed to do was walk to a certain mark at the top of the raked, wooden stage. It was cunningly designed to swoop upward away from the audience, culminating in a kind of frozen sine wave—a smooth, perfectly sanded wooden hill running from wing to wing at its crest. As I'd rehearsed it a hundred times, I'd get to my spot and tumble down the hill, then pop up and freeze among the rest of the company in the opening montage.

Standing backstage, waiting for the music to cue my tumbling act, I was overcome with terror. I could feel my heart pounding in my ears. It was like I was in a sensory deprivation tank, suspended, floating, totally isolated from everything and everyone around me. In his autobiography, Laurence Olivier says that just before every stage performance of his career, he was possessed by all-encompassing terror and nausea. But the moment he stepped onstage, the fear vanished and he was completely immersed in the character.

I brought my terror and nausea right along with me, thinking: *Walk to the spot. Find the spot. Then tumble. Easy peasy. Oh God... What is my first line? Wait—where is the spot? No! I can't do it. I want to go home. I want to die! Please let there be a blackout...*

The tympani drumming of blood in the ears and the clammy grip of terror kept up throughout the play. I said my lines to the Mechanicals, handing them their parchment scripts for *Pyramus and Thisbe*. Who knows what the audience saw or felt? But to me it was as if I'd been possessed by a text-to-speech program. Surely, I was the most mechanical Mechanical of all.

Next, I had a scene with Bottom the Weaver, another Mechanical, played by Vinnie, a good friend of mine and an actor so committed and passionate that his monologues often made me cry. The two of us were center stage, the sole focus of the play. Vinnie said his line, tossing it to me jauntily like an opening salvo in ping-pong, and stood there grinning, waiting for my response.

I said nothing. Every line in the scene had vanished from my brain. They must have been in there somewhere, of course, but no earthly means would restore them to my lips. Vinnie tried nodding energetically. He tried mouthing my lines. Nothing. Zip. Cortisol and adrenaline and a few other hormones had hijacked my body and among the three ancient options of fight, flight, or freeze, it had chosen number three.

There was bone-chilling horror in this, but also an eerie kind of peace, like that scene in *2001: A Space Odyssey* with the baby floating in space. We were all adrift together—the audience, Vinnie, and I—spinning in infinity. After what might have been two minutes, half an hour, or seven hundred years, Vinnie improvised something and we somehow made our escape.

Backstage, I opened a notebook, and began furiously scribbling a stick-figure comic. It was the scene that had just happened, with three identical panels conveying the infinite, frozen moment. I taped it up in the dressing room: a bit of self-deprecating humor, a lame attempt to save some face.

At intermission, Louis came backstage. He stood there, silently reading the comic. What on earth could I have been thinking? In what possible universe could the director of this high-profile, showcase performance have wanted to see a satire—by *me*—of the complete disaster I had just made of his play on opening night? He glanced grimly at the floor, shook his head slowly, and walked away.

Louis couldn't make much of me as an actor, but I think he was the best teacher I ever had. In one short speech he gave—the only time he ever strung more than three sentences together in class—he taught us everything there is to know about discipline. "Show up," he said. "It's the single best piece of advice I can give you—for this class, for college, for life. Just show up. I don't care how you're feeling—hungover, sick, exhausted on two hours' sleep—keep showing up."

A thousand times since then I've been struck by the deceptive simplicity of that teaching. It wasn't some empty platitude about the virtues of hard work. It was a promise that anywhere in our lives we didn't let doubt paralyze us, we'd grow. Faith and self-confidence, if they were lacking, would come in time, after we'd shown up often enough to learn that whatever we had to give was all we needed. We didn't need to be somebody else, somebody better, to reach for the things we wanted.

But after that opening night, I decided I was through with acting, or it was through with me. My head was full of words, but if they were suited to any action it didn't seem to be the kind I needed onstage. For now I'd just keep scrawling them in notebooks, turning them into song lyrics, and using them to talk back to the books I read.

It was my twenty-first birthday. I was legally an adult. It's worth emphasizing that all my heroes—all my models of manhood at the time—were self-destructive on a grand scale. There was Tom Waits of course, who with the help of his wife, Kathleen Brennan, would ultimately manage to pull himself out of the death spiral, reinvent himself musically, raise children, and get serious about yoga. There was Shane MacGowan of the Irish punk band The Pogues, an incandescent mess whose abuse of liquor and heroin would render him incomprehensible and unemployable (even by his own band) before thirty-five. And there was the Welsh poet Dylan Thomas. Enchanted by his book-length poem *A Child's Christmas in Wales*, I had memorized the whole thing to recite at Christmas for the extended family, whether they liked it or not.

Like few other poets, Thomas delighted in the musicality of language, and the recordings of him intoning his own work in his deep Welsh growl were like lullabies for me many nights that winter. He also delighted in whiskey, so much so that his drunken death had become an inextricable part of his legend. On a cold November night in 1953 he'd allegedly lined up eighteen shots of whiskey on the bar of the White Horse Tavern, his favorite haunt in New York's West Village, and downed them one after another. "Eighteen whiskeys! I think that's a record!" were supposedly his last words before the ambulance took him away. As the story went, he did not "go gentle into that good night."

I didn't realize it at the time, but the doomed artist archetype kept me close to John. John was too pure, too special for this world. If we were like brothers, then maybe I was destined for martyrdom, too. I took dark comfort in that. It was also a rebuke to my dad and the pressures he represented. In the midst of life, the doomed poet was in death—how could he be expected to plan ahead? To network?

With all this in the background, my drinking became sustainable drowning, of feelings and of self. But for a good long while, it also felt sexy and very grown up.

After the play, I invited the cast—friends and classmates from the studio—to join me in the West Village, at the White Horse Tavern. I downed four or five pints of Guinness in quick succession. Untroubled that I'd ruined opening night with my stage fright, or gracious enough to shake it off, the cast toasted my birthday with theatrical verve. I glanced over at the framed picture of Dylan Thomas above his customary table and was utterly happy.

Afterward, a few classmates followed me back to my apartment. One of them was Moira, smaller than me by a head, with a great, tangled, black-Irish mop of hair, flashing eyes, easy laughter, and sudden, surprising intensity. Her name, with its eerie and beautiful diphthong *oi*, meant "fate" in ancient Greek. She was a Pogues fan, too, drawn to the lyrical and the tragic, similarly adrift on the wine-dark sea. A week or two later, we'd be a couple.

We all drank some more and I played everyone a new song about *Hamlet*. They asked me to sing it again. Between the song, the guitar, myself, and my friends there was no space for doubt to creep in. No space for questions. The action fit the word and the word fit the action. For the first time since John died, I felt at home in my own skin, at peace with myself and gloriously alive.

Hamlet, Prince of Denmark [excerpt]

Hamlet wasn't much for conversation
In fact, he was a kind of a difficult guy to know
I would think that he was listening to me
Then he'd break into a soliloquy
"To be or not to be..." and off he'd go...

And leave me singing:
What has happened to Hamlet?
He used to be such fun
Now he only listens to the Cure and the Smiths
And he wears all black and he won't talk to anyone

Hamlet's end, as you might guess, was tragic
He took most of the court of Denmark with him, too
How do I know? I am his good friend Horatio.
And I'm the only one left alive to sing this song to you.

Goin' Out West

St. John's College is nestled in the foothills of the Sangre de Cristo (Blood of Christ) Mountains that Paul Simon mentions in the song "Hearts and Bones," about the "arc of [his] love affair" with the actress Carrie Fisher. At 7,300 feet, Santa Fe isn't "high desert," as I used to believe. It's on a semiarid steppe that gets around fourteen inches of rain and snow annually. High deserts typically get less than ten. Thanks to those four extra inches of rain, the warm, pink and orange sand of the mountains and the foothills is studded with piñons, round, fuzzy pine bushes about human height with the endearing vibe of an Ewok from *Star Wars: Return of the Jedi*. Between the piñons run arroyos, winding natural trenches made by runoff from the rainfall in the mountains. Newcomers to Santa Fe are warned never to walk in the arroyos. Dry and inviting as they are, they're prone to flash floods that can drown you.

In Bethesda, where Meri and I grew up, there's always a sense of enclosure. The suburbs were scooped out of the ancient woods and the woods always seem eager to reclaim them. As kids, we followed narrow trails down to the creek, out of view of civilization, but adult residents mainly commuted to work and back on the legendarily congested Beltway, then sheltered in place, their homes like fortresses. By the mid '90s, my parents and their neighbors were at war with a growing, displaced population of deer, swarming at night out of the remaining clumps of forest to eat their rhododendrons.

By contrast, the skies around Santa Fe are breathtakingly vast. From any vista you can see a rainstorm coming from two days away. St. John's is surrounded by gentle hiking trails up to Atalaya Mountain, and students are always camping and hanging out up there. For a lifelong Easterner, it's instantly liberating. Like some gold rush pioneer you feel the weight of history sloughing off your shoulders as you tilt your compass in the direction of the future.

From the moment her black hiking boots touched the parking lot, Meri was in her element. She bought a white pet rat that she trained to crawl up her sleeve, pop out at the collar, and lick her nose. Her dorm room quickly turned into a beanbag-chair-filled second home to an orbiting group of friends, many of them brilliant yet damaged and in need of refuge. With friends, she was instinctively, unconditionally generous with her time, attention, and any money she had. Her confidence was a renewable source of energy that she shared without arrogance or any strings attached.

Meri took her studies very, very seriously, approaching each great thinker in the canon as a therapist might approach a new patient, following their trains of thought, observing clues, building a working model of their mind. She loved the scientists and mathematicians most of all, telling me excitedly on the phone all about Galen's precocious (and gory) studies of anatomy and the bold electromagnetic experiments of Maxwell. Indifferent to math in high school, she became known around campus as a keen mathematical mind, famous for leaping up excitedly in the middle of a discussion about Pythagoras or Newton with some astonishing insight.

On weekends, she hiked and camped in the mountains with

JASON GOTS

Meri first sets foot on the St. John's College campus.

friends. Sometimes they took acid or mushrooms. More than once on psychedelics she had an experience of *unio mystica*—the sense of union with the divine in all things that's the heart of the practice of all mystical sects, from the Islamic Sufis to the Jewish Kabbalists, to the ancient Vedic priests of India. These instances of kenosis convinced her of the existence of a spiritual reality beyond current scientific understanding, though not necessarily incompatible with it.

Unlike me, Meri had no bad blood with science or scientists. Like her first great love, American democracy, science groped incrementally toward its distant aims. Democracy, as she understood it, stumbled—sometimes violently—in the direction of justice, while science bumbled and occasionally leapt its way toward truth.

As C. P. Snow points out in *The Two Cultures*, neither science nor the arts is immune to arrogance. Science is corrupted when it regards its current understanding as inviolable fact. Art is corrupted when it judges the rest of the world by its own aesthetic standards and ideals. But science as Meri loved it knew its own checkered history, acknowledged its own fallibility, and kept up its quest, undaunted. Her way of thinking and working was a revival of the lab science of our Pop Pop Joe, and the practical problem-solving of our Grandpa Jim, the engineer.

But as serious as Meri was about her scholarship, people always came first. Not only would she forgo a night's sleep to help someone through a breakup or a breakdown—she seemed to live for the opportunity.

Back in New York, in the winter of 1994, I was going through both. NYU was over, the cozy certainty and psychedelic magic of freshman year in Hayden Hall a distant memory. The doubts about acting and the pressure to earn a living had come together like opposing weather fronts to produce an acute and debilitating depression. By October, Moira had had all she could take of my suffering, which was no longer remotely romantic. She faced the same mighty challenge I did—that of starting an adult life in New York City—and I was emotional quicksand.

When she left, it was just me, Tom Waits, whiskey, and the 5 a.m. alarm clock for the coffee shop job in Newark, New Jersey, that I'd gotten by handshake from some guy I met at a party. I remember a pivotal, decisive battle one morning, lying there in my loft bed on Lafayette Street, every cell in my body demanding that I hurl the alarm clock to the floor, go back to sleep, and never return to work again. Then came a second voice, a hard-ass in my psyche who I now think of as "Sarge." *Get up, goddammit!* yelled Sarge. *You're a grown man now. Get your ass up and go to work!* Sarge is a thoroughgoing dickhead. I wouldn't wish him on my worst enemy. But this was a matter of survival, and survival is Sarge's specialty. I can't say I was ever happy in the job, but day after day, thanks to Sarge—anxiety, depression, sense of wounded entitlement, and all—I kept showing up.

One freezing cold Saturday in December, after wandering around the Village looking for a better job (my methods had not improved since Oakland) I stood at a pay phone on Lafayette Street and called home. I was at the end of my rope, exhausted, anxious, directionless, and alone. Until then, I'd been playing it cool with my folks, acting like I had everything under control the way I was supposed to. For half an hour straight I tried, through tears, to articulate the despair and confusion, the need for some counsel about how to move on from acting and build a meaningful life. When I finally paused for breath, my mom said laconically: "Geez... You sound like you're falling apart."

So I popped in another quarter and called Meri. This was a desperate last straw. I don't know how other brothers and their younger sisters behave but for all the love between us, there had always, also, been unspoken competition. I hated our parents' perception of Meri as the levelheaded one and me as the hopeless dreamer. And I knew Meri's attitudes about weakness and vulnerability in men. I didn't want the power dynamic to shift. I didn't want to risk losing her respect.

But I had nowhere else to turn. I've only ever had one or two close friends at a time, and John was dead. Ed and I were still officially friendly, but for the moment we were on different planets. He was immersed in work at NYU grad school to become an occupational therapist—a middle ground between his medical dreams of freshman year and the anthropology major he'd graduated college with. Other than worry, the only thing I was immersed in was literature—a bunch of old books that Ed hadn't read.

So I took the risk of being honest with Meri. For an hour and a half I kept pumping quarters into the pay phone as Meri tried to remind me who I was. "Are you kidding me? You're one of the smartest, most creative, kindest people I know! I've been bragging about you to all my friends. I play your tape all the time. Everybody loves the Hamlet song!" She gave me a hundred reasons to see this current, shitty situation as temporary. I took in as much of it as I could. And then she made a crazy suggestion: maybe I could come out to St. John's for graduate school. There was a new program starting up in Eastern classics—the great spiritual and literary books of India, China, and Japan.

In our family, taking off to India to "find yourself" was unthinkable. But a case for Eastern graduate school might be easier to make. A master's degree could take you in any number of directions. In the weeks that followed, I came to see St. John's as a kind of secular monastery—a refuge from the mess of my life in New York where I could submit for a while to the wise mentorship of Buddhist, Taoist, and Hindu scripture. I'd be with my sister, I'd get some perspective on things, and when I came back to the world, I'd come back on my own terms, planful and ready for action.

Road Trip, NYC to Santa Fe

The Pontiac Grand Safari. I'm not picky about cars, but this is not a machine any twenty-one-year-old wants to be seen in. It's ridiculous and yet somehow fitting that this aging, wood-paneled station wagon is my means of escape from New York City. I escaped suburbia for New York, and now suburbia has come like a soccer mom to shuttle me to a new refuge in Santa Fe. How much of an escape can I actually make in my parents' hand-me-down car?

I've never owned a car before, as will become obvious three days after this two-thousand-mile road trip ends, when a loud knocking will occur and the engine will seize forever because I don't know how or when to put oil in a car.

Ed is with me. We've emptied the Lafayette Street apartment, and I've left the keys in the hands of a friend who is supposed to return them to the landlord a couple days later, but who will instead give them to a heroin addict she knows from the local bar. The addict will squat there for two months until the sherriff rams the door open, and my father gets stuck with the bill.

But today I'm filled with expansive hope, ready to leave New York in the dust. Like the proverbial young man (and all those women the proverbs don't mention), I'm going west (to study the ideas of the East). I'm not seeking enlightenment—not yet, anyway. I'd be happy if the books and the change of scenery could help me find a little more peace of mind.

Ed and I have filled the car to bursting with my belongings (books, mostly), several boxes of two sugary cereals called Blueberry Morning and Banana-Something, and my overweight orange cat, Sophie, who will yowl unceasingly from the moment we leave New York until the moment we arrive at our destination. There won't be much meandering along the way. Ed's a busy guy, soon to start summer classes or an internship for his master's program. All these years later, he's still an occupational therapist—perfectly content with his calling. And there's the difference between me and Ed, in a nutshell.

We set out from New York in high spirits. We're young. We're buddies. And even in a station wagon, this is the Great American Road Trip. Ed is Puerto Rican Chinese, a little taller than me and more sturdily built. I've just dyed my hair blue and sea-plant green and tangled it with a comb into something that is entirely unlike the dreadlocks I was going for, in homage to Ani DiFranco.

So the sun's at our back, urging us westward, and traffic flows smoothly as we head out of the East Village toward the GW Bridge that will lift us out of the city. By now, Ed is also a card-carrying member of the Church of Tom Waits, so our first and only tourist stop, sometime before nightfall, will be Bardstown, Kentucky, which we mistakenly believe to be the home of the Maker's Mark bourbon distillery. It is, in fact, in nearby Loretto.

Here's how I imagine Bardstown: as you drive into the city limits, you see on your right a venerable old mansion next door to a huge, sturdy wooden warehouse. This is Maker's Mark, and all are welcome. On the porch, a Wilford Brimley type invites us to pull up a chair, telling us they "do things a little bit slower round here."

"Hey, Pete!" he calls out to a worker in overalls out of a Steinbeck novel: "Uncork the Ol' Faithful and let 'em have a taste!"

In reality, Bardstown is an industrial hellhole. Wherever we go, all we see is the forbidding, rusting metal exoskeletons of factories that could be churning out anything from whiskey to Drano. There are no signs inviting us to tour anything. *"Crap,"* I sigh, and we head for a state-run liquor store. There behind the counter sit two local guys, one with (I kid you not) a shotgun on his lap, eyeing us bemusedly.

"D-do you have bourbon?" I manage. *"Like, local bourbon?"*

"Heaven Hill," says one, pointing at the shelf.

"What's the difference between the brown label and the green one?"

Knowing nothing about whiskey, and getting no help from these guys, we decide the green one must be "fresher." Closer to the pure, unadulterated taste we've traveled so far to experience.

It's getting late, so we head for a motel. Our room is like something out of a Tennessee Williams play. A sad, peeling, laminated table. A low-hung, nicotine-yellowed lamp. Two beds, an ancient TV, and a generic painting of the sea. Ed and I sit at that table for hours, choking down this horrible rotgut. There is singing and backslapping and pissing off the balcony into the parking lot. At 5 a.m., Ed sets an alarm clock on the TV to wake us for an early start…two hours later. Ed's the kind of guy who remembers to set an alarm even after a night of guzzling Heaven Hill Green.

At seven, I awaken with what I can confidently say is the worst hangover I will ever have in my life. I can barely see, let alone stand. One eye simply won't open, so I power through it, imagining myself some kind of hearty pirate on the high seas, which conveniently also explains why the carpet is undulating.

Ed feels no better than I do, but after two cups of coffee he claims to be okay to drive. Around eleven, we stop at a breakfast chain restaurant somewhere in Tennessee. It's a gleaming mile of stainless steel, Sterno-heated trays heaped with suppurating sausages, hash browns, white gravy, and scrambled eggs. In my current state, salt and fat are exactly what I crave, and the coffee is having its intended effect of making me feel slightly less dead. I return from a trip to the trough for seconds to see a waitress leaning in to whisper something in Ed's ear.

"Y'all best hurry up and head on out of here," she tells him. Apparently there's a group of local boys who don't like Ed's brown skin and my fanciful hairdo. A couple more forkfuls of hash browns and we hurry on out of there, never to set foot in that town again.

From Odysseus all the way down to Ed and me, every literal journey's a life in miniature. You leave behind the comforts of home and strike off into the unknown. You meet (and become) surprising characters along the way. Danger and struggle, if you survive them, make for the best stories. But lately I've found myself questioning the whole "hero's journey" schtick. Every two-bit marketer knows that "conflict" is what gets our attention. Every producer knows that without a struggle, there's no story. Adversity's a teacher, to be sure. But is it the only way to learn and grow? Why are these the only stories we want to hear and tell? Why must all stories be stories of conquest? I can't help noting, with bell hooks, that these ancient macho archetypes are stifling, at the very least. Is it possible that all this fawning over myth (by way of Joseph Campbell and Jung) is an insidious form of conservatism, another way of reassuring ourselves—on the authority of ancient texts—that boys will always be heroes and girls will always be damsels in distress?

We fetishize struggle out of pride at having survived it. So struggle itself becomes a value, an expectation we pass along to our children. There's nothing wrong with resilience on the road to some goal worth striving for. But difficulty for its own sake is insanity. We get confused about this, force children to "buckle down" to meaningless busywork in school, make enduring drudgery part of the curriculum. At the end of an education, we shove young people out into the world unprepared to reconcile their dreams with the marketplace. In my four years at NYU there wasn't a single lecture on how real people made their living in theater or film. Instead, we heard rumors and braggadocio about the need to "hustle" and "grow a thick skin."

If our stories emphasize struggle over generosity, connection, and love, we perpetuate struggle in the world. That doesn't make us stronger, it makes us more callous and cruel.

We're on a tight schedule, Ed and I. So after breakfast we drive flat out the rest of the way, stopping only to take turns at the wheel.

The grad dorms at St. John's won't open until August. So I'll live with Meri for the summer in a house she's rented with some friends. Ed and I arrive around 8 p.m., the sun having beaten us west, hanging low and mellow at the horizon like a pendulous egg yolk. The southwestern landscape feels somehow "clean" to me, and I feel cleaner just being here.

Meri's nowhere in sight, and there seems to be some kind of rave going on. There are colored lights everywhere and dozens of people wandering in and out of the house, lying in the backyard among the cactuses, drinking and chatting on the stairs. A charming, affable, impeccably dressed thirtysomething who could be the actor Alan Cumming's twin brother greets me and Ed like long-lost cousins:

I'm Pete, but everyone calls me Petey. Are you Meri's brother, Jason? Oh my God, I've heard so much about you! It's wonderful to meet you! And this must be Ed. Welcome! It's madness here as always, but benevolent madness. It would be better to wait until tomorrow to unpack...

The only thing I unpack is Sophie, who happily trades the trauma of the Grand Safari for the trauma of this party. Petey guides us to what he says will be my bedroom and I set the cat up with food, water, and kitty litter, then head back out into the fray.

"Our friend Timothy is moving to Austin," says Petey. "This is his going-away party." I'm a little intimidated by all the strangers and by the professional DJ PA system and A/V setup, all of which turn out to belong to Timothy, who is, in fact, a rave DJ for a living. I'm a little hurt, too, perhaps, that my welcome to Santa Fe is mainly a goodbye to someone else, someone I've never heard of before. Timothy's leaving behind a generous parting gift, though: a little crate in the freezer holding twelve 1 oz dropper bottles of liquid LSD. Petey grins and offers me a dropperful.

Taking LSD like this, in a house full of strangers with thumping bass and a light show, is a clear violation of the Psychedelic Code Ed and I mostly adhered to in college. LSD was for introspection and interpersonal discovery, not for partying. I take a long, appraising look at this scene that for the next two months will be my home. Glance sideways at Ed, who looks disoriented, then back at Petey. *What the hell*, I think, tilting my head back like a baby chick, *when in Rome...*

Soon Ed absolutely has to go or he's going to miss his plane home. We hug like brothers on a dock somewhere, in some other century, one of them about to set off on a sea voyage from which he may never return. Although Ed's in motion and I'm staying put, I'm the one who's adrift. He catches his cab, taking with him my last, tenuous tie to New York and I'm swallowed whole by this strange, new life.

To this day, that was the craziest home I've ever lived in.

There was the aforementioned liquid LSD, cleaner and purer in its effects than anything we ever bought in Central Park.

Many nights I lay out in the cool of the desert backyard, gazing for seven or eight hours straight into the infinity of stars.

Also, I soon learned that Petey's main job was selling cocaine to high-end clients in Santa Fe and Albuquerque. He and his boyfriend, a married fiftysomething named Luis with slicked back, steel-gray hair, spent a lot of their time sitting at our breakfast table, sifting a giant mound of cocaine into baggies. At one point, at one of the many, many parties that seemed to pop up that summer like mushrooms after a rain shower, a very drunk Luis cornered me in the kitchen and said, "I bet you got a real sweet dick under those trousers." By then, nothing that happened in the house could faze me. "Honestly," I said, "when it's your own you just kind of get used to it, you know?"

Diane, a Navajo girl Meri had met at a rave and more or less adopted, slept on our couch, dreaming of renting a warehouse and throwing a rave of her own in order to earn enough money to one day sleep in a bed. Ultimately, she borrowed a thousand bucks from Meri, rented a bunch of audio equipment, then disappeared for good, leaving Meri penniless and stuck returning all those speakers, wires, and turntables to the store in her tiny Saturn.

This was the family Meri had assembled. She was the star around which this chaos revolved.

Throughout high school, Meri had been close with Mika, my parents' live-in housekeeper and nanny. Mika was born Michael, to a born-again Christian mother in Western Maryland. While living with us, Michael had a sex change operation and became Mika. I don't remember Michael well, but Mika was outspoken and wild. She smoked pot on our patio, danced on the weekends as "Aphrodite" in a Pittsburgh nightclub, and was always involved in some elaborate scheme/scam to get expensive jewelry or furniture for next to nothing. Once, soon after her operation, she casually flashed us her new breasts in the living room with pride. Unaccustomed as I was at seventeen to having new breasts flashed at me, Mika's happiness with her new body was infectious. It was strange and wonderful to see a person in her late thirties or early forties finally becoming herself.

Mika and Meri were besties, always smoking pot together (after school, while my folks were still at work) and laughing at something or other on TV. For Meri's senior prom, she gave my sister an elaborate makeover, dressing her in a brocaded gown like something out of *Sunset Boulevard*.

I think Meri's relationship with Mika taught her that the people we knew in the bubble of our upper-middle-class suburban homelife represented a very narrow slice of humanity. I think she became suspicious of lives that were too safe and tidy, with their messiness and violence swept under the rug. This biased her, sometimes, toward people with troubles, people in need of her help, as if they were more likely to keep her honest.

In the mostly benevolent chaos of that Santa Fe house, Meri moved with sunny grace, like the loving matriarch of some Old West gang of train robbers. Often, she'd be up before anyone else, cooking breakfast, or organizing the household into teams to clean up last night's mess. I was proud of her strength, amazed at how much she was able to carry without sinking.

Part of me imagined SWAT teams knocking the door off its hinges and dragging us all off to prison any minute. Another part wanted to follow Meri's lead and test the limits of my tolerance for a life that looked nothing like the one we'd both come from. The Psychedelic Code was out the window. Never mind "set and setting"; no one in that house ever took any drug in isolation. Beer flowed freely. Petey and Luis had what seemed like an infinite supply of free crystal MDMA and cocaine. We drank, we took the liquid LSD, then someone would pass around a mirror with lines of coke, or a pipe full of MDMA, mixed with weed.

I quickly learned that cocaine was not for me. For exactly

three minutes after taking it, I'd feel terrific and possess the oratorical skills of Winston Churchill. Then, suddenly, I'd be struck mute with crippling anxiety. Terrified of losing my bold, new personality forever, I'd snort another line. Two lines later, I'd sink into a deep depression. People would ask me if everything was okay. I'd mutter something and slink off to my room to wait it out.

The whole thing was so horrible, so undesirable that it seemed there was no possibility of my ever becoming addicted. Meri was different. She enjoyed cocaine casually. She could take it or leave it, like Mom Mom with a cup of coffee. I don't know if the difference was psychological, biological, or both; marijuana, too, sent me spiraling into doubt and paranoia. Some drugs just opened up the floodgates of the fear I hadn't yet conquered, and offered no support for dealing with it.

I discovered a group called Shakespeare in Santa Fe and got a nonspeaking role as a feather-festooned dancer in an outdoor production of *The Comedy of Errors*. One day close to opening night, two young women—friends of the Navajo girl—came from Phoenix holding large quantities of crystal meth. They shared it generously, hoping we'd buy some before they left. These were early days for crystal meth in America and it didn't yet have a PR problem. It was just something new and different.

For me, meth was like cocaine on a much longer time scale. For two nights straight, I stayed awake, regaling the cute drug dealers with tales from my life, which suddenly seemed as rich and fascinating to me as the *Arabian Nights*. The girls seemed captivated, too, and I thrived on their attention. I didn't eat. I didn't nap. I rarely even paused to breathe, or for a bathroom break. And eating was out of the question.

At the end of the third day, it was opening night. Twirling back and forth, capering down the aisle and onto the stage of the open-air theater, I was sure I was going to pass out. I'd collapse on the stage, the performance would be stopped and they'd rush me to the hospital, where I'd be arrested, then die of a heart attack.

Somehow, none of this happened. Afterward, Meri picked me up in her Saturn. I confessed to her what a useless, disgusting piece of shit I'd become. What a disgrace to our family name. I had managed to destroy my life before my first day of grad school. She gave me a hug and advised me to lay off the drugs for a while, take a shower, and have a nice, long sleep.

Jason as a dancer with Shakespeare in Santa Fe.

★ ★ ★

My life was bipolar that summer. When I wasn't assaulting the body with drugs or drink I was feeding the spirit with Buddhist and Hindu scripture. In preparation for the fall, I read the first book of the *Mahabharata*, the sprawling, dazzling, thirteen-thousand-page epic whose myths are the basis of Hinduism. All the Sanskrit names took some getting used to, but the book was like a soap opera on LSD—a kaleidoscopic chronicle of wonders centered on a family of superheroes. I was totally absorbed.

In Hindu cosmology, Brahman is the ultimate god—the source of all being. Unlike Vishnu and Ganesha and the hundreds of other, lesser gods that populate the *Mahabharata*, Brahman is like the God of the Hebrews: ultimate, faceless, and unknowable. Each living being contains something like a soul—a tiny spark of Brahman called "Atman." Over millennia of reincarnation into different bodies, what Atman wants most of all is to come home. To dissolve back into Brahman and end this long separation.

This was strikingly reminiscent of *tikkun olam*, a Jewish mystical belief I'd read about in college. According to the Kabbalistic mystic Isaac Luria, at the beginning of the universe a vessel containing the light of God shattered, showering sparks that became individual human souls. For him, spiritual work was the work of repair, of putting all these shards back together again.

In Hinduism, beings strive to purify themselves toward permanent reunion with Brahman. This is the purpose of Yoga, which refers to any physical, breathing, or meditative practice that teaches nonattachment to the things of this world. Through countless lifetimes, Atman inches ever closer to non-returning. Still adrift, still lost, I could relate to the longing to find some way back to the whole.

The Buddhist texts (Indian, too, but later than the *Mahabharata*) also talked about reincarnation, nonattachment, and non-returning. Gone were Atman and Brahman, but the goal was essentially the same: a state beyond the story arcs, the dramatic ups and downs of this world. With all the dramatic, chemical ups and downs of my life in Santa Fe, this philosophy made more and more sense to me, but I was powerless for the moment to put it into practice.

Over the next year and a half, the split widened further. My two closest friends in grad school—beautiful, sensitive souls both—were also addicts (one to heroin, the other to beer). What had started as a test of my tolerance and boundaries, an admiring attempt to keep up with Meri, became sadder and more desperate. I spent most days exhausted and hungover, swearing to myself I'd take that night off. But come sundown, I'd find myself at some bar again or in somebody's apartment, and one beer would somehow lead to ten.

I loved the reading, the writing, and the classes at school. There was no better feeling than sitting on a bench on campus in the shadow of the mountain, learning from Ssu-Ma Ch'ien's *Records of the Grand Historian* about the strengths and fatal weaknesses of ancient Chinese dynasties, thinking about how human nature is always torn between greed and generosity, the familiar and the unknown.

But in my own life, I was rootless and lost, even worse off than I'd been in New York. Meri knew where she was headed. After St. John's, she'd spend a year in a premed program somewhere learning organic chemistry, then continue on to medical school. What would I do? I wasn't an academic. I had no patience for secondary research and footnotes. My interest in texts was too broad and too personal for the game of trying to find some new angle on some obscure writer to distinguish myself in some subspecialty and hopefully get tenure. I was still writing songs. Still attached to the idea of being some kind of artist. Still scared and clueless about where to begin.

Rock bottom came in December of '95, close to my birthday. I asked the heroin-addict friend to get me an 8 ball (3.5 grams) of heroin and a needle. In what I recognize now as an act of mercy, he came back instead with cocaine, saying all the heroin in the county had temporarily run out.

I was disappointed, but determined. Whatever I was running toward or running away from, I wasn't done running yet. So, knowing everything I knew about myself and cocaine, I spent six hours one Saturday night alone at home, injecting it into my arm, followed by four hours of writhing around in a clammy death-sweat, curling up in a fetal position, listening to John Coltrane and begging a God I didn't believe in for redemption.

Meri,

I doubt I ever told you that story. I would have been too ashamed. For all the craziness you surrounded yourself with, you always seemed to have everything under control, at least back then. I was supposed to be your big brother and you'd rescued me from one hell already—how could I admit that I'd gone and made myself another?

But one thing Mom and Dad gave us both was a conscience. After that night, it hit me like a New York City garbage truck, one of those multiton iron rattletraps that periodically run down pedestrians while backing up or making a right turn: I might not know what to do with my life, but I wasn't going to throw it away at the end of a needle. I couldn't live my sister's life, die my best friend's death, or keep running forever for refuge from myself.

Part 3

The Body

Rather than adding something every day, lose something every day. Until you reach true nakedness, you cannot grow.

—Chiba Sensei, teacher of Ryugan Sensei of Brooklyn
Aikikai aikido dojo

October 2010

When the opponent comes at you, you don't resist. You don't punch back, meeting force with force. Instead, you absorb their energy, you become their energy and redirect it. Here words can only get in your way. The split second it takes to think "absorb" or "evade" is enough to break the flow. It's enough to take you out of the body, and that's when violence happens. That's when people get hurt.

My thick, canvas *gi* is heavy with sweat. My shoulder aches from practicing standing rolls—even the slightest hesitation and all 215 pounds of me, all that extra weight from the years before my son was born, all the drinking and the salty, fatty hangover foods—comes down with a *thunk* on the scapula.

Sensei is teaching a takedown in front of the class. He says nothing. Makes eye contact. Motions for me to come in. I like him and trust him, but there's fear in my body, so I'm tense and stiff as he catches my wrist and elbow, rotating the arm like a gate swinging open. The pain is searing, unbearable. Counterintuitively, I relax and the pain ceases. Slowly, he brings me down to the mat.

Brooklyn Aikikai is a small, family-run dojo in Gowanus, Brooklyn. The practice I'm learning, aikido, is relatively new, developed in the 1920s and '30s in Japan by Morihei Ueshiba. It's something more than a martial art. As a means of self-defense, in fact, it doesn't always fare well against other, more violent fighting techniques. It's better, perhaps, to think of it as a life-long spiritual practice, like tai chi or meditation. For Ueshiba, the most important battle is with the self.

♦

Back in college, at Circle in the Square, I had an acting teacher named Therese (Terry) Hayden. By the time I met her, she was in her early seventies and referred to herself dryly as "The Old Lady." In class, she was wise and irascible—an archetypical, Yoda-like mentor. Terry taught us that blockages anywhere, in body, voice, or emotional memory, were the enemy of art. The enemy of living, too.

There was one exercise where she'd have you stand in front of the class and just talk about anything. She'd observe for a while, then stop you. On more than one occasion I watched in awe as she told a student, "You're a middle child, aren't you? Always trying to please everybody," or, "Why are you afraid of your own body?" and they burst into tears of recognition and gratitude at finally being seen. Or seen through.

After one method acting exercise in which I crawled around the floor as a baby, trying (and mostly failing) to revisit scenes from my childhood, she commented, "You're very interesting. Very special indeed. But you have no connection to your body. You should take up swimming."

♦

There's a photograph of me, aged eleven or twelve, in a blue wrestling onesie with white piping. My limbs, just back from summer vacation, are a deep olive brown—the genetic legacy of the southern Italians on my mom's side. I stare down the camera with a look of smoldering determination, as if to say: *Come on, try me. Nobody messes with Jason Gots.* This picture was taken just moments before one of the greatest humiliations of my young sporting life.

Soccer hadn't worked out for me. Neither had flag football. So this winter, my folks had signed me up for wrestling. By the time I started, the season was already well underway. The team had been training for weeks and I'd joined just in time for the first tournament.

This probably took place in a high school gym, but I remember it as an Olympic stadium filled with tens of thousands of people. I remember the acrid smell of sweat and my own fear pheromones. I can still feel the dread in my solar plexus, that nerve center the yogis call the "heart chakra." There was a leaderboard. My name was up there, along with that of my opponent. Four matches to go and it would be my turn. Time for Jason Gots to reveal what he was all about.

I was supposed to "pin" the other guy. I wasn't sure whether this meant holding his shoulders down with my hands or sitting on him or what, but I did know I was supposed to be on top, rendering him immobile beneath me. When my turn came, I stepped onto the mat and attempted the aforementioned smoldering gaze. *Nobody messes with Jason Gots.*

My opponent was a boy about my age and height, with only one arm. In hindsight I realize there's another story here besides that of my own humiliation and subsequent backlash against my own body. This one-armed kid was a really good wrestler. I think he ended up winning first or second place in the tournament, in a sport for which you'd think two arms were the price of entry. For him, this match was probably yet another crucial validation of his wholeness. He needed and he deserved this win.

The bell rang, I glowered for a second and then *WHAM*, I found myself on my back, immobilized. In five seconds, he had pinned me. There's a terrible, narcotic calm in any moment when you realize there's no point in fighting back. All the fear and tension just leaves your body as you accept your inevitable defeat.

◆

For a few years in high school, John and I were rock climbers. St. Albans had an athletic program called Voyager that taught us first to "boulder"—climbing horizontally along the stone outer walls of the school—then drove us out to Carderock, Maryland, to climb a fifty-foot cliff face. There was such elegance and intimacy in the subtle dialogue between body and rock. The way we'd explore the surface with the high-friction rubber toes of our Scarpa shoes, sensing lip enough to shift our weight onto. The novel contortions necessary to ascend an overhang: you'd secure your hands, hook one leg above them, then hoist yourself up and over. The dry comfort of talc on the hands and the traces it left behind on the rock, ghost-markers of our passing, like ancient handprints in a cave.

◆

On a bright, cold day in early November, I arrived late for John's funeral at a family plot somewhere in Pennsylvania, just in time to see the ridiculous little metal canister—the first urn I'd ever seen—being lowered into the ground. I thought of John's dancer's body, its clarity of form, its grace, its topography a relief map of the man he'd become. I glanced again at the urn and had to stop myself from giggling. What was this tin can? What did it have to do with John? Why were we all even standing here?

◆

In Los Angeles sometime in the early aughts, Meri struggled down a basement staircase on a prosthetic leg that didn't fit quite right, carrying two giant laundry bags. Her husband was indisposed as usual or occupied with his schoolwork, which always took precedence over everything else. But Meri wasn't thinking about that—she was doing what she always did, using her enormous willpower to bulldoze her way through physical limitations. The laundry had to be done, and goddammit, she was going to do it. She'd lost some weight recently, so her leglet—the stump from her amputation—didn't suction as it should into the plastic cup at the top of the C-Leg. As she brought the prosthetic foot down on the second step, the leg wiggled, then buckled, and she tumbled headlong down the stairs. She'd had a couple beers. They may have contributed to the fall but they also relaxed the tension, the fear and resistance in her body that might have made the injury much worse. Banged up and bruised but more or less intact, she picked herself back up and started loading the machines.

◆

Sometime in May 1996, I followed Meri up the Atalaya Trail. She was twenty years old, strong and beautiful, her long hair dyed a striking orangey red. I was out of breath, in much worse shape than she was, barely keeping up.

"Look," she said, pointing out an especially bristly cactus. She made a goofy grimace like Marty Feldman in *Young Frankenstein*, hunching her shoulders and framing her face with spiky hands. "GET AWAY FROM MY WATER!" she shrieked. "That's how cactuses have to be, all the time. Everything wants their water. They're just holding on to it as tight as they can. Saguaro cactuses are big enough to share a little. They've got a kind of grudging arrangement with the Gila woodpecker. It can get past the spikes with its long beak. It digs a hole and hides out in there from the heat. Sometimes it eats and drinks a little from the inside." I had a flashback to Catholic church. *Take. Eat. This is my body. It is given up for you.* "Yeah," said Meri, "except for the Saguaro, it's not really a sacrifice. It hardly even notices."

We kept hiking. The only clue to the cancer she'd beaten eight years ago was a slight limp in her right leg. I got curious about it so she explained that every few years the metal prosthesis had to be lengthened to account for growth in the other leg. It was a minor surgical procedure—the doctor made an incision, went in and ratcheted it up a few turns. I thought about the chemo, the vomiting, the weight loss, the hair loss, the horrible-tasting canned nutritional shakes she had to drink to get her body weight back to normal. I watched her, full of life, climbing with happy determination toward the peak, and thought of every-thing she must have had to face—so early—about her body and herself to become what she was now. Her body moved in easy conversation with the natural world. The mountain seemed al-most to know and love her as she loved it. I was her brother. She had invited me. So my body belonged here, too.

◆

From the moment he was born in January of 2008, my son Emre's body was in constant motion. My wife, Demet, and I watched in fascination and sometimes terror as it discovered the world, exploring texture, experimenting with gravity. Watch-ing him, we relearned how a body negotiates space, how much motor memory we take for granted.

After food, the first preferences Emre's body showed were for adventure and speed. In his grandparents' apartment in Istan-bul, Turkey, when he was six months old, we hung a bouncing chair from an old, sturdy hook in the ceiling. Emre jumped and laughed for four hours straight, his fat little legs never seeming to tire. When he started to speak, one of his first words was *Go!* A strident command to run when I carried him on my shoulders.

His first cartoon hero was Sonic the Hedgehog, whose super-power, of course, is speed.

At two, his fingers found the strings of my guitar. His body and the body of one guitar or another have been inseparable ever since. The sounds the strings made vibrated the air, stirred the cilia in his ears, and awakened some structure in his brain that recognized music. At thirteen, he plays by ear, composes complex instrumentals in his head. All that restless motion channeled into melody, rhythm, and harmony, body speaking to body through song.

◆

On the aikido mat, all my words were useless. I had to shut up and listen to my body and the other bodies around me. I couldn't hear much at first. But with weeks and then months of practice a low hum began to emerge against the background noise of my chattering mind. Body language was slower and subtler, but it held essential information. Wisdom you could learn from. All the tension and fear that I'd tried to medicate with drink, drugs, and writing lived in specific parts of the body. Aikido offered direct physical feedback that helped you sense and work through them, letting go of these blockages and revealing your natural strength and ease.

How simple! How obvious! When trauma happens, it's the body that remembers. It's the body that keeps sending you threat signals years after the threat has passed. Talking and writing can help you explain how it feels, even figure out its origins, but healing begins in the body. In aikido, the aim was flow. With practice, you could feel when a move wasn't working, when something was off in your connection with your partner. So you stood up and tried it again.

This wasn't acting school. We weren't working toward some big performance or competing for a part. In aikido there were markers of progress, but even for a master, the work was ongoing. You were always imperfect, always in training. All you had to do was keep showing up.

The dojo itself was a body, too. The students and the sensei, Robert (also known as Ryugan), cared for the physical space as a community, cleaning the mat between sessions, sometimes coming by on a weekend to deep clean the apartment upstairs, where Sensei lived with his wife and his two-year-old son. I took on the job of vacuuming the *zafus* and *zabutons*, cushions a small group used each morning for Zen Buddhist meditation.

At first, a voice in my head balked at this. The voice of my dad, maybe, wondering whether we were somehow being taken advantage of. Wasn't I already paying for classes? Why couldn't Sensei just hire a housekeeper? But as I spent more time in this community, I saw that it wasn't like that at all. This voluntary work was itself a Zen practice for overcoming the ego. It forced you to see, then lay aside the transactional self that wondered, *What, exactly am I getting out of this?* You worked because there was work to be done. You were part of this community. This place was your home, too. And as hard as we worked, Sensei worked ten times harder, offering early morning meditation sessions and extra training at no charge, opening his home for community dinners, and taking seriously his responsibility for the personal growth of each student.

The voice in my head whispered, too, that hierarchical organizations always had the potential for corruption. In spiritual communities, where people often arrived wounded and made themselves vulnerable, wasn't the risk all the greater? How long before my dojo imploded in some sad scandal? But this was the first time in years I'd felt at home in my own body and in the larger body of a community. From all I could see, Robert was an ethically serious man, grateful to his students and committed to the health of this haven we were building together. How had my cynicism about communities served me in the past? It had kept me paranoid, isolated, and limited. Why not take the risk of trusting in others for once?

In addition to regular evening aikido, I started showing up at 6:30 a.m., three days a week, to sit in Zen meditation. Seven or eight of us sat in a row by candlelight in the darkened studio. Sensei clapped the traditional wooden blocks together, slowly at first, then faster and faster, bringing the mind to wakeful attention. For forty-five minutes, we sat in silence, cross-legged on the *zabutons*, spines relaxed but erect. While meditation in some Buddhist traditions involves elaborate visualization or close attention to the breath, the Zen command we followed was "just sit." Eyes gently closed, I was consciousness. I was nobody. I was everyone else in the room. It was another way of letting words go and sinking deeper into the body, of learning that inner and outer connection are a single, lifelong practice.

An Absence
of Care

Medical training in the United States is famously brutal. My father tells stories about operating on people during his residency after forty-eight hours on shift without sleep, nodding off with a scalpel in his hand. Two or three days after I was born, my mom—a woman trying to make her way in a male-dominated field—was back on rotations at the University of Southern California Medical School, treating patients. At the end of a hundred-hour med-student workweek in the early 2000s, a good friend of mine fell asleep at the wheel while rushing to the hospital on call, and woke up just in time to swerve away from oncoming traffic. These weren't rare exceptions; this was part of the culture, based—as more than one professor told my friend explicitly—on the belief that long work hours and limited sleep taught doctors endurance and resilience. That they toughened you up for the challenges of a medical career.

In fact, overwork and sleep deprivation pose life-threatening risks to the health of medical students and their patients. Loss of motor control (potentially deadly during surgery), clinical depression, memory loss, and impaired judgment are just a few of the many, well-documented costs of this culture. Physicians are supposed to be healers. Upon joining the profession, every doctor swears to the Hippocratic Oath: *do no harm*. It's an outrage that cruelty and indifference toward the body are at the heart of Western medical training.

It isn't necessarily surprising, though. In 1970, around the time my parents graduated, medical school classes were less than 10% female. Fifty years before that, the number was close to zero. It's reasonable to see this hazing culture as a legacy of patriarchal masculinity, a ritual girding of the loins for battle in the operating theater. For most of Western medical history, until the nineteenth-century rise of germ theory and bacteriology, the leaders of the profession didn't have much more to offer in the face of sickness, death, and patients' terror than bluster and bravado.

By the time Meri started at USC's Keck School of Medicine in the fall of 2000, female med students were no longer a rarity. But in some ways the culture had gotten even worse. In our lifetime, medical costs had skyrocketed in lockstep with the rise of the insurance industry. Mounting financial pressures had forced hospitals and clinics to streamline and automate their operations, increasing work hours for medical students and professionals but reducing patient contact to a minimum. All of this had predictably dehumanizing effects on doctors, patients, and teaching hospitals and programs like USC's.

In their third and fourth years of medical school, doctors-to-be rotate through various departments in the teaching hospital, taking notes, doing patient interviews, assisting with surgery, and getting exposure to various branches of medicine. As of this writing, no federal law limits the number of hours per week medical students can be required to work. The Accreditation Council for Graduate Medical Education sets the limit at eighty (averaged over a month), but the threat of losing accreditation, coupled with tight hospital budgets and staffing constraints likely incentivizes many schools to underreport.

But in spite of decades of lawsuits, student activism, and other forms of pushback, the system has been excruciatingly resistant to change. In 2000, the ACGME's eighty-hour policy hadn't yet taken effect. Meri's class regularly worked over ninety hours a week.

After St. John's, USC was a culture shock for Meri. Los Angeles was a sprawling, featureless, 24/7 traffic jam. Her professors (harried, overworked doctors themselves) had no time or patience for students' questions. Her fellow students were under too much pressure ever to hang out and become friends.

Empathy for patients came naturally to Meri. The detective work of pathology was exactly the kind of scientific investigation she lived for. But rote memorization was something else entirely. Even after all-night flash card sessions, her big-picture brain struggled to hold on to the minutiae of human anatomy. She faced punishing, three-hour exams that, for the first time in her life, gave her crippling test anxiety. The fact that her husband, Theodore—who had entered the program with her—had a photographic memory and breezed through these tests really didn't make this any easier. But this is what she'd signed up for, and she was determined to make it work.

My wife, Demet, and I stopped in LA for a few days in August 2003, a brief rest on our epic honeymoon road trip around the United States.

I could fill more than one book with thoughts and stories about Demet, my son, Emre, and our lives together. For the most part, in an act of brutal editorial self-discipline, I've left them out of this one. Still, a brief introduction is in order.

In the summer of 2001, less than a month before the towers fell and America was changed forever (at least in the minds of most Americans), Demet was on holiday from her philosophy master's program and visiting the US from Istanbul for the first time. Her best friend had won the green card lottery from Turkey a year before, arrived in New York with no place to live, and, in a set of circumstances worthy in its unlikelihood of the Infinite Improbability Drive from *The Hitchhiker's Guide to the Galaxy*, met and married my college friend Ed.

Demet stayed with them for a few weeks, then all three joined me in Nantucket in August, in my parents' empty vacation house. I was struck by her stillness and enigmatic self-possession. She was beautiful, too: small and catlike, with the Asiatic features of her ancestors, the Çerkez (Circassian) people of the Caucasus Mountains. When Demet went back to Turkey a week later, my heart went with her.

Between 2001 and 2003, we dated long-distance. Many snail mails were sent and much chatting done through ICQ—an internet texting app before there were smartphones. I visited Turkey, Demet visited America again, and then we were married in Bethesda, at my childhood home.

When people tell their love stories, they like to focus on appearances—"I spotted her from across the room," etc. But whether we know it or not, we're all looking for equilibrium. Demet is as practical and grounded as I am dreamy. As kind and loving as I can be critical. And among other things, for better and for worse, I bring playful, unpredictable energy to her life.

In 2003 Meri and Theodore were living in a small, two-story house in Burbank, near the Hollywood movie studios. Theodore spent most of our honeymoon visit in his bedroom, struggling with one or more of his personal demons. Since they met senior year at St. John's, Meri had vacillated between sharing her anxieties about his various struggles and covering for him.

One thing that never wavered, though, was her love for the man, which bordered on worship. She spent most of our visit telling stories about Theodore's academic brilliance, his pho-

tographic memory, and his wild, *Dukes of Hazzard*–style hi-
jinks with his lifelong best friend—a beer distributor from rural
Maryland.

Theodore was smart, to be sure. But Demet and I had always
found him pompous and arrogant. The first time we met, he
had leveled his gaze at me and asked: "Where do you see yourself in five years?" Left alone with Demet (a former philosophy student), he rattled off his knowledge of Wittgenstein, her
graduate specialty, then launched into his thoughts on Lacan,
whom she hadn't read. In their home in LA, we watched Meri
do all of the cooking and housekeeping and wondered whether
Theodore ever spoke half as highly of her as she did of him.

We're all looking for equilibrium. I think Meri was attracted
both to Theodore's outsize confidence and to the woundedness
it masked. He had enough of a spine, she hoped, to keep her
anger in check. And enough pain that she could spend the rest
of her life tending to it, and there would always be more healing to be done.

Meri's prosthetic knee joint was a scientific marvel. For twelve
years it supported the leg that carried her from Maryland to Santa
Fe, then back again for the year of premed classes in Baltimore,
then out to the other end of the continent. It drove her to devote her life to medicine. In every way, it dramatically changed
her life. But in the spring of her third year at USC, it finally
gave out. With no bone left in which to anchor the titanium
pin, amputation was the only option.

Psychologically, Meri was ready for it. The timing was tough
to predict in these cases, but she had long known the prosthesis
wouldn't last forever. She told me calmly how the surgery would
go and talked excitedly about the latest technology. If insurance
paid for the programmable leg she wanted, she'd be able to run,
ski, and ride horses with it, she said. In terms of strength, bal-

ance, and range of motion, it would be better than the natural leg she'd kept all those years.

She had the operation over spring break. It went smoothly enough, but for reasons that are still unclear, the surgeon didn't prescribe any physical therapy. The first time she tried on her new, cutting-edge, computerized leg, Meri fell flat on her face. With some practice, she was able to limp around the house, but skiing and horseback riding were fantastically distant notions. So was marching all over the hospital on rotations.

After an amputation, pain is inevitable. And Western medicine offers few options for treating extreme pain other than opiates and opioids—natural derivatives of the opium poppy like morphine and synthetic variants like hydrocodone. By 2003, America's opioid epidemic was in full swing. As has been thoroughly documented in the work of Pulitzer Prize–winning journalist Eric Eyre, who reported on the crisis from West Virginia, in Dr. Anna Lembke's *Drug Dealer, MD*, and in countless other books, newspaper articles, documentaries, and lawsuits, starting in the mid-1990s pharmaceutical companies aggressively marketed opioids to physicians, in many cases bribing doctors and criminally concealing the risks of their products.

Doctors then prescribed the drugs liberally and when legal prescriptions ran out or became prohibitively expensive, many addicted patients turned to the street or the Internet to feed their addictions. This led to a massive spike in overdoses and the economic and social devastation of entire regions of the US. According to the CDC, opioid overdoses killed 450,000 Americans between 1999 and 2018. Since then, growing public awareness has prompted a wave of civil and criminal cases against pharmaceutical giants and bipartisan federal legislation to regulate opioid prescription, research alternative forms of pain management, and support addicted patients' recovery.

This all started more than a decade too late for Meri. Soon after the operation, she began waking up in the night with searing pain in the right foot she'd lost. Phantom limb pain like this was a common problem in amputees, with no widely known treatment other than pain management with high-dose opioids. And the need for pain management could last a lifetime.

Since childhood, independence and toughness had been pillars of Meri's identity. During her middle school battle with cancer, pity was what she hated and rejected most vehemently of all—a crying grandma by her bedside could send her into spasms of rage. So in spite of the pain, the physical instability of the leg she didn't know how to use, and the unpredictable effects of the painkillers, she marched back out on rotations a few days after surgery.

I know this much about my sister; I'm sure she tried to mask any need for help and bluff her way through the pain. She would have shrugged off any sympathetic questions. But she had just had a serious, glaringly apparent, debilitating operation. Her professors and supervisors—professional healers all—had been informed of her situation, yet they treated her with undifferentiated intolerance, and sometimes open cruelty.

In one clinical class, for example, students had to stand at the back of the room for a long lecture. Meri was in obvious pain, but trying to conceal it. The professor called her out, demanding to know what her problem was. She apologized in tears, explaining that her leg was hurting. If she was such a "wimp," he said, she ought to consider a different career.

She struggled to keep up with the physical demands, delayed on her rounds by the hospital's broken elevators. The supervising interns criticized her mercilessly, calling her lazy and incompetent. One made it a kind of mission to toughen Meri up with all-night sessions spent writing and rewriting patient notes to her exacting specifications.

The administration wasn't much better. It soon became apparent that Meri was in no condition to continue her studies.

The only solution USC could offer was a full year's leave of absence, something Meri was hoping desperately to avoid. Theodore was on track to graduate in the spring, then headed for a postgraduate psychiatric residency at the University of Virginia. He wouldn't risk losing the job by trying to delay it. And Meri couldn't contemplate facing a year without him. After some negotiation, USC decided it would be best if she and the School of Medicine went their separate ways.

I picture Meri, stubborn, determined, limping along in the center of a whirlwind of forces arrayed against her: medical school culture; the pharmaceutical industry; Western medicine's reflexive tendency to throw pills at anything it doesn't yet understand. Self-reliant Meri, incapable of believing that anything other than her own willpower could decide her direction.

Like Job had done with God, she had placed her faith in medical science and for a while, she'd been richly rewarded. Then all at once, it let her down catastrophically. Among her professors, her surgeons, her colleagues, the school administration, and her husband the doctor-to-be—not one member of the medical community that surrounded her offered the help she needed, and the intervention she did receive (in the form of medication) derailed and ultimately may have ended her life.

Everyone's got plausible deniability. Nobody's liable for damages. There were multiple parties, mitigating circumstances, distributed and diluted culpability. But there were also a thousand missed opportunities for simple acts of kind awareness. And at the center of them, one brave yet vulnerable human being trying her best to stay in control.

Here is where I part ways with the certainty—the well-documented, infuriating arrogance—of Western medicine. No, I don't want smallpox back. No, I don't believe that everything Eastern is inherently wise. Yes, the scientific method is better than any other tool we have for testing what works and what doesn't. But in so many fundamental ways our medical culture is broken, characterized by a profound, systemic absence of *care*.

In some ways, positive change is on the horizon. Neurology and immunology are beginning to understand our health and our emotional lives as medically inseparable. The science of epigenetics is deepening our understanding of the interdependence of nature and nurture. It seems likely that the mainstreaming of and growing scientific interest in psychedelics, meditation, and yoga will transform for the better the treatment of trauma, anxiety, depression, and much more. America remains politically torn over health care, but there is near-universal recognition that the insurance industry is a disaster and our hospital systems are in desperate need of reform.

Today, as I sat down to write, a pop-up on my phone from the *New York Times* informed me that Purdue Pharma had pled guilty to criminal charges related to the sales and marketing of the opioid OxyContin, and agreed to an $8.2 billion settlement with the Justice Department for civil charges. It won't bring my sister back. It probably won't even prevent the next big medical scandal with devastating human costs. But it's a start.

The Valley and the Summit

Dear Meri,

One day on the way to Bobst Library to write, I passed a giant chalk-board some students had tied to the crossbars of a bit of scaffolding. At the top, in bubble letters, was the prompt, "What gives you hope?" There were lots of answers in many different hands, but in the center, bigger than the rest, someone had written: STORIES.

It's such a fine line between skepticism and cynicism. I'm skeptical of stories for the same reason I've loved them all my life: the mysterious power they have over us. It's about sequence and theme. Events follow one another in time, and a pattern emerges. The clearer the pattern be-comes, the more inevitable its momentum in seems.

In hindsight it looks like a crossroads, this moment in the first decade of the new millennium when you leave med school and I start life with my wife and son. In the arc of your story it looks like the beginning of a sad, slow decline. In mine, the start of a gradual climb out of darkness.

How real was this momentum? How necessary? We would have felt it even at the time. As much as you loved Emre, all the hoopla around his birth—a new beginning!—was also a painful reminder of the abrupt ending of your medical dreams, the growing distance between you and Theodore, and the fact that your medication made pregnancy impossible. I hate the parallels and want to reject this dual narrative. But siblings are like Einstein's entangled particles: separate us as far as you like; our stories are always invisibly intertwined.

All human stories end in death. So much of human history is the record of our epic, creative attempts to forget or deny this. But remembering, holding on to that fact—that's the only way I know out of the narrative grip. Ironically, it took a story to teach me this. Remember that book I sent you? The only one I ever bought you? Thich Nhat Hanh's Old Path White Clouds. *I don't know if you ever got a chance to read it. It set me on a path, and I thought it might offer you some comfort, at least.*

The book is that Vietnamese Buddhist master's lucid retelling of the Buddha's life, enlightenment, and teachings. More than any other text I know outside of the Pali Canon (a dense and challenging read), it captures the Buddha's humanity and his sense of humor (he had a great one). It lays out the Four Noble Truths and the Eightfold Path with simple yet searing clarity. And it's the story to untangle all stories, or maybe just to loosen their hold on us a bit.

Stories can be entertaining and fun. They can reconnect us with feelings we've locked away for years. They can be levers long enough to move the world. The Buddha told hundreds, maybe thousands of stories, each of them tailored to the specific understanding of his audience. Each of them a potential vehicle toward liberation. Stories aren't the problem, actually. The problem is that too often our stories tell us, rather than the other way around.

When someone you love dies, there's always guilt. Always the question of what you might have done differently. If you voice it, people tell you it isn't your fault, that you shouldn't dwell in regret. But so many other stories were possible, so many creative pathways out of the one you ended up stuck in. We could have recognized sooner the crippling effects of the drugs and addiction, found you alternative treatment for phantom limb pain, even if it meant scouring the globe. We could have confronted Theodore on his apparent failure to offer you the love and support you needed. All the things we did instead—convincing you to move to Florida, helping you format a résumé—none of them was the medicine you needed. Any happiness or peace I've found since then is haunted by that collective failure of imagination.

And that story, of what we did and what we didn't do, what we thought we knew and what we ought to have known, is yet another tempting off-ramp to cynicism.

We're all free already, but we fall into stories that convince us otherwise. For the Buddha (and his Hindu predecessors) this world was a valley of illusion. A stirred-up pond, cloudy with silt. It's worth every bit of time, creativity, patience, and love we have to dispel the illusion, to sit still enough to let the silt drift back down to the bottom.

Faced with the inevitability of old age, sickness, and death, the Buddha found hope in awakening. Awakening to our collective delusion. Awakening to compassion for every beautiful being bound up in these story-webs. If all things are interdependent, your suffering is my suffering, your freedom, my freedom.

Poet and natural philosopher Robert Macfarlane, author of Underland, *once talked to me about the views from the valley and the summit of a mountain. Within the valley, he said, you're in the body of the Earth. Lost in the story, but cradled by it, too. It's a place of wonder and discovery, but only one path forward is visible. The summit is lonely and isolated, but from there you can plot a course in any direction.*

I think we need both ways of seeing. In Buddhist terms, these are two views of "relative reality." We live in this relative world. The choices we make here have consequences. So I owe it to you, to myself, to my family, and to all beings everywhere to try and understand what happened to your life. That means retracing the valley step-by-step and also mapping out the terrain from above.

But I need a third eye also, a lens on "ultimate reality" that's both valley and summit at once. It's a perspective beyond stories, outside of linear time. I need it to stay close to the part of you no story could touch.

Just Show up

New York City, sometime in 1994, between college graduation and St. John's. On a second-floor walk-up on St. Mark's Place, across from a dingy pool hall where cover bands played "Stairway to Heaven" and "Wish You Were Here" with convincing enthusiasm for bridge-and-tunnel teens, lived Larry Bader. Once a week I made the pilgrimage from Lafayette Street to his apartment for a guitar lesson. Sometimes his puffy gray cat, Masha, was there, staring at me with her emerald green eyes. "The ex and I have a custody arrangement," said Larry, laconically. "It's mostly amicable."

That's the kind of guy Larry was—the kind who'd co-parent a cat after a breakup. In appearance, he was like Otto the bus driver from *The Simpsons*, his curly brown locks cascading down his shoulders from under a Sun Records baseball cap. Although the $20/hour guitar lessons suggested hard times, Larry was a serious bluesman. He'd been on the road with Mavis Staples and Bonnie Raitt. He practiced religiously, running scales and chord progressions up and down the guitar for hours each day. Unlike me, he kept his guitars humidified and polished. He changed the strings regularly. As far as I was concerned, Larry was discipline personified, and I was his disciple, here to make his ways my own.

★ ★ ★

Everyone I respected from John to Tom Waits seemed to know that discipline and practice were essential if you wanted to achieve anything. I knew I wanted discipline, but I didn't understand what it was, and what little I did know scared me to death. Mom's discipline—my first model—was terrifying. Its demands were insatiable, relentlessly perfectionist, and rooted in self-denial. I tried to keep up, to meet her expectations, but in the end the message was always the same: *You're weak. You're a quitter. You'll never be good enough.*

I knew this old story was holding me back. I sensed that this discipline monster was something I needed to face and make peace with. But I still had a long way to go.

This is from a journal I kept around that time. It's self-inflating and self-deflating, wise and confused. I wish I could reach through its pages to hug that kid and tell him to take a deep breath. Tell him he was more or less on the right track:

There is this thing of discipline. I think I know less about it than perhaps I should…

Q. Is it possible to alter one's Nature?

A. …it should be possible through an act of will, by continually disproving our own assumptions concerning what we can and cannot do, right? If we become discouraged, we may decide (because history carries weight), that we have failed once again and were foolish to think we could be anything other than weak or lazy.

So I bought sturdy, new boots. They are an external representation of an internal desire for reliability, stability, and strength. They are also a lot like Tom Waits's boots in a poster I saw. They are also "manly," and in keeping with my search for Manhood over the past few years. Heh heh. I know my own motives so well...

So. Discipline. I suppose I have been in many ways more disciplined in the last few months than usual. I have read five Nabokov books, *Karamazov*, *The Republic*, *Phaedrus*...

Now, here's the other thing. Are these ideas silly? No. We know for a fact they are not. If my sole reason for reading these books was to convince myself that I am a disciplined person, then, yes, they would be. But motives are complex. I also read Plato to be closer to Meri, who is so far away.

I will practice guitar because it will make me a better guitar player. The discipline will bring peace. It will make me feel like a Real Man. It passes the time. Richard Thompson does it and he is a hero of mine. It is a prayer. A sacrifice.

Don't be so quick to judge. Everything is deeper and shallower than it seems.

Discipline has two parts, both of which I struggled with. First, you had to decide where you wanted to go. Like the Cheshire Cat says, whichever direction you choose, you're bound to end up somewhere. But somewhere wasn't good enough for me; I always got hung up on the destination. Take guitar: my heroes (Tom Waits, Ani DiFranco, Richard Thompson, Paul Simon) were poetic lyricists and spontaneous, soulful singers. I started to worry that too much practice would make my playing stiff and mechanical. If I was truly a songwriter, shouldn't it all just come to me naturally?

This was ridiculous, of course. Richard Thompson was one of the most technically accomplished guitarists alive. Paul Simon practiced constantly. Ani DiFranco's fingerpicking was percussive, melodic, complex instrumental perfection itself. Even drunk, Tom Waits had the chops to improvise his way through a forty-five-minute jazz piano set. Their passion and their presence was amplified by discipline, not diminished by it.

The second part of discipline is consistency. *Keep showing up.* You learn more from the daily struggle with yourself than you do from the technical skills you acquire. Here, too, I quibbled endlessly with myself, got lost in Talmudic sophistry. The question I was stuck on was, *How much is enough?* The inner Mom said there was no limit. No reasonable amount of daily practice. That if you were really committed, you'd practice every waking moment. At that, the inner child threw its hands up in disgust and stalked out of the room.

Larry and I listened to Taj Mahal's "You're Gonna Need Somebody on Your Bond" and Freddie King's "Me and My Guitar," blues barn burners from two living masters. He taught me the pentatonic scales, essential to blues, and had me try to figure out the lead guitar on both songs. At home, practice was a mix of learning leads, practicing scales, and jamming along with slower players like Lightnin' Hopkins and John Lee Hooker.

I did try to practice; all these years later my fingers still know the scales Larry taught me. But I couldn't stop the inner child from rebelling against the inner drill sergeant. After a month or two of this internal battle I started to dread the arrival of practice time. Where in all this hassle was the spontaneity? The fun? The music?

In relationships with women, I was faithful and typically monogamous. When it came to discipline, I had serious problems with commitment. It never took long before any structure started to feel like a cage.

I grew up assuming that discipline always had to feel like work. If you felt like doing it, it wasn't really practice. Reading and writing always came naturally to me, so I never thought of them as disciplines. Like mother, like son.

In high school I could spend hours writing a few lines of a sonnet because it felt like a puzzle, or a game. In college and grad school it was journaling and song lyrics. The right words, when I found them, released a burst of inner energy that could keep me euphoric for days. There was a lot of work involved. There were times when my mind, reaching irritably for a rhyme or the right image, started to feel like a wrung-out sponge. But the reward was so profound, so personally fulfilling, that nothing could have stopped me from making the effort.

Reading was rewarding work, too. It offered a different kind of hope and momentum. That year before St. John's, while I was commuting to the coffee bar in Newark, it was a way of connecting to Meri, who was out in Santa Fe reading many of the same books, and to brilliant minds from the past. As an undergrad I'd studied English and dramatic literature, but philosophy, Russian lit, and most of twentieth-century prose had passed me by. Filling in those gaps was a worthy challenge. And like writing, it was self-sustaining. As soon as you tuned into the rhythms of Faulkner's or Nabokov's prose, or to Socrates's relentless questioning, the ideas and the music of the language set the neural net on fire while the hands scrambled to keep up, underlining memorable turns of phrase and scribbling thoughts and questions in the margins.

Of course it took discipline. The reading demanded attention, engagement, and effort. It was a daily practice. *The Brothers Karamazov* was long, sometimes densely philosophical, and full of characters with complex Russian names and diminutives that kept me flipping back to the family tree in the front of the book. But Dostoevsky was like Shakespeare, able to shift in an instant between grubby detail and archetypal truth. The character study of the three brothers, driven respectively by heart, mind, and spirit, was almost unbearably moving and wise. I felt myself in the presence of a great teacher, which fueled the effort with joy and the thrill of learning.

Dostoevsky led to Tolstoy, then to Gogol, then to Nabokov.

Genius is a much-abused word. Even when used in good faith, it means very different things to different people. To me, Vladimir Nabokov is a genius because his prose sings with a music that signals the entrance of something new into the world. Again and again while reading his memoir *Speak, Memory,* I was struck with the sense of peering through some hidden veil into the realm of angels, or some place so close to the source of Beauty itself that it ought to be forbidden to enter lest it blind you or drive you mad. I plowed through eight or ten of his books in a row, hoping it was true what an older, admired schoolmate had once told me: that we absorb the voices of the writers we love, and that's how we find our own.

When it came to the discipline of writing, Nabokov set a witheringly high bar. As if dominating literature in two languages wasn't enough, he was also a chess master and an obsessive lepidopterist with multiple species of moths and butterflies named after him. He famously stuck to an unwavering daily routine, writing his novels on narrowly lined index cards, filling a box with them, then going back to revise them meticulously. His genius was inseparable from his commitment to the structure that supported its careful refinement. A structure that to my twenty-one-year-old mind seemed utterly incongruous with the magic of his prose. How boring! How unbelievably bourgeois and suburban! This kind of thing was exactly what I'd left Bethesda to escape!

Journalists had to pull these kinds of details out of Nabokov like a dentist extracting wisdom teeth. He found "process" talk unbearably tedious, preferring instead to keep his magician's art hidden behind the concealing cloth. I get it. Does it add to *Ulysses* to learn that James Joyce liked to chew on the ends of his pencils? But hiding the seams creates a second, possibly unintended illusion: that art just happens. That there's no work or discipline involved.

There's peril in both directions. It's interesting and sometimes instructive to learn how your favorite writers work, but it can be daunting, even damaging to a young writer trying to develop her own process. Right discipline is any practice you can sustain, and that also sustains you. It's always personal and idiosyncratic. Rilke famously wrote the fifty-five *Sonnets to Orpheus*, some of the most sublime poetry ever composed, in three weeks. *The Lord of the Rings* took Tolkien sixteen years.

The *Ānāpānasati Sutta* is the Buddha's discourse on breath meditation, or mindfulness of breathing. At various points in the scriptures he says that among all the "skillful means" of meditation he taught, the hundreds of creative and varied strategies for cultivating concentration and wisdom, *ānāpānasati* on its own is sufficient to lead to enlightenment.

In its simplest form, it's about noticing the sensations of the breath as it goes in and out, and maintaining that awareness over time. If you've ever tried this, you know that it's much harder than it sounds at first. You become annoyed by the whiny sound of your inner voice going "in...out...in...out." Your attention gets so rigid that your jaw starts to ache. You can't stop thinking about French fries or sex or some email you forgot to send.

In *A Path with Heart*, Buddhist teacher Jack Kornfield likens the untrained mind to a puppy. When it wanders away into trouble, screaming and cursing won't do either of you much good. Better to pick it up lovingly and try again. Repeat that action often enough, and the puppy will learn.

Discipline as I now understand it now isn't about learning to endure pain. It isn't about suffering stoically. It's about gradually opening up to life as a process you can't fully control or predict. It's about embracing and learning how to work with change.

Ānāpānasati is every discipline in microcosm. It's a structure that reveals and refines you. It takes patience, self-compassion, commitment, and time. On the days when you don't "feel up to it," nothing is gained by powering through the meditation with gritted teeth and a resentful heart, or on the other hand deciding to sit this one out. However you feel, whoever you are today, you just show up and work with what you've got. Repeat that action day after day, year after year and you'll learn to focus more on what's present in the body, less on your opinions about how you ought to feel. You'll connect more deeply to yourself and to others. You'll learn that acceptance is the foundation of growth.

In 2009 and 2010—soon after Emre was born—I got serious in a new way about finding a spiritual path. Maybe it was the fact that first thing each morning I saw his gray-green eyes looking into mine expectantly, absorbing my moods, learning how to regulate his own. Maybe it was the fact that the responsibilities and challenges of adulthood had brought all the old demons bubbling up to the surface—anxieties, doubts, and insecurities so intense that a liter of vodka a week was barely enough to keep them at bay.

Until then, life had been an either/or proposition. Either the muse graced you or you didn't make art. Either you died young, like John, in a blaze of glory, or you lived a long, dull, suburban existence, boosting the yearly stats of the Christmas shopping season. But now I was somebody's first model of what it meant to be a man. I thought about how my relationship with my own father still overshadowed my life. Emre, Demet, and I were in this together, for decades to come. I couldn't afford to be cavalier and noncommittal anymore, to keep on numbing my demons rather than learning to exorcise them. I needed hope. I needed to believe that growth and healing were possible over the long term. I needed a path long, deep, and wide enough to contain my whole life.

It's a miracle that I landed on Buddhism. In spite of the ongoing inner culture war with my father, I had internalized a Western materialist scientific worldview. In spite of Meri's recent experiences with USC and pain management, I was skeptical bordering on cynical about any form of healing other than Western medicine. Buddhism's metaphysical ideas about karma, reincarnation, and Nirvana—the final liberation from suffering that's the ultimate goal of the path—left me cold and hostile. I had to do mental gymnastics to hold on to the parts I found useful and inspiring while glossing over the bits that triggered the inner bullshit detector.

As always, I started with the books. I cast a wide net at first, reading modern classics by Suzuki Roshi, Chögyam Trungpa, Pema Chödrön, Joseph Goldstein, and more. It was a potpourri of three major strains—Zen, Tibetan, and Theravadan traditions—by some of their most influential teachers in the West. When this historical "fifth wave" of Buddhist teaching started in the US in the late '60s, it faced some of the same challenges I was now struggling with. Earlier waves had adapted to different challenges. When Buddhism arrived in China around the first century, CE, for example, it encountered a culture without the monastic, renunciant traditions of India. There was no Chinese infrastructure to support believers who wanted to leave home, take a vow of poverty, and devote their lives to spiritual practice. Everybody worked. So Chan Buddhism focused many of its meditative practices on everyday tasks like washing rice.

In 1960s America, hierarchical traditions like Zen—well adapted to feudal Japan—had to respond to the antiauthoritarian attitudes of their new, young American acolytes. These same young people, many of them refugees from the organized monotheisms of their parents, were less open than Eastern Buddhists to talk of miracles and *devas* (lesser deities in Buddhist and Hindu cosmology). This forced the fifth wave teachers to reexamine the scriptures, focusing in on what Buddhist scholar

Robert Thurman, echoing the Dalai Lama, calls Buddhism's "inner science": its ethical and psychological practices for gaining insight into the self and the spiritual nature of reality for the sake of freedom from suffering.

This wasn't simple apologism or rebranding for marketing purposes. The Buddha is explicit in the scriptures that abstruse debates about metaphysics aren't the point. He's equally clear that you're not supposed to take his word for anything. To gain insight, you have to see for yourself.

I followed the fifth wave teachers back to some of their ancient sources, like the Zen essays of Dōgen or (in the Tibetan tradition) Shantideva's *Way of the Bodhisattva*. There were some ideas I could relate to and some I emphatically could not. Zen's austerity and militaristic intensity scared me. It felt too close to the kind of discipline I grew up with and was still trying to recover from. Shantideva's vow to "liberate all beings, no matter how numberless," seemed impossibly lofty and idealistic—I could barely understand how to liberate myself.

There was a kind of tectonic historical split between early Buddhism, the Theravadan traditions of India and Burma that emphasized the inner work of spiritual growth, and the later Mayahana ones that emphasized the practice of compassion for others. But all traditions shared the Four Noble Truths and the Eightfold Path.

In Thich Nhat Hanh's *Old Path White Clouds*, the steps of the path and the nature of the Buddha came through clearly. As a spiritual guide, I found him smart, funny, courageous, and relatable. Not a god to be worshipped, but a spiritual hero worth listening to. The more closely I looked into the Eightfold Path, the more it seemed to offer what I was looking for—a systematic yet flexible framework for growth. And as for lifelong immersion and intellectual stimulation, Buddhism had twenty-five hundred years of cultural history and literature—art, schools of practice, scripture, philosophical commentary, oral teaching, poetry—a corpus as rich and varied as humanity itself.

But if I was allergic to the metaphysics, I was equally suspicious of spiritual organizations. Since sangha, or spiritual community, is one of the three basic pillars of Buddhist practice, that posed a problem. The more I read, the clearer it seemed that there was only so far you could go without a good teacher and a community of "spiritual friends" to support your growth. But from the Catholic Church of my childhood to any number of well-documented "cult" scandals, it seemed like there was something inherent in the structure and power dynamics of these organizations that led to corruption.

Still, I saw enough value in the ideas and practices to investigate for myself. So I started window-shopping—sitting at a Zen temple, a Theravadan Vipassanā (insight meditation) center, with Tibetan Buddhists from the Kadampa and the Gelugpa traditions, with a group that fused Western psychology with Tibetan Buddhism, and with the Zen practitioners at my aikido studio.

The inner critic was loud. People come to these groups from such a wide variety of backgrounds and for so many different reasons. How was I supposed to see them as my *community*? I came seeking inner peace, equanimity, and compassion. Instead, I often found myself on high alert for any sign of superstitiousness (crystals, beads) or fake, saccharine piety. I disliked beatific permagrins, the sight of anyone bowing to a statue or a teacher, expensive-looking linen outfits (beware of all enterprises that require new clothes), and Sanskrit tattoos. Based on these surface trappings, I resented any "phony" yogis I encountered, resented myself for resenting them, and despaired of ever finding a sangha I could trust. I often left those gatherings less at peace than I'd arrived.

In some communities it was immediately apparent that certain students were closer to the leader or leaders than others, and that they enjoyed a special "insider" status: an invisible but undeniable aura of spiritual importance. One group in particular seemed to be a kind of elaborate pyramid scheme designed to draw people more and more deeply in (to more and more expensive trainings) with the promise of esoteric knowledge available only to the chosen few. In this sense, it was no different from the Masons, Tony Robbins, or, for that matter, Herbalife.

These early brushes with sangha were frustrating but illuminating. The right community, like the right discipline, is the one you can live with. I was drawn to small groups more than to massive ones, could connect more easily with simple practices like *ānāpānasati* or Zen sitting than with complex Tibetan tantric visualizations of Manjushri—the deity of wisdom—or Avalokiteshvara, the bodhisattva of compassion. Over time and with the help of meditation, I learned to relax my critical grip a little, focusing more on the benefits of the practice and the people I connected with than on the minor things that annoyed me.

A note of caution. There's a famous quote from Walter Kotschnig, an early twentieth-century Austrian Jewish academic and diplomat: *"Let's keep our minds open, by all means...but [not] so open that [our] brains fall out!"* Power abuse in spiritual communities is not a minor thing. It's wise to be wary of spiritual leaders who create a climate of nepotism, demand obedience, or claim to have unique access to enlightenment. But there's a middle ground between blind submission and wholesale rejection of any community whatsoever.

If there were a Nobel Prize for spiritual practitioners, or even, let's say, a medal at the fair in Queens County (where I live), I doubt I would win. There have been years when I meditated consistently for forty-five minutes a day and years when I couldn't bring myself to meditate at all. In 2020, I finally got it together to sign up for a weeklong meditation retreat, then COVID canceled it. Basic Buddhist ethics—at least as central to Buddhism as meditation—advocate avoiding "idle chatter" and "intoxicants that lead to heedlessness." Anyone who knows me could tell you that idle chatter is a core part of my personality. And in the decade since Emre was born, I've struggled to live nondestructively with alcohol, sometimes quitting it altogether for a year or more, sometimes sticking to rules like "only on weekends, and then no more than three drinks at a time." But there's always a part of me, once I start, that could happily go on drinking all night, seeking kenosis in oblivion.

I'm not a perfect Buddhist, by any means. But Buddhism is undeniably a central part of my life. When I wake up at 3 a.m., worried about my son or our finances, meditation helps me see and let go of my thoughts before they spiral out of control. Buddhist meditation (with and without the addition of psychedelics) has helped me work through childhood trauma and become a better father and husband. The practice of *mettā* (loving-kindness, goodwill) has helped me meet the inner drill sergeant with more compassion and redirect his protective energies more productively.

The concept of sunyata, or emptiness, has helped me understand that the self isn't as real as it likes to believe. Just as my apparently solid body is also a quantum field of oddly behaving forces and particles, my opinions, expectations, and self-image are fictions—useful at times, at other times completely at odds with reality. The concept of *pratītyasamutpāda*, or "dependent origination," has taught me that to the extent that beings do exist, we're interconnected. This aligns with the globalist, humanist values Mom Mom passed down and shapes the way I think about everything, from grocery shopping to presidential elections.

More than anything else perhaps, Buddhism teaches me fundamental lessons about the discipline and practice of living. For example, that suffering and struggle are universal, no matter how privileged or personally upbeat you might be. In addition to everyday frustrations like traffic jams and computer viruses, we all face loss, old age, sickness, and death. So the right orientation toward everyone, yourself included, is compassion. Everything is part of this spiritual practice. Applied to meditation, work, and relationships, compassion means not quitting in shame the hundredth or the thousandth time you lose your way. Nobody's perfect. Showing up sometimes just means beginning again.

Everything Is Not Okay

Meri and I used to joke about the "Manis women"—the informal network of Mom, her three sisters, and their mother, my grandma Beatrice Manis. If an uncle went rogue, gambling away the family's savings, or one of the nine first cousins started hanging out with the wrong crowd, the Manis women formed like Voltron, sharing ideas and resources in marathon phone sessions at any time of day or night until the problem was solved.

Solutionism came naturally to me and Meri, too. Like our other family passion, explaining, it was a double-edged sword. There's clarity and simplicity in filtering for the relevant details, diagnosing the problem, and jumping into action. But some problems aren't so easily understood, let alone solved. Sometimes what's needed most is deep and careful listening. Sometimes the impulse to fix the problem is born of impatience with the messiness of other people's lives and pride in your own good sense. When the zeal for a quick solution takes over, it's always worth asking yourself: *Who am I really serving here?*

★ ★ ★

[A phone call, some Sunday in late 2005, New York ← → Charlottesville]

Me: Hey, Mer!

Meri: Hey, J!

Me: How's life in the Deep South?

Meri: Nothing like Graceland. People are so down-to-earth!

Me: That's what they show you at first. Then the dark underbelly reveals itself.

Meri: Probably. But the UVA campus is beautiful. There are flowers everywhere.

Me: Why, flowers seem nothing to me but a foul and pestilent congregation of vapors.

Meri: Shut up.

Me: So, like, what are you doing while Theodore is learning to use the brain scrambler?

Meri: It's not a brain scrambler. Transcranial magnetic stimulation is nothing like the old days, when they zapped people with a thousand volts and hoped for the best.

Me: No. By contrast, it produces highly functional zombies.

Meri: It doesn't produce zombies. It works on people nothing else has helped. People with severe anxiety and depression.

Me: But *how* does it work?

Meri: They don't know.

Me: So they just zap the brain and hope for the best.

Meri: Not exactly...

...but kind of.

Me: And what are you gonna do while he's busy scrambling brains?

Meri: I'm thinking of going to UVA, too. Getting a master's in public health. In elder advocacy.

Me: Yeah?

Meri: Yeah. When I was on rotations, working with the old people is what I liked best.

Me: You were always so good with Pop Pop.

Meri: Can you imagine? Ten years living with that stroke? Going from programming computers, analyzing DNA, and scuba diving all over the world to barely being able to communicate?

Me: You know what? I don't know what elder advocacy is.

Meri: Elder abuse is rampant in the US. Something like five million people a year. They get abused in care facilities. They get lost and totally confused navigating the medical system. And there's basically no one on their side.

Me: I think you'd be awesome at this.

In retrospect, it seems obvious that the abrupt end to medical school had been a crushing blow. But Meri's self-assurance functioned as a kind of Jedi mind trick. The potentially worried gaze slid right off her, like "Nothing to see here, folks. Pass on." So I took it at face value that she was doing okay.

Virginia was much stricter than LA when it came to prescription opioids. Doctors refused to prescribe the massive doses of hydrocodone Meri was by then dependent on to manage the phantom limb pain. Not only that, they suggested that she go into treatment for addiction. I think her family and friends all saw the situation from Meri's perspective: the pain was real. Phantom limb sufferers were always being dismissed either as hypochondriacs or drug addicts lying to get a fix. Unscrupulous doctors and people looking for drugs to sell or abuse were taking advantage of the system, making things difficult for people like Meri with genuine medical needs. Meri advocates all, we were relieved that (for the time being at least) her LA physician was willing to keep prescribing.

I didn't know much about opioids and it didn't occur to me that long-term dependency on these drugs was dangerous enough to warrant a serious search for alternatives. Anyway, the Jedi mind trick convinced me that Meri had already done all the possible research and there was no better option available. She had read about "mirror therapy"—then a relatively new treatment that took advantage of the brain's "mirror neurons," using a mirror to trick the brain into seeing a healthy, pain-free limb in place of the missing one. It was interesting, she said, but still rare and experimental. And after all, the meds seemed to be working.

And things really did look fine for a while. She got the master's degree. She got an administrative job at a grant-funded program tracking drug users in treatment. The organization was a total shambles and Meri ended up radically rethinking the data collection process, doing a heroic job of trying to get years of chaos and neglect under control. Ultimately government auditors came in, fired her boss, and shut the place down for mismanagement. From what I could see, in that job Meri was at her fiercest and finest—well organized, energized by a seemingly impossible challenge, and motivated to help people in need.

When Theodore's residency ended, he got a job at a clinic in Chicago. Before they left Virginia in 2009, the physician in Charlottesville helped her transition from hydrocodone to methadone, an opioid that kills pain without producing the euphoric highs that can drive a demand for ever-increasing dosages. Methadone is milder in its effects than hydrocodone, but it's still addictive and can have potentially deadly side effects, including neurological changes and heart arrhythmias.

[A phone call, January 2011, New York ← → Bethesda]

Me: Hey, Mom!

Mom: Hi! How's that kid doing?

Me: Not napping. Not ever. Robustly ready to play from 5:30 a.m. until bedtime. I'm looking forward to college.

Listen. I'm worried about Meri. I didn't want to say anything when we were home for Christmas, but she's not right.

Mom: I know.

Me: Is it the meds? I mean, she's fine for most of the day, but then it's like a switch goes off. She starts talking really slowly, repeating herself. She doesn't hear anything you say, then she stops making sense entirely. It's like she's dreaming or something.

Mom: We were thinking it might be an interaction with alcohol. It usually happens after one or two beers.

Me: Maybe. If that's the case, then she really shouldn't drink. Like, ever. But who can talk to her? I think I need to try. I don't think she's even aware of it. What if this happens with colleagues? Not that she's working...

Mom: It's hard. She sends off hundreds of résumés and never hears anything back.

Me: They say nobody gets hired that way anymore. They say you have to "network." I've had five jobs since I got back to New York and I still have no idea what the hell networking is. How is she supposed to figure it out after spending five years at home taking care of her dog?

In high school, Meri was the levelheaded one and I was the artsy flake. After college, I fell apart and she was the only one who offered me refuge. Now, for the first time in our lives, it looked like she might need my help. She wasn't asking for it, and if I knew her, she wouldn't easily accept it. But these dissociative states she'd been getting into—I'd never seen anything like them. They were utterly terrifying.

I talked to her. At first, she was humiliated and started crying. I tried to explain that there was nothing to be ashamed of. It was obviously chemical, obviously something we could and should get under control. She agreed that alcohol might be the trigger. I shifted into a firm, big-brotherly tone of voice—something new in our relationship. I asked if she'd promise me she wouldn't drink. She promised.

Over the next couple years, every time I saw her the problem was worse. Sometimes she drank, in spite of the promise, but sometimes when she wasn't drinking, the states came on anyway. Drinking made them worse, perhaps, but it wasn't definitively the cause. At a Christmas dinner with my parents' friends she'd suddenly get hostile, attacking someone for a stupid offhand comment we'd normally chalk up to the generation gap. In the middle of playing video games with Emre she'd completely lose touch with reality. I'd find him urging her to pick up her controller and drive her virtual motorbike out of a ditch while she babbled incoherently to herself. I talked to her about it multiple times. Talked to my parents and Theodore. I urged her to talk to her doctors, maybe look into different medication, but nothing helped.

In the process, our relationship shifted. Now I wore the stable sense of confidence and she was the person in need. She told me admiringly (mixed with what sounded like envy) that I never seemed to have any trouble getting a job. I had to laugh. Since graduate school I had been a freelance actor recording Shakespeare on CD-ROMs, a barista, a deli guy, a waiter, a bartender, an unlicensed (but legal, long story) speech therapist, a middle school and community college English teacher, a 30-something intern intern then editorial assistant at a publishing company, a writer of children's books for kids in Korea learning English, and a writer-editor for an online think tank of "big ideas" and professional learning. I was almost forty years old, my career made little sense to me or anybody else, and my parents had repeatedly had to bail me out for the rent and other expenses of living in New York. But since Charlottesville, in spite of the master's degree from a respected university, Meri hadn't been able to find any work at all.

[A phone call, January 2011, New York ← → Chicago]

Meri: Hey, J!

Me: Heya, sis! You sound out of breath.

Meri: I'm walking Cali. This neighborhood is filthy. I can't believe all the litter. I'm gonna organize a cleanup.

Me: Yeah? How do you do that?

Meri: I'll just put posters everywhere and have a meeting. It's ridiculous. I think people just need to be reminded that we're all sharing these sidewalks and parks. Maybe if they see their neighbors out here picking up their trash, they'll feel guilty and stop littering.

Me: Maybe. Or maybe they'll double down on their assholery.

Hey. Can I talk to you about something?

Meri: Sure.

Me: I've been thinking about your job situation. I have an idea. I'm definitely not Mr. Career, but what if we had a regular meeting once a week just to systematically strategize about this thing until you're on your feet? I read this book recently, *What Color Is Your Parachute?* Basically you break down all your interests and skills and then make a plan for how to move your career in the direction you want to go. I know this stuff sucks. I think it sucks extra to do it alone.

Meri: Yeah. I'd like that.

Me: We could make a shared spreadsheet on Google Docs. Like, keep track of all our ideas.

Meri: Okay.

So we set a weekly calendar reminder. For the time being we stopped talking about the dissociation, which seemed impossible to solve. I fantasized that if only we could break the big goal (getting a job) down into smaller, more achievable goals, she'd start to feel the momentum and everything else would snap into place. We talked through her "skill set" and the causes and missions that mattered to her. Made spreadsheets of all the places in Chicago she might consider volunteering; after all these years, volunteering seemed like a good way to get used to the workplace again, and a possible pathway to a job.

In spite of my long-standing, well-documented contempt for our nation of relentlessly cheery self-branders, networkers, and careerists, for the relentless bombardment, everywhere you turn, of advice for managing your time and your life more efficiently, I transformed myself into my sister's career coach. Looking back, I doubt spreadsheets are what she needed from me. With the dissociative states unaddressed, she was hardly in a position to work anywhere. And in Chicago, she was completely isolated. Since the amputation, Theodore had drifted away from her emotionally, focusing all his energy on his career. I didn't know this, because she hadn't told me and I hadn't asked. Rather than a career coach, what she probably needed was someone to listen. A brother's invitation to get down to the things she really needed to say.

We managed to find her a volunteer gig, grant writing for a nonprofit, but it didn't last long. She couldn't explain why in any way that made sense to me. It seemed likely that she'd dissociated more than once at work.

[A phone call, some Saturday night, fall 2013, New York ←
→ Chicago]

Me: Hey, sis! Just enjoying some beers out here on the balcony, looking out over the brutalist hellscape of Astoria, Queens, and thinking of you.

Meri: (long pause) Hey, J.

Me: What's going on?

Meri: Theodore and I split up.

Me: What?

Meri: Yeah. (deep breath)

He was fucking an intern. I found her texts on his phone.

Me: What?

Meri: She mentioned me. She knew my name. She knew how to spell my fucking name.

Me: Jesus.

I'm so sorry. That motherfucker.

Meri: I haven't been easy to live with. I drink and scream at him for hours like Mom. I started going to AA.

Me: Really? How much were you drinking?

Meri: Enough. I lost my driver's license for a while.

Me: How did I not know any of this?

Meri: It's embarrassing. But AA is great. It really makes you look closely at your life. And the other people are amazing. I feel so connected to this community. One of my friends there, Bruce, is gonna help me move out. He's this huge, incredibly funny guy covered in ironic tattoos, like flamingoes.

Me: How can we be embarrassed to talk to each other? I'm your brother. How could I not know that all this was going on?

Hey, can we just stay on the phone for a while? I've got all night.

There were many more phone calls after that. More listening, less solutionism. AA didn't last long, and sometimes we both drank while we talked. Sometimes I saw this as self-serving on my part. Thought maybe the big brotherly thing to do would be to try to hold her to sobriety by abstaining myself. More often, though, it just seemed like a way to be there with my sister, rather than standing in authority over her. Meri talked about gardening, Cali, and small acts of kindness she had done for her neighbors or they'd done for her, because that was her happiness: those moments of care and connection.

Sometimes, several beers in, she'd reach a point of despair, crying about the uselessness of her life. With AA behind her, she knew no one in Chicago. She felt broken and unlovable, washed up at thirty-five. She talked in earnest about running away to Alaska. Starting over, far from anyone who knew her. I imagined her out there in a cannery, limping around the salmon-slick floors on the prosthesis that still didn't fit right, and once again, I got scared.

In a flurry of phone calls to my parents, I argued strenuously that she wasn't safe on her own. I thought we should convince her to move down to Florida to be close to family, at least until her life was back on track. They agreed, and together we kept repeating the idea until Meri finally gave in. Gotses can be very convincing. We just don't always know what we're talking about. I didn't see it at the time, but moving to Florida, trading whatever independence she'd had for the ever-present concern and supervision of my parents and their friends, was yet another unacceptable blow to her dignity.

Agnosis

December 2014

Meri had been busy in preparation for our annual Christmas visit. Clambering up on a rickety stepladder (and probably falling off more than once), she had bolted the steel cable of a zip line to two trees in the backyard of her single-story house. It was for Emre. For his seventh birthday the previous January, she had planted a little mango tree, which we hadn't seen yet. Just a week before our arrival, it had produced a single, tiny mango.

The whole plane ride south, he was vibrating with excitement: "Can we go see the zip line? Right when we land? Can we?" So we dropped our suitcases at my parents' house and drove the ten minutes to Meri's place. You could tell immediately which one was hers. The front yard was lush with flowers. There were buckets and shovels and bags of fertilizer lying around, ready for tomorrow's installment of her never-ending yard work. After a quick tour of the interior (cozy, cheerfully decorated with sunflower art, very Meri), she took us through to the backyard. "I'm in a fight with the neighbor," she said, pointing to a bush whose roots were growing under the fence. "He's an asshole. I love his girlfriend, but he's an asshole and he wants me to rip out this bush because it's partly on his property. Look at his yard! It's not like he's doing anything with it."

Emre was already zip-lining. Climbing up the stepladder, giggling as he sped diagonally across the yard, walking the mechanism back with the rope and doing it all over again. Cali, Meri's German shepherd mix, now thirteen or fourteen years old but infused with a burst of puppy energy by Emre's frenetic presence, ran around cheerfully barking. Demet, Meri, and I sat around the metal table next to her house, opened three beers, turned on her Bluetooth speaker and put on A Tribe Called Quest.

As the sun went down, Meri invited Emre for a sleepover. Emre vibrated with excitement: "Can I? Can I?" Demet and I exchanged a glance. Meri's dissociative states had become less frequent recently, but her moods could still be volatile. I wondered if he'd be safe with her, and hated myself for thinking it. "I think he should stay with his grandparents tonight," I said. "It's his first night here and everything."

Demet and Emre drove back to my folks' place and I stayed on to hang out with Meri. Someone could pick me up later. Tribe gave way to Nas which led to The Roots which led, incongruously yet somehow perfectly, to Paul Simon's *Rhythm of the Saints*. I didn't question her drinking anymore. I was her brother, not her counselor. We sat together like we'd done a million times since she was a high school senior, commenting on life as if from a lofty summit. A six-pack in, the conversation shifted.

Meri: I think there's something that ties it all together.

Me: Like what?

Meri: A force. An intelligence. I don't know. Nature is too extraordinary. I know you always hated math but when you get into calculus you really start to see the mysterious structure of things.

Me: I mean, I used to think like that, but—

Meri: But what?

Me: You know Demet studied philosophy. She's pretty logical-minded. I used to argue with her but she's convinced me that it makes no sense to talk about this kind of thing. We don't know what happens after death, but all the evidence we do have suggests that nothing happens. What of "me" could possibly persist after I die?

Meri: You sound like Dad.

Me: Ouch.

Meri: It's so arrogant! So unbelievably arrogant!

Me: Hey! I don't think it's arrogant. I think it's reasonable.

Meri: You have no idea. No fucking clue. We understand like .01 % of that [waving at the sky] and this [pointing to herself]. How smug and stupid is it to make these kinds of claims?

Me: You're making claims, too. You're gesturing toward God.

Meri: No I'm not.

Me: Yes, you are. You're suggesting there's a kind of divine intelligence that holds everything together. That's intelligent design theory. You should move to Kansas.

Meri: No. I'm saying I don't know what it is. I don't dare try to describe it or put a name on it. But I sense it.

Me: No. No… I get it. I do know what you mean.

Meri: I'm saying that we have two choices. To open out to the vastness of the 99.98% we don't understand—to orient ourselves toward that wonder and mystery—or to cling miserably to the bit we do know, insisting that's all there is.

Me: I never understood math. But when Ed and I used to trip, I saw the 99.98%. I had the humbling and awe-inspiring experience of feeling, viscerally, how little I know. But these years have been a slog. I'm trying to make a living. Every waking minute is filled up with work, or thinking about work, or taking care of Emre.

Meri: Yeah, but look at him! He's a consciousness. He's asking questions, absorbing everything, spotting patterns. He walks, he talks, he plays guitar! He's a fucking miracle.

Me: (quoting Hamlet) "And yet, to me, what is this quintessence of dust?" I just keep vacillating back and forth. I just read this book by Daniel Dennett. He's a philosopher of consciousness with grounding in neuroscience, evolution, and computer science. He traces consciousness all the way back to random molecules banging together to form bigger molecules. He shows how everything that we think is so mysterious and marvelous is just an "emergent property" of complex structures, which are themselves just layers of simpler structures, which come from randomness and chaos. When people get all starry-eyed about the mysteries of consciousness, he's fond of saying, "it's in the meat."

Meri: Remember how Dad used to talk about the cats? They're just rubbing against you to mark their territory. They're cuddling with you because they're looking for warmth. Like what animals feel can't be anything like love. Like we're not animals, too.

Me: I know what awe feels like, and I want that feeling. I need that feeling. Without it, I'm a cramped, critical little creature. Less arrogant, I think, than depressed. I need to believe that life and reality are more than "the meat." But it's so hard to stay open like that. My mind is so impatient. So ready to put words to things and tie them up in neat packages.

Meri: Including yourself.

Me: Sure. Including myself.

We got quiet for a bit. Paul sang: *"and sometimes, even music cannot substitute for tears."* And that's the last real conversation with my sister I can remember.

March 21, 2015, was a Saturday. Emre, Demet, and I were at our next-door neighbors' for a casual dinner party. Emre was on the couch, showing off a new guitar piece he'd composed. I was drinking seltzer and nodding politely as someone talked about real estate (a subject I know nothing about), when my phone rang. It was Dad. "Hey, Pops!" I answered, keeping things breezy and lighthearted as we tried to do with each other these days. "Hi, Jason," he said, then paused for a couple seconds. "Meri died. Mom found her in her bed."

I went numb. I managed to mutter something like, "Okay. Okay. Thank you, Dad. I'm so sorry…" He said something about memorial arrangements and the medical examiner. Neither of us had any language for this, any way of connecting to our own feelings in this moment, let alone with one another. I wish I could say I collapsed into my bed and lay there weeping until grief had run its course. I wish I could say I did anything other than immediately start working out the logistics of getting to Florida. It was as if Meri's death wasn't even news to me. As if it had been scheduled long before.

I've worn myself thin with guilt over how hard it's been to grieve for her. When the tears did come, they came most often for the imaginary life she might have lived, rather than the real one she lost. A writer once told me that writers write because they're stuck on the outside of life, observing everything at a distance, trying to find some way in. That may be true, but it doesn't explain how we get stuck there in the first place.

I don't know what closure is. Or mourning, either, to be honest. Here I am, years later, still looking for—something. It's like wandering around a vast and vaguely familiar mansion in a dream, rattling every doorknob on some urgent but undefined mission.

For a long time I consoled myself with the thought that I had learned something important from her death—something about the preciousness of life. I tried to borrow some of her courage to live my own life more fully. I still do. But people don't die for the benefit of our personal growth. There's no lesson here. No neat binding into which the story will fit. No way, finally, to bring her back to life or to let her go, either.

Forgiveness

March 16, 2020

Hey Meri,

In one week, it'll be five years since your death. Last night and
the night before that, I sat in ayahuasca ceremonies in a dance
studio in Brooklyn. Since the first one, in the yurt upstate, back
in the spring of 2017, I've come at least a dozen times to kneel
on a pillow before the *ayahuascero* and receive a plastic shot glass
full of this viscous, bittersweet, nasty-tasting liquid—sometimes
mustard yellow and sometimes pomegranate red—and then, half
an hour or so later, to dive into the realms of deep consciousness.

I wish I could have shared ayahuasca with you. I think it
might have helped you more than all those phone conversations
or any doctor you saw since middle school. It might have broken down some of the stubborn self-reliance that wasn't serving
you anymore, leading to insights that could have saved your life.

The *ayahuascero*—let's call him Ramon—is a no-frills kind of
guy. He shows up in jeans and sneakers. In the winter he wears
a Canada Goose coat. The altar at the front of the room is simple and traditional. In a small metal bowl, there's a stick of palo
santo wood that's burned as incense ("for balancing," one of the

helpers told me). It's got a lovely, somewhat medicinal smell. There's a bottle of *agua de florida*—an alcohol-based, citrusy liquid that's splashed on the hands and sometimes the face for the dual purpose, I suppose, of refreshing and sanitizing. There's a hand-rolled, fat cigarette filled with uncut tobacco leaf. Ramon uses this ceremonially, taking a few puffs and blowing smoke in the four cardinal directions and over the open bottle of ayahuasca. The *medicina* itself is in a plastic water bottle, its Poland Spring label removed.

Unlike the group I first sat with in the Catskills, Ramon isn't creating an overtly religious experience here. He doesn't call himself a shaman or expect any special devotion—he's what the Buddha would have called a "spiritual friend," a knowledgeable guide with twenty-seven-plus years' experience leading these kinds of ceremonies. His role is to create a spiritual setting and conditions of safety within which this sometimes-challenging work can unfold.

Periodically while in the throes of the experience I'll look up to see Ramon walking softly back and forth, checking gently on each person, shaking a rattle made of hundreds of nutshells or seed pods, and he'll strike me as a sort of kindly Smurf from another dimension—an earth spirit of friendly care. Throughout the ceremony he sings *icaros*—traditional songs in a sequence aligned with the stages of the journey, from entry, to peak intensity, to reflective calm, to return. He has a beautiful, rich bass voice. The songs are a touchstone of courage when the emotions get too intense. They remind you to stay calm. That you're spacious enough to handle whatever the *medicina* might bring you.

You and I are both products of the Western medical/scientific worldview, so I can't quite believe and wouldn't try to convince you that it's magic. But without question, it has mysterious powers to unstick the stuck parts of ourselves and bring what's been hidden, forgotten, and silently poisoning our lives to light. It's medicine of a kind no MD can (yet) prescribe and that so many of us sorely need. I can't quite believe in anthropomorphic plant spirits, but I know for a fact that it's a great teacher, or a tool that enables us to teach ourselves.

Saturday night's session was a struggle, as the first night of a two-night session often is, and I can't say I emerged from it with much clarity. I struggled mainly with political guilt—the question of what it means to live in these times, when the planet and so many vulnerable lives are under existential threat, and whether it's sufficient to focus on work and family, protecting myself as I sometimes do from the barrage of bad news on the internet. As Kae Tempest puts it in her poem "Three Sided Coin,"

> *So where is the good heart to go but inwards?*
> *Why not lock all the doors and bolt all the windows?*

These last few years have been intense for my family. I've been pouring all the energy I thought I could muster into holding our life together. Meanwhile, the pressure outside has been building. A white supremacist driving into a protest in Charlottesville. The murder of one unarmed Black person after another by police. Global warming. Mass extinction. The tipping point of a global pandemic. For the most part I've swallowed it, reasoning that I'd be wasting my time trying to be Greta Thunberg or Shaun King. That my work lay in bringing light to my tiny corner of the world.

But ayahuasca's an emetic in more ways than one. Things don't stay swallowed. That first night brought all the pressure, the sorrow, and the guilt over my own political paralysis bubbling to the surface.

In some traditions, it's recommended that you come into an ayahuasca journey with an intention. As psychedelic therapist Françoise Bourzat points out in her book *Consciousness Medicine*, consciousness-expanding journeys of all kinds, from mushroom ceremonies in Mexico to sweat lodges in Arizona, to ayahuasca retreats in the jungles of the Amazon can benefit from intention setting, which is why so many vasly different cultures through-out history have incorporated it into their healing practices.

The intention can be something you want to work on, learn more about, or answer concretely. You can't control what the *medicina* brings you, but the intention acts like a wish that can lend structure to the experience.

My intention going into this weekend was about insecurity. That was always a big difference between us—your courage and my self-doubt. This time, I was looking for answers: Where did this insecurity come from? This sense that at the very center of my being, there's a gaping hole—a lack I can never quite fill. It's harmful to my work and to all of my relationships. How can I grow out of it?

Although Saturday felt painful and inconclusive, on Sunday night I settled into the ceremonial space feeling strong, happy, and ready to get to work. The cup Ramon handed me felt less full than usual, and a little fear response kicked in. I found my-self wondering whether it wouldn't be enough to give me what I'd come for. I told myself to relax. There's always an oppor-tunity, midceremony, to take a second cup. And no matter the dose, the *medicina* always hits me hard.

From my first experiences with psychedelics, I've had a prej-udice against the idea of "visuals." I've met too many, mostly male, recreational psychedelic users who are essentially look-ing for a light show. The idea of staring for eight hours awe-struck at a video of fractals has always struck me as ridiculous and superficial—a waste of an opportunity for deeper insight. This prejudice made me resistant, blinding me to the possibility that visuals might be another powerful means by which these substances sometimes communicate, or help us communicate with ourselves.

The visuals that hit me full force at the start of my Sunday night journey were horrible. An infinitude of cartoonish, garish, candy-colored, interlocking shapes and forms, reminiscent of the way R. Crumb's imagination vomits forth all the detritus of the culture. They were a swarming, relentless kaleidoscope of advertising, social media, the whole grotesquerie of self-branding, self-promoting capitalism. I felt fear and revulsion. The distilled essence of alienation and distrust.

But with the *medicina* (as in life) fear is always a learning opportunity. I started a breath meditation, worked on releasing the defensive tension. The thought occurred to me that the *medicina* had brought me face-to-face with the feelings of aversion and critical judgment that so often dominate my life.

So I tried to lean into the visions. I tried to trust in the experience. The skeptical part of my brain kept arising in resistance, annoyed at having to deal with this ugly commercial bullshit. But the more I relaxed, the more sublime and beautiful the visions became.

The skeptic fought back: *It's not paranoia if it's true! These are all the things you hate in the world, for good reason. Critical discernment is a form of wisdom. Don't open your mind so wide that your brains fall out!* But this was a subtler lesson. Not that everything in the world is beautiful and good. But that fear and aversion make monsters, even of would-be heroes.

At some point the visions subsided and I cycled, moment to moment, through waves of trust and distrust. I remembered "Internal Family Systems Therapy," a psychotherapeutic approach from the 1980s that focuses on subpersonalities of the mind—inner protectors, inner nurturers, and so on. Lying there on my air mattress it occurred to me (and not for the first time) that I've got a kind of hypervigilant inner soldier. He's on active duty all the time. Often, he wakes me up at 4 or 5 a.m. and won't let me get back to sleep. He monitors Emre for any sign of sloth. He monitors Demet for any sign that she might not be as driven as I am to grow and progress. In doing so, he drives everyone (myself included) crazy.

I felt a sudden wave of compassion for the soldier. I decided to name him "Sarge." I saw that Sarge was an aspect of my conscience. He was trying to keep me and my family safe and strong. He wanted to protect us from sliding into entropy and decay. At times, his vigilance had shielded me from alcoholism or worse. Sarge wasn't my enemy: he was just confused about his jurisdiction. About where his protection was needed, and when. I wondered where he came from and what he was so afraid of.

Then I went back to our childhood. Just like the night, three years earlier, when I talked to you in that yurt, this recollection was somewhere between a dream and a dissociative state. Part of me was in the Brooklyn dance studio, part was back in my childhood relationship with Mom. I felt my terror at her uncontrollable rage. Her casual indifference and cruelty. I felt how much it hurt—how small and empty and hated it made me feel.

I saw Sarge rising up to protect my heart from her, sometimes at the cost of my ability to feel anything at all.

Then something shifted. The lens of compassion I'd turned on Sarge and on my frightened inner child panned over to Mom. *But she was so afraid,* I thought. *She must have been so afraid.* I understood that the rage and the coldness were Mom's own inner soldiers, protecting her from the powerlessness she must have felt so much of the time in those years. Worries about the business, about losing the house, about your cancer... She rarely slept. She woke early to run her seven miles a day, trying to keep herself strong and always at the ready.

I took it all in at once: my pain, her fear. I understood that both could be true—that I didn't have to ignore one to see the other. I'm allowed to feel hurt. I'm allowed to feel angry. And I'm also allowed to forgive her. I understood something I only half heard when the playwright V Ensler said it to me on *Think Again.* Forgiveness, she said, isn't about forgetting. But until you can find a way to forgive, you keep repeating the original violence, taking it out on others and yourself.

Sometimes ayahuasca gives me a mantra. In my first ceremonies, the theme was acceptance, so the mantras were "welcome, friend" and "yes." This time, the phrase "be a friend to yourself" swam into my consciousness. It felt like a profound directive. Sarge is obsessed with rooting out weakness. If I want to sit down and watch TV, even after an exhausting and productive workweek, he tells me I'm slacking. He reminds me of all the important emails I've failed to send. He goes further, haranguing me for being fundamentally lazy and incapable of seeing anything through. He compares me to successful people, people I admire like Old Mr. Nabokov, assuring me that *they* do not have time to sit on their butts watching TV. That they don't just sit around waiting for their careers to happen.

Be a friend to yourself. I explored what that might mean. I started trying on pet names I'd never in a million years use for myself: *sweetie, dear one, angel.* Suddenly I was laughing out loud: Jonathan Van Ness of Netflix's *Queer Eye* had appeared before me. If you've never seen that show, Jonathan is a beautician, and a sparkly outfit-wearing, nonbinary bodhisattva of self-esteem, always telling everybody they're gorgeous and referring to their hair as "she," as in *"She's feeling a little down today! She just needs some szhooshing up!"* With everyone they (Jonathan) meet, they always radiate pure goodness, pure *mettā*, directly from the heart.

Jonathan told me to be a friend to myself. *"You're a beautiful soul, honey! You need to know that!"* And as crazy as it seemed that it was them of all people, a TV personality I'd never met in person, it made perfect sense. I allowed myself to bathe in their affirmation. *You are a beautiful soul, honey. You are a beautiful soul...*

In the ceremony, self-love isn't a fortune-cookie concept. It's a thing you enact. A way to remind your personal Sarge that we aren't perpetually at war. In daily life I tell myself it's humility I practice, but more often it's self-humiliation. *Be a friend to yourself* is something I need to practice.

Coming back into my body in the later stages of the ceremony, I noticed how shame and insecurity live in my posture. I kept catching myself hunched over and curling inward—shoulders, chest, fingers, even my head. As I stood to make a trip to the bathroom, I thought, *Walk with dignity*. I remembered Alexander Technique from my NYU movement classes, and imagined an invisible string pulling upward from the crown of my head, my skeleton hanging loose and free. I realized how invisible I normally try to make myself out of fear of overwhelming others or taking up space I don't deserve. I realized there was a middle ground. *Self-confidence and care of others aren't enemies. They're mutually necessary.* I stood tall and surveyed the room. *Whatever you fear, whatever you lack, walk tall in dignity and beauty on this earth.*

I don't believe ayahuasca healed my insecurity in one night, nor would any *ayahuascero* worthy of the role suggest that it could. Like any psychedelic, ayahuasca gives you information you need to put into practice. It's up to me now to remember these lessons and use them in my daily life.

Maybe five months later, in the middle of some chitchat with Mom about Emre, I took a deep breath and said: "Can I talk to you about something? It's kind of heavy."

"Sure," she said.

"So… I don't even know where to start," I said. "I was wondering, you know, it seems like you've come a long way since I was a kid. You and I have a much better relationship. You're an amazing Nona." (Her preferred, personalized spelling of the Italian term for grandmother.) "But when I think back to childhood, most of what I remember is screaming and cruelty. Cold discipline. Or maybe that's not entirely fair—there were the encouraging good-morning notes taped under my bedroom light switch…the scavenger hunts for Thursday's 'special breakfast'…

all the presents and candy at Christmas and Easter…all those forms of love at a comfortable distance. I just can't remember a single hug or a kind word."

Mom started with an apology. "I'm so very sorry for all of that. Meri and I talked about it years ago. She was very angry and confrontational."

"Yeah," I said, "that's how she was. I think her anger insulated her. I internalized everything and made it my own problem."

"You were great kids. Both of you. There was so much stress—that's not an excuse, at all—but there were so many worries. And I was already a very anxious person. You didn't deserve that at all. You deserved so much better."

A few weeks earlier I'd given Dad a book I'd read by an MD about ayahuasca's healing properties, and she had read it, too. Now I shared the whole story about the ceremony back in March, about Sarge and her and Jonathan Van Ness (who took some explaining). I'm supposed to be a writer, Meri, but I know you know there are no words that can express what it felt like to have that conversation after all these years.

"You know," I said, "this book I'm writing brings up a lot of heavy stuff. It goes back to everything we've been talking about. I don't want to hurt you. I want to tell the truth, but I love you and I don't want to hurt you."

"It's okay," she said. "You just write the book you need to write."

Right Livelihood

Long before I knew anything about Buddhist ethics, it was a problem for me that almost every job I ever had seemed to involve some kind of ethical compromise. And in every case, management seemed to justify this on some pragmatic basis; it was inevitable because of politics, or the nature of the business. One job was with an internationally known speech therapy clinic. After a week of training us, it set unlicensed (and therefore cheap) "clinicians" loose to do therapy with children and adults with a huge range of learning difficulties and developmental disorders. My last patient there was a child with autism so severe that he spent every session under the table reciting entire episodes of *Scooby-Doo*, verbatim, while I waved little pictures at him of mouths pronouncing different consonants and vowels. When I finally gave up on the program and showed an interest in *Scooby-Doo*, he hugged me and wouldn't let go.

Buddhism has the concept of "right livelihood." One of the early steps on the Eightfold Path, it's based on the principle that the work you take to sustain your life shouldn't compromise you ethically. Right livelihood, along with *right speech* and *right view* are the elements of *sīla*, the ethical foundations of the Buddhist path. Without *sīla*, meditation is considered pointless.

Your mind and heart are torn in too many directions by doubt, remorse, and/or the repercussions of past negative actions. *Sīla* is the necessary substrate for mental focus and spiritual growth.

In June 2015, two months after Meri's death, I started a podcast. I was working at the time for a media company called Big Think, where I'd been for about five years. Big Think was best known as a kind of eclectic online brain tickler full of video interviews with titles like "Are You a Psychopath? Take the Test," and "What if Einstein Was Wrong?" Big name public intellectuals like Elon Musk regularly rolled through. So, occasionally, did smug public criminals like Roger Stone. The company was a small, busy start-up, so my job as editor, then (briefly) managing editor was like fourteen jobs rolled into one.

In terms of "right livelihood," Big Think was a mixed bag. Some of the work—like producing a series in which Bill Nye (the erstwhile Science Guy) answered questions from kids and adults all over the world—felt gratifying and useful. Other parts felt ethically wrong to me, like the time I was asked to convince a guy who made and distributed plans for 3D printable automatic weapons to write a blog for us.

Controversy attracts attention. By 2015, social media and smartphones had made attention harder and harder to get and to hold, so clickbait proliferated at companies like Big Think as they competed for market share. It was the nature of the business, and it was corrosive in ways that by 2020 would threaten Western democracy and erode people's faith in a shared basis for evaluating reality itself. I pushed back wherever I could, driving my bosses crazy. Other times I bit my tongue to keep my job—the closest I'd ever come to making a living I could live with.

The first season of the podcast *Serial* in 2014, with its millions of downloads per episode, had convinced every media company to start its own podcast. When my bosses brought up the idea of a Big Think podcast, I may literally have jumped out of my chair at the company meeting, shouting: "Me! Me! I want to do it!"

The Russian learning theorist Lev Vygotsky wrote about what he called the "zone of proximal development." It's the space just outside of your comfort zone in any area, just beyond what you've already mastered. With "scaffolding" or support, the ZPD is your room to grow. I had never hosted a radio show or done much public speaking since that disastrous NYU production of *A Midsummer Night's Dream*. But something told me that this podcast was right in my ZPD. And maybe one step closer to right livelihood.

I came up with the name *Think Again* and we decided it would be a weekly show. After some initial back-and-forth with management, I had total, unsupervised control over its production. If I could muster up the courage, here was an opportunity, finally, to make something that really mattered to me and share it with the world.

My close friend and creative brother-from-another-mother Eric Sanders helped me plan it all out. In Meri's spirit, we designed *Think Again* to welcome the unknown with experimental curiosity. There was a destabilizing surprise twist intended to provoke spontaneous, unlikely conversations: in the middle of each episode the guest and I would watch a video clip or two on a random "big idea," then talk about it. The clip was chosen by the video team, and was a surprise to both of us.

In some ways, the show aimed in the opposite direction from so much of "big idea" media at the time. Rather than mining guests' ideas for little, clickable nuggets of usefulness, it was like a St. John's seminar—an open-ended conversation for the sake of intellectual discovery and delight. Within weeks of the first planning meeting, I found myself chatting with former Black Flag front man and spoken word artist, Henry Rollins, about gun control and the concept of "genius," and with author Salman Rushdie about the physics of black holes.

For Big Think, the podcast was supposed to be a small, low-cost experiment—something I did a few hours a week among many other responsibilities. But between booking, preparing for conversations, taping, producing, and social media marketing, running a weekly talk show took up half the workweek. Also, most of my guests had just published a book—a book I intended to read. I had invited them out of interest in their work, I wanted to learn from them, and it felt disrespectful to both of us just to come up with questions based on the publicist's crib sheet. Pretty soon I was hard pressed to care about or focus on anything at work other than Think Again. But my energy for the podcast was boundless.

Between 2015 and 2020, there were roughly 220 original episodes—shows that weren't compilations or reruns. Some guests were filmmakers, so that's at least two hundred books and twenty films I might not otherwise have seen or read, full of mind-and-heart-expanding ideas. And that's 220 intense, one-on-one encounters with extraordinary people.

Everyone's extraordinary. But not everyone knows it. And temperament and life circumstances can block, to varying degrees, people's ability to fully realize or express themselves. Most of the guests on Think Again were people who had grown into their voices and were trying to do meaningful work in the world. And the precious time I spent engaging with them and their ideas helped me to grow into my own voice.

From the writers I talked to, many of them literary heroes of mine, I learned crucial lessons about craft. When I sat down to write this book, I remembered something the Turkish novelist Orhan Pamuk had told me: that writers must learn above all else to navigate their own mental and emotional lives like master sailors, keeping to a schedule but staying sensitive to the ebb and flow of their own energy—learning to work with, rather than against it. Struggling to revise my manuscript, I remembered that Lauren Groff had the courage, after writing a four-hundred-page first draft, to throw the whole thing away and start from scratch.

From Buddhist master teachers like Sharon Salzberg, Joseph Goldstein, Norman Fischer, and more, I got answers to some of my most vexing questions about the dharma. Goldstein told me he sees enlightenment as a process of "lightening up," and tries not to worry about when or whether he'll reach the end. Sharon Salzberg reminded me that being free of attachment isn't the same as being free of humanity; even after enlightenment, after penetrating the deepest nature of reality, the Buddha was reportedly moved to tears by the loss of a dear friend.

Equally important, some guests helped me open outward and engage more deeply in social issues, after a lifetime spent turned anxiously inward. Historian Jill Lepore and her book *These Truths* unpacked the deep history of the fault lines in the American experiment—the broken promises we're still fighting over today. Ibram X. Kendi, author of *How to Be an Antiracist*, illuminated the history of whiteness and how to take an active and effective role in fighting racial injustice. From philosopher Robert Macfarlane, I gained perspective into deep time and the beauty of our ailing planet. Cambridge Analytica whistle-blower Chris Wylie woke me up to the pernicious power of social media as a tool for spreading disinformation and polarizing culture. From V Ensler, author of *The Vagina Monologues* and *The Apology*, an imagined letter from her father from beyond the grave about the sexual and emotional abuse he put her through in childhood, I learned more than I can ever express or repay about what true forgiveness means.

I often felt terrified in an interview, overcome with self-doubt. My ego would go to war with itself, expecting perfection, disappointed with the reality as I tried to stammer out some long-winded question. Editing these conversations each week, listening for hours at a time to my absurd giggle and neurotic overuse of the word *like* was excruciating. At these times I remembered Meri, tried to channel her courage and self possession. In her voice, I reminded myself that everyone—the most brilliant podcast guest included—sees only a tiny sliver of the big picture. We're all precious, we're all imperfect, and the right attitude in the face of our vast ignorance isn't fear, but rather openness, humility, and wonder. I came to understand that self-doubt is itself a form of egoism—a defensive way of turning inward and away from the world.

In this attitude, I tried to be a stand-in for the audience, sending the St. John's–like message that big ideas, complex questions, and the joys of thoughtful conversation for its own sake weren't just for experts, they were for everybody. I hoped that some people would feel welcome, for the first time maybe, at intellectual tables to which they weren't always invited.

That first year was rocky, but by the second, the show had started to find its voice. I worked on striking a balance between listening and opening new conversational spaces with questions and personal stories. I talked about Meri's death. I talked about Emre and online gaming. Soon, I started getting emails from all over the world, from college students, professionals, and retirees in many different fields. A new dad in Australia wrote that the show helped him "make sense of an increasingly nonsensical world." A professor of sociology wrote that the show had rekindled a love of learning that the narrowly specialized world of academia had almost extinguished in him. A young woman wrote that *Think Again* was a lifeline for her in a time of terrible isolation and pain. For the first time in my life, I felt connected to a wider human community, not just in theory but in practice. The show translated ideas and values that mattered to me into something tangible that made a difference in people's lives.

Without Big Think, of course, the show would never have existed. My bosses proposed the idea and gave me total freedom to make exactly the podcast I wanted to. They supported me in getting technical training and going to podcast conferences. I used Big Think video clips for the surprise conversation starters and relied on the company's brand name to book many of the better-known guests. But as the show took over my life and took on a life of its own, Big Think faced increasing financial difficulties, and paying a full-time podcaster made less and less business sense. After five of the most challenging and rewarding years I'd ever known, the closest I'd ever come to "right liveli-hood," it became clear that it was time to move on.

Money

If we value freedom, what we need is time *to figure out who we should be and what matters to us. This requires time to educate ourselves and to deliberate on what should count as meaningful activities for us—both individually and collectively—rather than being prescribed what should count as meaningful activities by what happens to be profitable for a capitalist at the moment. The latter is serfdom, not freedom.*

The key to the critique of capitalism is therefore the reevaluation *of value. The foundation of capitalism is the measure of wealth in terms of socially necessary labor time. In contrast, the overcoming of capitalism requires that we measure our wealth in terms of what I call* socially available free time. *As long as our measure of wealth is socially necessary labor time, machine technologies cannot produce any value for us by virtue of their own operations. The technologies that could make us wealthier—that could give us more time to lead our lives—are instead employed to exploit human labor even when such labor is not needed.*

—Martin Hägglund, *This Life*

In his monumental work *This Life*, philosopher Martin Häaglund writes about the fundamental problem of capitalism. In capitalist culture, money becomes the universal measure of value—a proxy for the worth of any thing, act, or person. Is Jeff Bezos "worth" more than Maya Angelou? A day spent slaughtering cows more than a day with your kid in the park? Under capitalism, the answer is a definitive "yes."

A common objection, he points out, to any critique of capitalism, is that no better alternative exists. Would you have us go back to the Dark Ages? Was Communist Russia or Cuba Marx's promised utopia? This is like excusing the toll of alcoholism—drunk-driving deaths, cirrhosis of the liver, generations of trauma—on the basis that we haven't found a more efficient tool than alcohol for dealing with stress.

What do I value? Beautiful things, mostly made of words. Connection with people. I have never had much success translating any of this into value under capitalism.

The money my parents have made from their business bought me time to read, travel, and ask big questions about what's worth doing with what Hägglund calls "our one, precious life." At the same time, it made me intolerant of making a living at any job that isn't perfectly aligned with these deeper values. As a result of this and other circumstances, I've been dependent on that family money, off and on, for most of my life.

In 2016, just as *Think Again* was taking off, Demet fell into a crippling depression and her solo law practice was in danger of collapse. My Big Think income wasn't nearly enough to support us and we reached the point where we could no longer pay our rent. After months of struggle and secrecy, I called home in desperation, told my folks the whole story and asked for their help. They've been helping us financially ever since.

It's sometimes hard not to see this as a conclusive defeat in the battle Dad and I started in high school. A repudiation of my values under capitalism. After all, art and beauty have never quite managed to pay the bills. In my more vulnerable moments, this fact threatens to undermine everything I think I've learned, to devalue every bit of hard-earned wisdom I've been trying to write about here.

I can imagine other people's lives, but I only have direct access to my own. I don't know what I might have done under different circumstances, whether facing hardship without a safety net would have made me stronger and more independent than I am, or whether it would have broken me. Would I be more practical? More driven to brand and network and market and promote my podcast on social media? I'll never know. None of us has any choice but to work with the life we have, and resist the "near enemies" that lead to ingratitude and despair.

Laypeople who commit to Buddhism take five precepts, or vows—promising to refrain from things like killing and "intoxicants that lead to heedlessness" (I don't believe, as some Buddhists do, that psychedelics fit that description, but that's a conversation for another time). As with all Buddhist ethics, the precepts are meant as protection against regrets and attachments that can slow spiritual growth.

The precept against stealing is subtler than the equivalent Biblical commandment. Buddhists promise not to take "what isn't freely given."

My relationship with my father is much better now than it was in high school. The older we both get, the more urgent repairing this relationship seems, to both of us, I think. In some ways, the hardships of recent years and the opportunity they gave him to help us brought us closer together. He has been kind and gracious through all of it. But as we both know well, it was never "freely given." How could it be? It has been difficult and painful for him to see his son in this situation, contrary to the basic values of financial self-reliance he'd hoped to pass on. And I've asked for and accepted that help at a cost to our relationship; a misunderstanding that I sometimes worry may never fully heal.

Those last few years, Meri found herself in the same situation—financially dependent on our parents and full of self-judgment and doubt. What I told her then is what I'd like to tell myself now: it's just a situation. It's not the whole story. It's a situation under capitalism, and situations (and systems) always change.

★ ★ ★

And there's another way to look at it. Another, simpler perspective I sometimes feel we're coming to, my Dad and I; whatever difficulty or discomfort it may have come with, this bailout was (and is) an act of generosity. Of kindness. Of love. And when I'm not all twisted up in knots of self-recrimination, the natural response to that is gratitude. Not the sickly-sweet Oscars-thank-you kind of gratitude, but the kind that accepts that in some way or other, sometime or other, all of us need help from someone and all of us will offer it. That kind of gratitude is yet another form of love.

Box of Notebooks

I woke up at 3 a.m. one day in early March 2018, with a terrible sense of urgency. This was a new kind of pain—a wormhole back to the moment when college was ending, when the pressure to grow up and build a career collided like a freight train with the relative simplicity of life with Lisa, then Moira, with my pen and my books and my guitar. It might sound maudlin to modern ears, but the old word *keening* is the only one strong enough to describe what I was feeling. I keened for all the years since then, all the time I'd spent—as Paul Simon puts it—"tumbling in turmoil."

For all those years, no matter how bad things had gotten, I'd been trying to move forward. Telling myself—without knowing I was doing it—that happiness or clarity was just around the corner. But that night, for some reason, the exhaustion of all that hopeful storytelling, all that desperate rewriting, swept over me like a tsunami, and with it came a yearning, for once, just to let my life be what it was.

Unable to sleep, I took my guitar and a notebook into the walk-in closet we sometimes used as an office and wrote the first verse and the chorus of a new song:

I'd like to tell the truth for once
As if it's even possible
Without all of the filigree
And Cordovan geometry
About how there was never
A container that could fit
All the love and all the emptiness
I tried to stuff inside of it

How angry and how disappointed
Every effort made me
Every promising new prototype
And radical discovery
Every reinvention, every sliver of redemption
That got stuffed into a notebook
Too embarrassing to mention

And I think I might be ready
Yeah, I guess it must be time
To open up that old box of spiral notebooks

At the bottom of another closet sat a literal box of notebooks, some spiral-bound, some marble, full of all the thoughts, poems, bits of short stories and song lyrics from high school through college. I don't think I'd touched any of them since I wrote them. Metaphorically and actually, the box was full of unfinished business.

Over the next few months, I opened it again and again, rereading old writing on many of the same themes I still wrestle with—the themes I've written about in this book. I was surprised to hear a voice from twenty-five years ago that I recognized clearly as my own.

Some things I found in the box of notebooks:

- A postcard from John I didn't know I had, to which (brace yourself) he had taped a bit of his actual earwax as a joke that from anyone else would have been creepy as hell but from him (and I'm afraid you'll have to take my word for this) was somehow just goofy and sweet. Also, if cloning ever becomes commonplace, there may be some ethical questions to wrestle with...

- A hundred pages of a stick figure comic I drew about an antihero with a wiggling eyeball for a head, on tragicomical adventures that sometimes resembled my life in college, sometimes borrowed from Shakespeare, and sometimes looked like nothing else I've ever seen.

- The script for a musical I wrote twenty years ago in a dark vaudevillian style that still shows up in my fiction.

- Song lyrics and poems going all the way back to high school, the skeletons of first drafts still visible under the flesh and skin of careful, patient revision.

- Quiet, thoughtful journal entries, rage-filled diatribes in invented character voices, direct-address letters to Meri, to my parents, and to friends that I clearly wrote with no intention of sending, ever...

For years, I had dismissed the whole box as an undifferentiated, embarrassing mass of self-pity. Instead, I found in it an extraordinary variety of strivings and creative, hopeful attempts—some more skillful than others, of course—to make sense of my life and bear witness to it. A thousand little acts of love.

The cover page of Jason's long-lost comic book.

Opening it meant facing the fact that growth isn't linear. It's not a radical act of transformation or resurrection. There is no clear-cut *before* and *after*. In many ways, I'm the same person I've always been, and integrity demands that I don't pretend otherwise.

Somatic therapist Resmaa Menakem writes about "dirty pain" and "clean pain." Dirty pain is trauma avoided, repressed, or de-

303

Two among many notebooks in the box.

nied. In other words, trauma unmourned. Clean pain is suffering metabolized—faced directly with compassion and released.

It's so tempting to lock your life away in little boxes. So easy, in the face of pain and uncertainty, to edit your story into something neater and more presentable, something more like all those pretty stories you've read or seen in a movie or heard other people tell about themselves. It's a very human thing to do, and—credit where credit is due—it's a kind of creative act. You're just trying to make yourself happier, or safer, or more beautiful.

Paradoxically, though, that act of revision can hide the very thing in you that has the greatest potential to give hope and help and happiness to others. That precious, inimitable voice that sang so effortlessly at age three, or twenty.

I think we owe it to ourselves and one another to keep the box of notebooks open.

For me, since that morning, part of this work has involved making art central to my life again, rather than something locked away in those notebooks, "too embarrassing to mention." I met a beatmaker through Reddit and we started collaborating on new songs. I started writing fiction again—dozens of short stories and, with my friend Eric, two pilots for fiction podcasts, pitching them to producers in New York and LA. My dear friend Jason Viseltear, a luthier, invited me to give a concert in his Lower East Side violin shop. I invited old friends and new and played songs from college through the new one, about the box of notebooks. And in May 2020, I ended *Think Again* and started a new podcast called *Clever Creature*, an "experimental variety show" of short fiction, conversation, and songs.

Writing this book was a deeper dive into the box of notebooks, another attempt to "try and tell the truth for once" about Meri and John and myself.

> My sister she was honest
> But she couldn't make it work
> She was swimming in the quicksand
> She was drowning just in sight of land
>
> And I reached out my hand
> And it was strong but it was slippery
> Like words after I write them down
> Like love when it's a memory
>
> I think maybe I'm ready
> Yeah, I guess it must be time
> To open up that
> Box of spiral notebooks

The NYU library was a great place to write before COVID confined me to Emre's bedroom. The planned meditation retreat in Massachusetts was the perfect culmination of years of practice, until it was canceled due to lockdown. Yet the only real threat to thriving in the absence of these "just right" stories was the idea that things were going awry—that life might be souring from a tale of hard-won triumph into a series of unfortunate events.

On a regular schedule for over a year I sat down to write this book. Sometimes I was happy to work within the outline I originally came up with. Sometimes I struggled against it, broke it to pieces, lopped off limbs, and reassembled what was left. Discipline demands only that you show up, not that you pretend to be someone you aren't. How do you find room to breathe within the structure? How do you explore the space from different angles? By changing tense, through time travel, through direct address? Sometimes a doorway presents itself. Sometimes you just have to start anywhere and grope your way through.

As long as we're alive (and depending on which Buddhist you talk to, maybe long after that) the real business of living never ends. That's the work of mourning our losses, of opening ourselves to gratitude, forgiveness, and love. When the story no longer looks predictable and linear, when it branches out in every direction at once, that might be a good indication you're starting to see things more clearly.

The Concert in Central Park

By the time we get to Central Park, around 11 a.m., you can't get within a hundred feet of the stage. Still, it's a really good spot. Right in the middle, close enough to see Paul's face.

Overhead, seagulls are swooping around in anticipation of dropped salami and potato chips. They've flown upriver from the New York Harbor, but Meri's here and we're both thinking of Nantucket and the sea.

John and Lisa are here, too. This may be the only day the four of us will ever spend together. Paul Simon's concert in the summer of 1991 is free, and it's a historic moment—almost exactly a decade since Simon and Garfunkel's Concert in Central Park, the album of which Meri and I have both listened to so many times that we've memorized Paul's patter between songs. Paul will be here on his own—well, without Art Garfunkel, anyway. Things are bad between them, apparently. I don't really want to know.

Paul's bringing along maybe a dozen Brazilian and African musicians who worked with him on *Graceland* and the latest album, *Rhythm of the Saints*, along with US band members he's toured with for years. Anticipation is high. By the time the show starts, there will be almost fifty thousand people here. It won't start until sundown, but we're up for the twelve-hour picnic. We spread out our blankets, iced tea, and snacks, and settle in.

Meri: This is so surreal. I can't believe this is actually happening.

Me: I hope Art's doing okay. He lives over on Central Park East. I once delivered a package to him. Well, to his doorman. He'll hear the whole thing.

John: I'm sure he's over it by now.

Meri: I doubt it. What has he done since then? A Christmas album?

Lisa: Poor Art. He sang such nice harmonies!

Me: Can you imagine? They were buddies from high school. They dated girls together. Got famous together. And then Paul's like, "Sorry, dude, I'm outta here. Gotta do my own thing." I'd never do that to you, John.

John: Nor I. We will never break up the band.

Me: No way. We will just keep evolving.

Lisa: Like Spinal Tap.

Me: Not like Spinal Tap! Way more durable than Spinal Tap. We'll be like Brian Eno or something.

John: Just dissolving into digital bits of ambient glory.

Meri: I'm starving. Is anybody else starving?

Lisa: We've got pesto and eggplant sandwiches on home-made ciabatta.

Meri: What? You are a goddess.

Me: She's an earth spirit. A dryad, maybe.

Lisa: I like that. I can totally be a dryad. Reclining on a carpet of moss.

Meri: I'd like to be a fire spirit, I think.

Me: That makes sense. And John's air, for sure.

That leaves water. Maybe I can be water?

Meri and I wonder about the setlist. We hope he'll play some of the old tunes, like "America."

Meri: Driving up here, I kept hearing that line about the cars on the New Jersey Turnpike looking for America. It gave me goose bumps.

Me: Well, you know what *American* spells…

Both of us together: A Meri Can!

She remembers the bit in the '81 concert album where Paul thanks the mayor, then the Parks Department, then the Central

Park pot dealers who, he says, are donating half of their revenue to the city tonight. And we remember the one essential thing we forgot to bring along: weed.

No problem—nobody sells "loose joints" anymore, but we can get a couple dime bags over in Sheep Meadow and rolling papers at some deli on Central Park West. Lisa lights an American Spirit. John lies on his back, his hands behind his head and elbows butterflied out, looking up at the sky. And Meri and I head for the periphery.

When we get back maybe forty-five minutes later, our pockets bulging with fragrant buds, the field is blocked off with wooden police barricades. Inside the barriers, the crowd has already gotten so thick you can't see past the first two or three rows of bodies. Behind us, outside the barricades, stands a battalion of porta potties—the only restrooms in sight. Two of New York's Finest and Beefiest stand in front of us, guarding the field. They hold wide John Wayne stances, arms folded across their chests.

Me: Our friends are in there.

Cop 1: NO ONE gets in!

Me: But our friends are in there. We came together. We have to get back to them.

Cop 2: Did he stutter? We have our orders. NO ONE gets in.

Panic rises in my chest. I turn to confer with Meri. This is a disaster! These are pre–cell phone days and we have no way of letting John and Lisa know what's going on.

Cop 1 (joking to Cop 2): If shit goes down, guess where I'm gonna be?

Cop 2: Where?

Cop 1: Up in that tree. Two barrels pointed straight down!

Meri: Excuse me, Officer? How many people are expected at this show?

Cop 1: Fifty thousand, give or take.

Meri: Okay. So you've got fifty thousand people in there. Nobody can get in or out. And the toilets are out here. What do you think's gonna happen when all those people need to go to the bathroom?

Cop 1: We got our orders! Nobody gets—

Meri grabs my hand and ducks under the barricade, disappearing into the crowd. I follow behind her, feeling the brush of a hand across my back as one of the cops tries and fails to catch hold of my shirt.

Meri leading the way, we assert a path back to the safety of our picnic blanket.

As the cool of the evening comes on and the sun sinks down below the Hudson River, the opening guitar riff for "The Coast" slices through the 85% humidity like a razor blade. Paul sings:

> *This is a lonely life*
> *Sorrows everywhere you turn*

I look over at John. He's smiling beatifically, swaying with his eyes closed and his face turned up toward the music like some medieval saint infused with the Holy Spirit. The stage lights illuminate Lisa's glorious tangle of hair and Meri's angular, joyful dancing. These are the people I love most in the world. I want arms long enough to draw them all together, to hold them so tight that we can never be pulled apart.

The weed is doing its job, too, silencing the self-reflexive chatter in my head, dissolving the barriers between me and these fifty thousand strangers, between me and the stage. Our bodies are woven by the batuque samba drums of Grupo Cultural Olodum into a single organism in rhythmic motion. I feel deep, spiritual gratitude for this music, for this unlikely union of African and Brazilian drummers and guitarists and the little Jewish singer from Queens.

What I hear, what I believe we all hear, is the harmony and tension between distinct voices, histories, sorrows, and longings that have improbably found common cause in this time and place. Whoever we are, they're our sorrows, too, from the first shock of birth through the bad news from the doctor that the tumor's inoperable. And they're our joys—it's the birthright of our bodies to dance like this, any way the song moves them.

Acknowledgments

It's hard not to think of gratitude as a debt, but when you frame it that way you introduce a grim responsibility that has little, I think, to do with gratitude. Debt decays to guilt, which decays to resentment, which (in my case, anyway) decays to the idea that it's easier just to avoid entanglements altogether. And we must embrace entanglement—right?—or else we're hardly alive.

Below are some of the many people to whom I'm grateful as this book (my first) is published.

Mom and Dad: For the monumental act of love you have done for me in reading this book, enduring all my painful opinions about our shared past, and—impossibly, miraculously—going beyond all that to express your admiration for the writing and your support for its publication. You have taught me a profound lesson in what love is—one I'll be unpacking for the rest of my life. And for everything else, of course. Meri should see us now.

Demet: Without your patience, kindness, and wisdom, I would never have allowed myself the freedom to grow in the ways that made me the person who could write this book. And through the long, difficult months of the pandemic, when hope was in short supply for so many reasons both universal and particular to

our life together, you reminded me that this work was both possible and necessary. Let's keep tending this garden we've made.
Together, there's nothing we can't do or become.

Peter: You appeared out of nowhere and invited me to dream
this book into being. It's one I needed to write but couldn't
have written without your encouragement. I'm grateful for the
breadth of your vision, which made room for a story that's only
tangentially related to the podcast that first caught your attention. Grateful, too, for your patience and gentle encouragement
as an editor working with an anxious, self-conscious, first-time
author who might have been scared into silence by any other
approach.

Eric, my brother-from-another-mother: In so many ways, as I
know you know, this book has evolved from our long conversations over the past twenty years. Conversations about art, ambition, money, family, and every other goddamn thing under
the sun. Thank you for your unconditional love and support,
and for everything your optimism and boundless creative energy have taught me—among so many other lessons, the freedom to say "fuck it" and just make whatever you want to make,
even though you'll never be George Eliot or Q-Tip or Virginia
Woolf or Shakespeare or David Foster Wallace or Tom Waits.

Emre, my boy: Every day you teach me how to be a better
man, both by the example of your big, beautiful heart and by
the worthy challenge of being dad to a kid with such epic emotional and intellectual range. In learning how to help you and
when to shut up and stand back in reverent silence as you grow
into yourself, I learn the true meaning of life (which is also, of
course, forty-two).

Ed: Your unwavering love and faith in me, when I often have
so little for/in myself, is a beacon in my darkest hours. You see
me, which is (as you'd put it) remarkable, given how very dif-

ferent we are—as different as Earth and Air, which I guess is what drew us together and has kept us together so long. Here's to us one day on a Brighton Beach bench in our flat caps, with Russian dumplings and beer.

Amanda: For that blend of joy, positivity, and honesty that's yours alone. For being one of the most levelheaded and (somehow at the same time) playful people I know. And for coming to the calm, heroic rescue of an anxious first-time author.

Bill: For your wonderful laugh, which hasn't changed since we first met in Oakland. For reveling with me in music and poetry. For listening so closely at such a distance.

Sarah: For being the best listener, ever. For seeing right through us. For healing what might otherwise have been beyond repair.

Rob: For all the listening to and the sharing of beautiful words and music. "Blessing" breaks my heart every time I hear or sing it, which is often. For the depth of your heart and mind, which inspire me deeply. For a precious new friendship, late-ish in life for making true, new friends.

Anais: For your willingness to help when you didn't know if life would allow you to and then for helping anyway, even as your world sprung back to busy life. For your songs, which are medicine and your gift to everyone—may they grow forever green.

Gish: For your warmth and intelligence, the joy of two conversations with you full of laughter, and the beautiful, reassuring reflections—the first (aside from those of my editor) I got after two years of wrestling alone with words in a pandemic bedroom.

Neil: For your long-ago decision never to become one of those "Do you know who I am" people. You're my hero of creative freedom and human kindness. What a glorious, playful shapeshifter, unafraid to let all the things you love speak through you.

Tom G: For knowing much better than I ever will how to find humor and joy in the unbearable.

Tom W: For playing in the sandbox with your skulls and your bones, making that glorious noise. And for loving all the little things lost, and Kathleen B, for playing with him.

Terry: For your inspired madness. Keep on tilting at all the windmills.

Sharon, Joseph, Ajahns Amaro and Sucitto, Caroline Jones, and all my other teachers in the dharma: For your smart and unpretentious transmission of the medicine.

Karen: We met only once, but I was moved by your presence—your heart—to trust you with a delicate and possibly cheeky request. And oh, how you came through...

MLP: For being your real, beautiful, unpredictable self, one of the few courageous enough to hang out in the not knowing.

Nicole, Jason, Chris—dear friends and early readers: For the years of friendship and deepest trust, and for telling me the truth as you know it.

Libby: For the warm embrace of your presence from the moment we met. For your openness and invaluable help with this project. Your tarot reading was right—it hasn't always been easy, but it's never been boring.

Lisa B: For growing up with me for a while all those years ago, for revisiting all the old revenants more recently over the phone, and for your love and kindness in giving this book your blessing as it dusts off all the skeletons in hopes that they may dance again.

Lisa M: For your trust and your support on this project that's as personal to you in some ways as it is to me. You were nothing but openness and sunlight itself, just as I remember you from Glen Echo days.

Matt, Alex, Tobe: For telling me stories a brother might not ever otherwise get to hear.

Nathan: For your kindness, decency, and openness, which didn't have to coexist with your enormous talents, but somehow do.

My students: You remind me over and over again just how vast the possibilities are.

The good people at Hanover Square (and I won't mention names because I haven't met you all yet and don't want to leave anyone out): For your warmth, hand-holding, and masterful execution of things I wouldn't have the first clue how to do without you.

Abby: For swooping in at the eleventh hour at the behest of a friend and saving the day.

And everyone and everything else I've forgotten to mention. Every author, friend, singer-songwriter...for everyone who's ever done me an act of kindness that restored hope when it was flagging, thank you.